THE CHARISMA
EFFECT

THE CHARISMA EFFECT

Desmond Guilfoyle

The McGraw-Hill Companies, Inc.

Sydney New York San Francisco Auckland
Bangkok Bogotá Caracas Hong Kong
Kuala Lumpur Lisbon London Madrid
Mexico City Milan New Delhi San Juan
Seoul Singapore Taipei Toronto

McGraw·Hill Australia

A Division of The McGraw·Hill Companies

Text © 2002 Desmond Guilfoyle

Illustrations and design © 2002 McGraw-Hill Australia Pty Ltd

Additional owners of copyright are acknowledged on the Acknowledgments page.

National Library of Australia Cataloguing-in-Publication data:
Guilfoyle, Desmond.
The charisma effect : how to captivate an audience and deliver a winning message.
Includes index.
ISBN 0 074 71144 X.
1. Public speaking – Handbooks, manuals, etc. 2. Oral communication. I. Title.
808.5

Published in Australia by
McGraw-Hill Australia Pty Ltd
4 Barcoo Street, Roseville NSW 2069, Australia
Acquisitions Editor: Javier Dopico
Production Editor: Rosemary McDonald
Editor: Christine Eslick
Indexer: Diane Harriman
Proofreader: Tim Learner
Interior design: Wing Ping Tong
Cover design: Melanie Feddersen
Illustrator: Alan Laver, Shelly Communications
Typeset in Bembo by Wing Ping Tong
Printed on 80 gsm woodfree by Pantech Ltd, Hong Kong

CONTENTS

ACKNOWLEDGMENTS

This book grew out of years of people-watching, and its pages would be empty without the help of those hundreds of public figures who were both willing and unsuspecting targets of my modelling experiments. I honour them for their immense talent and the richness of the pickings they provided. I apologise for pilfering some of their best kept secrets.

I wish to acknowledge Ailsa West for providing the soil in which this project initially took root. I also owe much to my friend and colleague Charmaine Anderson for supporting my work in the field and encouraging me to be excessive.

John Grinder, PhD, more than anyone showed me how to unravel the mysteries of patterning and pattern detection. I wish to thank Tad James, PhD, for his immeasurable contributions to my knowledge and understanding of modelling, meta-programs and the hypnotic effects of language. Avinoam Sapir is a genius who transformed psycho-linguistics and content analysis into an indispensable form of nourishment for me.

I am indebted to Rex Steven Sikes for providing the perfect hook for the material I gathered over the years. My agent, Sheila Drummond, astonished me with her professionalism and the ease with which she placed my manuscript. I wish to thank my acquisitions editor, Javier Dopico, for his priceless advice on transforming dry academic text into a reader friendly book. I also owe a debt to Liz Byrski, Chung Chin Lung, Gail Phillips, PhD, Geoff Duncan, and others too many to mention for humouring, encouraging and supporting me.

WHAT IS THE CHARISMA EFFECT?

One of the greatest diseases is to be nobody to anybody.
Mother Teresa

Bob Hawke did it, Winston Churchill did it to the limit, Maggie Tabberer does it, Michael Jordan does it and manages it with supreme elegance, Tiger Woods is now acquiring it, and it comes out of Oprah Winfrey's pores. Jana Wendt still does it, Ray Martin could do it if he expressed a tad more emotion, Richard Branson does it on good days, but John Howard and Paul Keating never did it and never will. A fair number of CEOs, men of the cloth, sports men and women, the odd politician and many other highly visible and not so visible Australians do 'it', so why can't you?

Of course, off-the-scale charisma quotients may not be what you require to gain the visibility, status and authority needed to succeed in your field of influence. You may have little desire to become another Nelson Mandela or Mother Teresa, but you may well be wondering what more you have to do to give your career or vocation the boost it deserves.

You may question why some of your contemporaries are more persuasive, eloquent, popular or magnetic. You may be perplexed over your failure to get good ideas across the line, or agonise over the low levels of enthusiasm generated by your presentations and speeches. You may want to be a leader and not a follower, and you're unsure of what to do to improve your leadership profile and build your charisma quotient.

The processes, techniques and ideas you encounter in this book can give you the edge you're looking for. They are the result of observation and modelling of the behaviours of hundreds of successful public figures and broadcasters I have worked with and met over nearly thirty years. The more than thirty thousand interviews I conducted as a current affairs presenter provided rich territory in which to observe charismatic public figures and performers first-hand.

1

For the past twenty years I have studied charisma and persuasion as an adjunct to my broadcasting activities. I have noticed recurring patterns of behaviour in many of the most successful and persuasive of the public figures, entertainers, artists, politicians, academics and other famous people I've had the pleasure of interviewing. I, like many others, had fallen for the mischievous piece of fiction that you're either born with 'it' or you're not. The evidence I've gathered over two decades challenges the fanciful notion that charisma is the physical manifestation of some mysterious gift from the gods or a yet undiscovered charisma gene. My research and experience suggest that charismatic communication is learn-able and do-able.

This book explores the mechanics and mindsets of doing charismatic communication. It draws together elements of form, content structure, modes of delivery and self-design to create a working model of the charismatic communicator. As you turn its pages you will discover how to do charismatic communication. You will learn how to employ the techniques, strategies, behaviours and internal processes charismatic communicators adopt to become leaders of people or opinion-makers.

The word 'charisma' is derived from the ancient Greek and means 'the gift of grace or favour'. Grace and favours are bestowed, as you know, as a result of, or in response to, things that are said or done. You don't have charisma— other people award it to you. Charisma can be seen essentially as the result of a series of sophisticated transactions between individuals and groups through a given medium.

Charismatic personalities share many common and distinguishing features. They *adopt* specific strategies and *learn* particular behaviours to achieve the total magnetic package known as charismatic communication. Through repetition, these strategies and behaviours become natural and habitual.

The remarkable thing is that you can acquire and develop charismatic behaviours by drawing on the internal resources and abilities you have now. You have what it takes already: there is no need to wait around for the invention of charisma gene therapy. The key to developing a charismatic aura is to creatively mine and manage your internal resources: your imagination, your powers of observation, your ability to learn and your infinite capacity to read and respond to given situations. What you will discover is that charismatic communication and influence begin with enhancing your knowledge, experience and practice of specific sets of behaviours, and repeating them until they become automatic.

Charismatic speakers and performers instinctively know, however, that they can't expect the grace and favour of their colleagues, contemporaries, subordinates or audiences until they have created a shared or mutual space in which the charisma transaction can take place. The following case studies explore this all-important first step in developing the underpinning attitudes and mindsets so common in first-rate charismatic communicators.

STEPHEN'S STORY

Stephen is an intelligent and creative upper-level executive who can turn his energy and enthusiasm off and on like a tap. Stroking egos with the natural ease of a Hairdresser to the Stars, Stephen lights up with lethal charm when around those he wants to impress. He is articulate and stylish: an original ideas man who has learned a number of persuasion techniques through experience and reading books.

He displays an unnatural knack of recognising the psychological weaknesses of his superiors and adopting roles that feed and support their delusions and neuroses. He struggles with super-human effort to connect emotionally with senior and influential executives in his organisation. He is grovelling, sycophantic and terrified of their power.

He shows little hesitation, however, in delivering incriminating reports on his peers and is valued by his immediate superiors as a kind of agent in the field. There are times when his repetition of their cruel or casually insensitive observations about colleagues and subordinates is rendered so faithfully that you'd swear he was an instrument through which they expressed their psychic pain. His ability to click into the language and behaviours of this inner circle reveals sensory awareness of the highest order.

Stephen receives much needed approval and patronage in return for his services. His bosses see him as a loyal and reliable lieutenant who does their bidding without question: as someone they can control. He is, by all appearances, a successful 'leader' in a large organisation, and he may appear very familiar to you. His ascent of the executive ladder has been rapid, but it isn't too hard to imagine a descent of equal and dramatic haste. While his immediate superiors view him as reliable, charming and innovative, his staff are unified in their scorn. Ask those who have worked for him to describe his character and you'd discover no discernible difference in charisma quotient between him and Pol Pot.

It is far more comfortable to be on top of Stephen than under him. His reputation for sucking up to superiors and being disinterested in the welfare and needs of his colleagues and subordinates often leads to the eruption of open hatred at the mere mention of his name. His peers and underlings see him as self-serving and manipulative, dangerous and autocratic: hardly the qualities that motivate subordinates to give 100 per cent. Hence, he invites, at best, a form of malicious obedience and, at times, a swell of breathless impatience over 'when someone on high is going to wake up to this man'.

You will never hear Stephen articulating an idealistic vision of the future of his organisation. That's far too risky. You will never see him aligning staff needs with corporate goals because he doesn't appear to have taken the time to think about the values and aspirations of the people who work under him. And you certainly won't find him fighting an honourable battle on behalf of his staff just because it's the 'right thing to do'.

Stephen's rise in his organisation mirrors the crude self-interest and indecent naivety of parts of its upper management structure. He practises what can generously be called 'upward charisma'. He invests most of his charm and other wiles in 'love-bombing' those superiors he imagines can help him most. He engages many of the behaviours employed by genuine charismatic communicators, but for narrow and self-serving purposes. He has no greater vision than that of protecting and enhancing his personal interests and, tragically, his superiors support and nurture such behaviour.

Stephen is a menace to the future prospects of both himself and his organisation. One day he may well have to face the wrath of his masters. Ultimately, the balance sheet will overshadow his courtly sleights of mouth and fawning behaviour: nothing will save him from the consequences of estranging those who are charged with delivering on the bottom line.

You have to lament such a pitiful waste of charisma and persuasion potential. Many of Stephen's behaviours could be usefully employed in improving the performance and profit of his organisation and guaranteeing his future. The lesson Stephen can choose to learn is that love-bombing produces lasting results only when deployed consistently, sincerely and passionately: a lesson well learned by Sandra.

SANDRA'S STORY

Sandra is a senior executive in a leading financial services company. The first thing that attracts attention to Sandra is her appearance. She was once described by a colleague as looking like 'a badly arranged bouquet of flowers being buffeted by the wind'. Her hair is the colour of copper wiring and erupts at interesting angles, while her lively, green eyes shine preternaturally from a landscape of pale skin and freckles. Her favourite business colours are aqua and cobalt blue, and her colourful scarves create both scandal and sensation. She has what her co-workers describe as 'the vibe', a unique, enchanting quality that draws people to her.

Sandra was recruited at thirty-five after having self-financed her Masters in commerce and was one of the first females to parachute into a senior executive position within the company. This caused resentment in a number of males who had been working for the company for some years. Within three months, Sandra had won her detractors over, not with captivating clichés and hollow charm, but through her ability to create and enter a shared reality. She is endowed with boundless curiosity, and her questions are uncommonly thoughtful, original and sensitive. Her awareness of the sensibilities, values and aspirations of her colleagues and staff is unequalled in the company. She consistently steps into the shoes of staff and clients to the extent that people report she makes them feel very special and important.

One of Sandra's favourite sayings is 'Why compete when we can help each other get what we want?'. She isn't shy in putting out for what she wants for her division to staff or, indeed, her superiors. She is a passionate devotee of principle-centred leadership, basing her style on empowerment and interpersonal trust. As a leader, Sandra sees herself as part navigator, part facilitator and part developer. She has a special relationship with younger staff members, to the point where her sense of dress has become a fashion statement for young women in the company. Many 'just want to be like Sandra'. 'Sandra uniforms' have reached almost epidemic proportions.

'My mother died when I was nine so I had to mother myself. I came to appreciate how encouragement, belief and kindness spur you on. The important people around me encouraged, and sometimes forced, me to take responsibility. They helped me to become stronger and more self-confident at a fairly early age. The thing I learned most was that if you want something to happen you have to put your head, heart and soul into it. If it involves other people, their heads, hearts and souls have to be in it too. The only way you can get that kind of commitment is to connect it to something bigger and demonstrate a benefit for everyone concerned.'

Sandra's presentations to clients are legendary. There is competition among her colleagues to be part of her presentation team just to witness 'how she pulls it off'. Her CEO never misses a major presentation. 'Her ideas are bold and certainly not mainstream, and yet she has this knack of connecting them to people's higher intentions. There are times when I think I'm sitting in a revivalist meeting, and when I look around I see groups of business hard-heads on the verge of shouting "Praise the Lord!".'

Common ground is a key factor in Sandra's modus operandi. Her language style is earthy, direct and uncomplicated. Superiors, colleagues and clients alike trust her. She talks continuously about doing 'the right thing' for her people, her company and her clients. Her charismatic behaviours have integrated smoothly into her management style and she prods and challenges people to 'come on board and share the spoils'.

Sandra's results illustrate that building collective identity, being genuinely curious about people, reinforcing individual contribution and worth, speaking plainly and powerfully, and operating consistently from a strong value system are the 'secrets' that give her an edge in a highly competitive industry.

ETHICAL CHARISMA

People would walk through hot coals for Sandra as much as they would probably like to barbecue Stephen slowly over them. Yet both possess high charisma quotients. The difference is that over time Sandra has engineered an identity and a set of congruent capabilities and behaviours that harness human potential and direct it towards mutually satisfying ends. Stephen squanders his charisma quotient on a relentless quest for approval and status from an in-group he desperately wants to be part of.

Sandra learned through experience that power and influence have to be earned through authentic relationships with those who are stakeholders in her business and personal environment. She also learned that persuasion is dependent on meeting people's needs, of understanding values and aspirations, and of engendering trust across the board. Stephen has taken some of the techniques of persuasion and used them to manipulate a small cell of people for his personal ends. Would you care to guess whose use-by date is approaching rapidly?

Stephen and Sandra both embody 'it', the so-called indefinable X factor attributed to charismatic leadership down the ages. They both practise sets of very special behaviours that appear to give them a distinct advantage in their personal and professional endeavours. You've noticed, however, a huge dissimilarity in both the way they employ those behaviours and the ends towards which they are directed.

Sure, you can live by Stephen's example and exercise your charismatic powers to manipulate others for your own ends, to satisfy your lust for power and inflate your personal vanity, but it almost seems to be the nature of things for events to catch up with unethical and egocentric leaders. Some leaders use their charismatic abilities productively while others are ultimately destroyed by theirs, destroying others in the process.

Contemporary history is peppered with examples of unethical charismatic leaders beguiling followers and ushering them down a path of suffering and wretchedness. The general lesson appears to be that those who *develop* their followers fare much better than those who attempt to *enslave* them. Adolf Hitler, Jim Jones, David Koresh, Bagwan Shree Rajnish and Shoko Asahara all succeeded in transforming their followers into vassals before disaster befell them. Over the last few decades, a rogue's gallery of lesser business, political and religious figures has emulated their behaviours with equally distressing results.

The late fugitive Christopher Skase used his not inconsiderable charisma quotient to build an empire, only to have it collapse into a heap of human misery. Junk bond king Michael Milken employed his charismatic talents to build up a covey of disciples who reportedly would have jumped off a cliff for him. They followed their leader's instructions devotedly and leapt into financial ruin. Had there been no locks on the gates, a few of them may have followed him into gaol.

Ethical charismatic leaders are notable for talking up their audiences and followers. They demonstrate abilities to inspire people to extraordinary effort by expressing a belief in the capacity of their followers to realise personal potential. They seek to empower their followers by furnishing them with ideas and opportunities for personal and vocational success. This contrasts with other so-called gurus, cult leaders and fundamentalists of all hues who demand compliance with rigid behavioural formulas that undermine choice and link self-worth to their whims and opinions.

Trust is a major component of charismatic communication. A real test of charisma and influence is whether people will continue to follow charismatic leaders or speakers when they commit a major blunder or demonstrate human weakness. If Stephen made a major blunder his execution would be swift, but if Sandra committed one, chances are she would have enough charisma credits in the bank to cover the inevitable withdrawal.

Bill Clinton's notorious sexual exploits had little effect on his popularity because his charisma balance was well in the black. The Republicans backed down from an all-out offensive against Clinton because of fear that their campaign would bolster support for him. Clinton left the presidency as one of the most popular presidents of all time. While Clinton may well have had the sexual acumen of a gerbil, history will probably recall that his policies, speeches and personal interventions were informed by a strong identification with Middle America and empathy for the victims and vanquished of American society.

One of the reasons why the Sandras, and indeed the Clintons, of this world wield so much influence and enjoy such high levels of support is that they have built their identity around principles of empowerment and inclusion. They have also learned that self-presentation in its various forms is the art of aligning information about themselves, their vision and their views about the world with the reasonable expectations of target individuals and groups. There appear to be six key factors that govern whether the shelf lives of charismatic communicators will be long or short, and whether they and their followers will triumph or collapse into a mass of recrimination and ruin:

1. Power. Is it exercised to enable or disable?
2. Personal vision. Is it responsive to or dismissive of the interests of followers?
3. Communication. Is it two-way or one-way?
4. Stimulation. Does it empower or enslave?
5. Goals. Do they help people realise personal ambition or are they designed to fulfil the leader's ambitions?
6. Ethics. Do they support fairness, integrity and taking risks for the greater good, or do they serve the self-interests of the leader?

These six factors can be constant reminders that charismatic communication requires more than smoke, mirrors and the gift of the gab. They demand you give yourself a few moral lessons, not for the sake of upholding dogma or things your mother taught you, but for self-preservation, the preservation of others and the sheer worthiness, practicality and usefulness of an ethical approach.

It's useful, for example, to build your identity on values of keeping your word, honesty, empathy, prudence, self-awareness and good ethics, not because you'll go to hell if you don't, but because people follow those who personify such values and invest trust in them over long periods of time. It's also useful to incorporate into your vision the hopes, dreams and aspirations of those you are seeking to persuade, to offer opportunities for them to develop, and to pay attention to collective interests over self-interest. You embrace those values and behaviours not necessarily because of the number of heavenly credits you can earn by doing so, but because they deliver loyalty, support and better mutual outcomes. In Sandra's words, if you invite others to 'come on board and share the spoils' long-term success may well be your reward.

The models and techniques described in this book are extremely potent and can, if used inappropriately, severely affect the professional and personal relationships you have established and may form. Like most communication techniques they are in themselves neutral. In the minds and mouths of people, they can produce an index of outcomes from highly rewarding to positively ruinous. You can 'use' the methods you'll learn to manipulate those around you into doing things they wouldn't ordinarily do, if you want. You can seek to shaft others with technique, but be aware you'll probably only do this for a time before you and your reputation, and maybe other people, begin to suffer.

YOUR 'IT' QUOTIENT

Having embraced the simple but powerful precepts above, it's time for you to assess how much of 'it' you have right now. Do the following quiz rapidly by allowing the answers to come to you without too much conscious thought and evaluation. You may agree with both answers, but one will undoubtedly have a little more meaning for you, so note the option that most (more than 51 per cent) describes the person you are. Do the quiz rapidly.

1. I AM CONCERNED MOST ABOUT:
(a) what is happening right now and how it should be managed
(b) future events and issues that may have to be addressed

2. I CONSIDER MYSELF:
(a) a global person who prefers mostly to think about the Big Picture
(b) a specifics person who likes to think about detail and process

3. I FIND IT:
(a) very easy to step into people's shoes and understand what it feels like to be them
(b) sometimes tiresome and quite difficult to imagine what others are feeling and thinking

4. GENERALLY, I SPEND SOME OF MY TIME:
(a) analysing past mistakes and missed opportunities
(b) focusing on what has been achieved

5. I AM MORE INTERESTED IN:
(a) preserving and extolling the virtues and values that have made us what we are
(b) inventing new practices and conventions that reflect today's environment

6. I BELIEVE:
(a) that complex ideas require detailed explanation in order not to trivialise them
(b) it's entirely possible to condense complex ideas into simple yet powerful models

7. THE BEST WAY TO CONVINCE SOMEONE IS TO:
(a) find their emotional hot buttons and link your message to their needs
(b) use the power of reason and logic to mount a solid argument

8. MY EXPERIENCE TELLS ME THAT:
(a) there are many ways in which high risk can be managed
(b) fools step in where angels fear to tread

9. I AM MOTIVATED BY:
(a) a personal vision supported by deep beliefs and values
(b) my history and culture and the general beliefs and values supporting it

10. I OFTEN QUESTION:
(a) how things can be improved and made even better
(b) why something is being done

11. IN DEBATES AND DISCUSSIONS, I:
(a) link my point of view to what I know are my opponents' ideals and coach the opponents towards my way of thinking
(b) try to blow the opposing argument out of the water by showing its proponents where they are wrong

12. I AM A PERSON WHO:
(a) blows up sometimes but cools down into a holding mood
(b) keeps destructive emotions and impulses pretty well under control

13. I BELIEVE:
(a) a person has to have a very clear sense of who they are and who they want to be
(b) you are who you are and you may as well make the best of it

14. I LEAN TOWARDS THE VIEW THAT:
(a) curiosity killed the cat
(b) you can never be too curious

15. I THINK THIS QUESTIONNAIRE IS:
(a) pathetic
(b) quite intriguing

The answers that more accurately reflect charisma potential are:
1. (b); 2. (a); 3. (a); 4. (a); 5. (b); 6. (b); 7. (a); 8. (a); 9. (a); 10. (b); 11. (a); 12. (b); 13. (a); 14. (b); 15. (b).

If you scored between 0 and 4, you need a fair amount of development work to expand your charisma potential. A score between 5 and 8 indicates that you have developed some good charisma building blocks and now need to move to the next level. A score of 9 to 12 reveals high charisma potential. You are already employing charismatic behaviours and further refining of your behaviours and approaches will yield excellent results. If you scored 12 or above, your charisma potential is exceptional. You are probably thinking and behaving charismatically in many environments and may simply need to hone your abilities further.

FORMS OF CHARISMA

Over the past two decades leadership research based on the idea that leadership and charisma are *perceptual* phenomena has flourished. What this means in everyday language is that charismatic communication and persuasion are ultimately determined by the perceptions of audiences, followers and contemporaries. This may have only just occurred to you and is in stark contrast to the popular misconception that people *have* charisma and influence and strut their stuff like flamingos during the mating season.

Strong evidence supports the theory that charisma and influence are the dividends of specific ways of thinking and behaving. Put another way, distinctive thinking patterns and behaviours are the *means* and charisma and influence are the outcomes, or *ends*, determined by a panel of judges, namely the people who come in contact with a person doing charisma and influence.

This is not to say that people do not award charisma halos to individuals as a result of achievement and/or position in society. Members of royal, presidential and prime ministerial families (and their pets) are often awarded the prize for no greater reason than their position. They may have the behaviours and thinking patterns of cane toads but people, and the media in particular, *attribute* charisma to them.

In some cases there can also be a contagious element to charisma. Perceptions of charisma can sweep through a population like a bad strain of the flu. Princess Diana, for example, represents a classic case of someone being awarded charisma, not because of any particular attributes and behaviours associated with charismatic performance, but perhaps because of an absence of them. A highly privileged, sweet and somewhat intellectually dull kindergarten teacher with severe personality problems and looks no better than average, Diana managed to capture the imagination of the Anglo-Saxon world. The attribution of charisma may have had little to do with Diana and more to do with the people who caught the charisma bug through images manipulated by the mass media.

Contagious charisma such as the Diana epidemic is like an engineered virus that dwells in the minds and hearts of followers. The media, because of its insatiable need for heroes and villains, engineers the virus prototype from the raw materials available and disperses it through the airwaves to often unsuspecting hosts. The virus fulfils the emotional needs, fantasies and dreams of the masses, and a fission-like process occurs creating a charismatic sensation. The contagion model also supports the theory that charisma is a result of perceptual processes in the heads of followers, rather than a mystical state of being.

People can be awarded charisma for doing weird things, such as being first to the top of a particularly high mountain or sailing solo around the world four times. They can take on the mantle of the demonic charismatic by butchering other charismatic figures or committing a series of heinous murders. Achievers, especially in the entertainment, modelling and sporting worlds, are also labelled charismatic because many people attribute a rise to the top of the entertainment pile, a beautiful collagen-inflated face on an emaciated body or the winning of a race to charisma.

In the case of corporate success, there may at times be more reason for attributing charisma. In a 1999 study of over one hundred different empirical tests, researchers concluded that business leaders who demonstrate behavioural charisma have significant and positive effects on their organisations, contemporaries and followers. Other studies show CEOs awarded the charisma prize by followers are more effective than transactional leaders (leaders who trade benefits to get the job done).

The evidence suggests that the phenomenon of charisma can arise from a broad range of circumstances, events, behavioural elements and follower characteristics. Charisma can be attributed to someone if they do or are something special, are in the right place at the right time, are involved in crises, personify the fantasies and dependency needs of the masses through media exposure, participate in real-life dramas, or have a special place in the collective consciousness of followers.

Research also suggests that 'behavioural charisma' (thinking and behaving in ways that match universal charisma prototypes) is as common, or more common, at the present time than other forms of charisma. In the case of charisma you can either be immaculately conceived as a chicken, or grow into one from an egg.

WHO, HOW AND WHO

In your initiation into the art and practice of behavioural charisma, you will encounter ideas, techniques and suggestions on how to work with audiences and contemporaries to create your identity as an influential leader. An important step in doing behavioural charisma is to recognise that there are three crucial areas you need to address when increasing your capabilities as a charismatic communicator. This book is divided into sections that mirror these critical components. They are:

1. the source of the communication (who says it)
2. the nature of the communication (how it is said)
3. the characteristics of the audience (who hears it)

Who says it

Personal credibility is established by such things as prior history, grooming, style of dress, facial expressions, tone of voice, congruence of emotions, expertise, word of mouth and so on. Notice that expertise appears near the end of the list rather than at the beginning.

The evidence shows that people tend to believe people who *appear* to be authoritative and trustworthy. It makes sense to the average person to pay attention to the appearance of speakers because it often represents the only information available on which they can make a judgment. So, if you look and sound the part, you substantially increase the likelihood of being given the part.

Appearances can thus be a deciding factor in establishing your initial credibility. However, looking the part is one thing, being the part is another. To do charisma effectively over time you need to buy into and duplicate the successful thinking patterns, values, beliefs and actions of charismatic role models. There are many books that have been written on appearance, style and grooming, so this section will focus on developing the tonal, structural and identity components of trustworthiness and authority.

How it's said

How something is said is an essential factor in charismatic performance and persuasion. How you structure and deliver your content can in many instances be more important than the content itself.

The form and structure of delivering a message have been shown to outweigh content in numerous studies. In the 1990s, studies of leader rhetoric at the University of Southern California and others strongly suggested that word structure, use of symbols and expression are deciding factors in the extent to which people will become aroused, inspired and committed to a leader's message. Conversely, the literature also shows that weak delivery severely erodes the power of a message, no matter how inspirational or visionary the content may be.

You will learn how to structure and voice your content, and to ethically embed emotion-based messages. You will come to know when emotion is more effective in gaining acceptance of an idea than reason-based or logical approaches.

Charismatic speakers are usually highly skilled rhetoricians who have a fascinating propensity to operate outside the domain of pack rhetoric. You will learn how to rise above the cheap rhetorical devices of political discourse and the carping approaches of single-issue bigots. You will discover more elegant communication methods than assaulting your audience's cochleae by engaging in voice-to-voice combat with your opponents. You will encounter ways to structure and deliver information to achieve the purpose of leading listeners and followers to specific conclusions.

Who hears it

Charismatic communicators recognise that meaning is the outcome of human intercourse. Throughout this book you will encounter ways in which to work with your listeners to create and shape the definitions that lead to meaning. You will realise the value of communicating in 'shared space'. You will begin to appreciate that relevance to the experience, values, needs, fears, hopes and aspirations of your audiences, followers or subordinates is a deciding factor in the persuasion process. You will build up a repertoire of rhetorical devices, behaviours and ways of thinking that enable you to enter the reality of those you wish to impress or convince.

Charismatic behaviours can elevate levels of self-esteem in an audience. Isn't this what you describe as morale? You can probably recall instances where you have left a particularly rousing and magical meeting or speech feeling better about the world, your future and yourself, can't you?

You will encounter techniques designed to make your content directly relevant to each individual member of an audience. Many speakers demonstrate by their performances a belief that the new and novel can simply be dumped on an audience without any need to connect content to what people know, understand or need. You will learn how to make your rhetoric more acceptable and persuasive when talking about change.

The three themes above are mutually dependent and intersect in many parts of this book. They are an inseparable trio. Overlook one and your efforts may fail, but integrate the trio into your daily communications and watch your star rise towards the heavens!

1 WHO SAYS IT

SELF-DESIGN AND PREPARATION

1 MANAGING IMPRESSIONS

You never have more than one opportunity to manage
a first impression.

Please look at the following candidates and ask yourself whom you would
invite as the final guest to make up an intimate dinner party of six.
Consider the options and allow yourself to distinguish what feelings and
attitudes you have about each of the categories of person. Choose one of
the options below, and know to some extent why you made the choice:

- a very funny woman with a reputation for being a great raconteur
- a respected actress who is a celebrity
- a blond television star with a hit series
- a female author of a recent bestseller
- a left-wing feminist with strong views on social engineering
- a lesbian

Would it surprise you to know that all of the labels above refer to the
same person, Ellen DeGeneris? You can see that each label highlights
different aspects of DeGeneris and allows you to form a particular
impression of her. Certain thoughts and emotions were triggered in you
when you looked at each category and helped you make your choice. Each
category exists as a statement that is true in its limited way, but it
depreciates and omits other attributes that would give you a broader and
perhaps truer impression of DeGeneris as a person.

We label and judge people we meet within a timeframe of ten seconds
to four minutes. It works something like this. You meet someone, and in a
matter of milliseconds you begin to experience a surge of information
from the encounter. You can't process all the data consciously, so you rely

on mental categories you've developed over time. Those categories, or pigeonholes, can be positive, negative or sometimes ambiguous when you feel unsure about the person you've met. The feelings you have about the person are quite arbitrary and can be unfair.

We engage in this form of categorisation with varying degrees of partiality and prejudice. No one can truly categorise another human being accurately. Categorisation by those who meet us will depend on a huge number of variables: preferences, biases, generalisations, personal history, memories, attitudes and states of mind, to name a few.

If you didn't use categorisation as mental shorthand, you couldn't exist as an organised and social being. Without the aid of mental categories as the normal basis for pre-judgment of people, objects and events, you would spend much of your time paralysed by the sheer intensity and volume of information you would need to process. You have a natural predisposition to pigeonholing, so you may as well understand it, get used to it and work with the opportunities it presents.

When we pigeonhole a person, thing or situation, we highlight some attributes, play down other attributes and discard attributes that don't conform to the way our mental categories permit us to look at the world. Every description of every person, thing or situation is a result of the highlighting, downplaying and discarding of information. Take a few prototypes for a spin and you'll soon begin to realise how they influence your judgment.

You can undoubtedly recall instances where you have met someone and, within seconds, chose not to want to know him or her. What was it about them that left you uninterested and unavailable? Perhaps you experienced a hint of aversion or dislike? Conceivably, you never engaged in a rational and conscious assessment of them as a person. There was something about them that didn't quite add up, wasn't there? Whatever it was, it was enough for you to dismiss any notion of getting to know and understand them. What happened? The answer is that the person you rejected didn't comply with some category or pigeonhole buried deep in your unconscious mind.

Occasionally when we meet people something about them reminds us of someone else or an experience from our past. A particular facial or physical expression, vocal nuance or tone of voice can trigger immediate aversion or attraction responses. Even handshakes can trigger instant impressions and judgment. Think about your personal categories for handshakes. What impressions and judgments do you sense yourself making about people with limp handshakes? How do you automatically respond when someone reaches out, palm-down, and invites you to shake their hand in the submissive palm-up position? Have you ever twisted their hand back into the normal position and noticed a flicker of re-evaluation in their eyes?

Now, think of a time when you were introduced to someone you instantly 'clicked' with. Go back to your memory of that occasion and begin to notice how you clicked with them. What was it about them that pressed your buttons? What did you say about them after the meeting? You may have attributed certain qualities to them: warm, friendly, interesting, honest, open. How did you come to those impressions, and did you really have the opportunity and time to make such a detailed assessment? It's more likely, isn't it, that the person conformed to a ready-made category or pigeonhole in your mind and the 'click' occurred when a match was automatically made?

A fascinating side issue of our tendency to match people against categories and form instant impressions is that people customarily attribute their conclusions and subsequent behaviours to conscious mental processing. Although it may typically appear as if we are engaging in the conscious management of our responses and behaviours, the reality more than often is the opposite. Many of the actions we take in social settings are believed to reflect the inaccessible and often unfathomable workings of the unconscious mind. We may attribute our impressions and responses to conscious thought, but routinely they are simple justifications after the fact.

Knowing that people will pigeonhole you is a useful piece of information to possess and presents a number of opportunities. What do you think they could be? American researchers Lord and Maher offer some fascinating insights into the pigeonholing process as it applies to leadership. They modelled the cognitive maps (pigeonholes) people use in categorising individuals as leaders or followers. Called the Recognition Model, it identifies general preconceived ideas we have about the qualities that make people leaders. We rate intelligence, honesty, integrity, uniqueness, generosity and 'presence' as key features in desirable leaders.

The research suggests that there are widely shared prototypes on the qualities that constitute leadership. Individuals who 'fit' universal categories or pigeonholes, who look and sound the part in a particular culture, will be more readily embraced by audiences than those who don't. In practical terms what this means is that if you want people to take notice of what you say, you have to project an image that meets as closely as possible the expectations of your audience.

As the DeGeneris example demonstrates, you may have to highlight some attributes, downplay others, and discard characteristics that are not in alignment with shared prototypes. This will allow you to be seen in a particular light and will enhance your power to persuade. Appreciating the importance of categories and conforming to people's expectations is a fundamental trait of charismatic communicators.

LOOKING THE PART

When people encounter you as a leader, speaker, or media spokesperson for the first time, they will rapidly scrutinise your looks and appearance and form an impression in seconds. They will scan your face and eyes first, make a judgment and move on to your body. This quick appraisal is usually followed by attention to your clothing and manner of dress, on which further assessments are made. They will then tune in to your voice and notice your vocal quality and tone. If you fit their categories and you're given the thumbs up, they may then choose to listen to what you're actually saying.

The first step in impression management is to look the part by matching shared expectations of what someone in your position and speaking context should look like. Context is an all-important factor in making decisions about appearance. For example, if you were speaking to a group of neo-hippies at a Centrelink seminar on vocational training, you would be ill advised to turn up in an Armani suit, perfectly matching accessories and a dazzling gold Rolex. You would have a better chance of getting heard by resurrecting an old T-shirt, slipping on a well-worn pair of jeans and fatiguing your hundred-dollar hairstyle. Similarly, if you were talking to an assembly of Victorian wool growers on their turf about growing more fine wool, you might want to acquire a pair of R M Williams boots and speak as slowly as they do.

On most occasions, however, the business wardrobe creates positive impressions of respectability and trustworthiness. Researchers in the United States put this proposition to the test and found that people are much more likely to trust a person wearing the business uniform than a person wearing casual garb. They placed a clean-cut 30-year-old man wearing the classic business uniform at a busy Texas intersection and instructed him to walk against the traffic lights. Then, they dressed him in slacks and a blazer and told him to perform the same task.

Guess what? The researchers found that three and a half times as many pedestrians followed the suited subject into this law-breaking foray than followed the casually dressed subject. The right uniform in the right place convinced people to place their trust in a total stranger to the extent of risking prosecution.

Written advice on grooming and corporate style is extensive and comprehensive. The books are easy to find in libraries and bookshop chains. So, rather than wasting your time reinventing the wheel, you will concentrate on other significant areas of impression management that have either been underplayed or continue to require attention and reinforcement.

Body

We live in a highly body-conscious society. Studies have shown that, at some level, people view the bodies of those they encounter as external representations of internal 'substance'. Category bias (discrimination) plays a large part in the impressions people form. Obesity, spare tyres and beer bellies are often viewed as signs of weakness or a lack of self-control, and sometimes as a signal of avarice. Fat politicians with leadership aspirations, for example, fight constant battles to keep their waistline below the circumference of a football field because they know that voters will make unconscious assessments involving body management and managing the country.

While we can't escape the body blueprint in our genes, we can make the best of our appearance. We may be offended when people form impressions and make judgments on how we maintain our bodies, but the fact remains that people generally view our physical appearance as a metaphor for our personality and character.

Research shows that good-looking people have many social advantages unavailable to those of lesser looks. If anything, the impact of looks has been underestimated in the past. People tend to display a positive reaction to good looks, which transfers into favourable perceptions about the people who have them. Goodish looking people have been found more able to change attitudes and get what they want from others. Generally, they're seen to be more kind, talented, honest and smart.

Even good-looking criminals get off lightly. In a study conducted in Pennsylvania in the United States, researchers used a standard rating process to evaluate the physical attractiveness of seventy-four accused males at the beginning of their court cases. At the end of the trials, sentences were reviewed and it was found that better looking defendants got significantly lighter sentences. Moreover, better looking criminals were more than twice as likely to avoid a jail sentence than those who were rated as not good-looking.

Should we all give up now and leave the beautiful people to walk the catwalk of public life? Of course not! You don't have to be good-looking to look good as a total package. The imbalance can be addressed by developing other attributes, much as blind people compensate with enhanced senses of smell, touch and hearing. The lesson is that not-so-good-looking people have to overcome any physical setbacks with qualities such as healthiness, integrity, originality, consistency, generosity, and better and more elegant persuasion techniques.

THE SAMENESS PRINCIPLE

You may wonder if there are broader applications of the tendency of people to award status on the basis of fitting particular pigeonholes. You are now about to discover a powerful factor that can lead to group bonding, often for the most unimportant and trivial of reasons.

One secret of group motivation may lie in a phenomenon that causes individuals from diverse backgrounds and typology to act in concert as a group on the flimsiest of pretexts, even when they don't know each other. The sameness principle dictates that even superficial similarities can have the effect of motivating individuals to act like groups: to support individuals who appear to be of the same ilk, to defend the group from external pressures and to embrace its symbols, rituals and beliefs.

The lesson is that if you can get people to form an impression of even insignificant sameness, they will build a bond on that tenuous link. They will do what a group does: seeing itself as special, reinforcing the self-esteem of its members, exaggerating its differences with other groups, reserving special generosity for bona fide members, seeking to gain privileges and status for the group and creating competitors or (unfortunately) enemies of outsiders.

You see, hear and experience group behaviour in most areas of your life. In the workplace, for example, superficial similarities give rise to various forms of group expression. Management versus workers, technicians versus the technically naïve, young Turks versus old farts, all are examples of behaviour being driven by a sense of superficial sameness with others. Look around at the personal fiefdoms in any organisation and notice how people can be drawn into supporting specific agendas and goals by virtue of some superficial affinity. Observe how the goals of particular fiefdoms may often be contrary to the broader objectives of the organisation. Pay attention to overt or implied demands on group members to authenticate their membership of the group to maintain group unity.

Authentication often requires members of groups to make personal sacrifices and embrace 'approved' values and attitudes in place of individual freedoms. Notice also how other fiefdoms are identified as competitors, and superficial differences are consciously or unconsciously exploited to manipulate highly negative impressions of 'outsiders'. If you've ever been banished from a cherished group (family, peer, social or otherwise) as a punishment, you will readily identify with the agony of not belonging. Make no mistake, if you really want to belong to a group you'll discover yourself taking on its beliefs and values over time. If you don't, then exile, invisibility or marginalisation will be your punishment.

The office politico instinctively recognises the sameness phenomenon. Appeals such as 'We women/men have to stick together', 'We have to keep an eye out for the old guard or they will stifle us', 'They [management] will try and pick us off one by one', 'Our journalistic independence is under attack', 'Production is being sacrificed to save the sales department' and the like can be powerful influencing tools in the hands of today's impression manipulators.

Such appeals to superficial sameness are no different from appeals to sameness on the national and international stages by alleged statesmen and stateswomen. How is it that an Albanian and a Serbian can live together for a lifetime as neighbours, sharing fundamental and important similarities, and be called to battle by the cynical exploitation of superficial differences in religious heritage and received history? Sameness is often used as an influencing tool to motivate the 'troops' against perceived or imaginary threats from illusory outsiders. Often perpetrators will build their power base on it.

But, can we employ the sameness principle with integrity and for mutual rewards? A clue that may help us in our quest is that behaviour is informed, or driven, by people's values, beliefs and attitudes. The values, beliefs and attitudes people embrace are often associated with specific words or descriptions. These words connect the value to its expression and form an emotional trigger. If individuals are motivated by superficial samenesses, such as nationality, religion, race or voting preferences, that are cynically linked to the important human need to belong, can we find other more fundamental and high-level similarities and align them to outcomes that benefit all members of an audience, group or team?

Sameness as a mental skill

If a majority of people are motivated by sameness in the context of group behaviour, then does it not make sense to elicit sameness from, and reflect it to, a group of unique individuals brought together as an audience or team? Knowing as you do how shared values and beliefs represent the highest order of sameness, would high-order sameness not neutralise the more cynical and self-serving appeals to low-order sameness?

When you begin to elicit high-order sameness you make an amazing discovery and it is this: people from most walks of life are fragmented by low-order sameness but united by high-order sameness. The truly incredible revelation you will experience is that the highest ideals, beliefs and principles of the majority of people are shared. Conflict is often brought about by the way people go about realising their highest intentions, not the highest intentions themselves.

Often, we define the success of a team or group by the absence of conflict and the achievement of mutual outcomes. If opposing groups of people were to undergo a process of discovering common high-order sameness—in place of individual and group 'demands' (and more than often superficial sameness)—wouldn't that enable a relationship to be built around common values and criteria? If differences were put aside in favour of discovering high-order similarity, wouldn't you have a basis for cooperation, discussion and group solidarity?

Building support around shared high-order sameness can give your ideas a durability and purpose that transcend the shaky alliances of ideas built on superficial sameness, the personality of the leader, personal authority and the like. If you examine highly successful movements of opinion you can, among other things, notice the following:

■ strong expressions of solidarity
■ consistent focus on 'common bonds' (shared values)
■ shared values that reinforce and generally do not bear down on the values of individuals
■ rewards based on, or linked to, shared values
■ an emphasis on supporting the 'relationships' between other groups
■ respect of individual needs and differences
■ a commitment to agreed processes
■ clearly established outcomes or goals which have been 'filtered' through the group's high-order value system

Ask yourself this question. Which of the above are not dependent somewhat on shared high-order sameness? None?

Understanding the abstract of high-order sameness is one thing. Putting it into practice is another. So, how *do* you do high-order sameness? A good way of learning how to do it is to take a deeper look at conflict. Conflict is what undoes solidarity and unity of purpose. Behind any disagreement, struggle or difference is a likely conflict of the *expression* of beliefs or values.

Often, the expression of a conflict leads people astray. This is an extremely important factor to understand and utilise in public-speaking contexts. The television, newspapers and radio are full of people getting side-tracked by trivia. There is a fair amount of evidence suggesting that in the phoney wars of political and social debate there is often a deliberate attempt to bog debates down in the trivial expression of so-called differences.

So, how can you overcome the negative effects of trivial sameness and difference and introduce high-order sameness? Below is a case study that deals with a conflict between two people. The same principles can apply to group and 'tribal' conflicts. Review the dialogue and follow the counsellor's techniques as he goes beyond the *stated* disagreement to unearth high-order sameness. Notice how he deals with the superficial differences fuelling the conflict.

Radio presenter (RP): I'm sick to death of X. I feel I'm working with a Nazi. Every time I want to do talkback he says no.

Counsellor (CR): If he said yes, what would that deliver to you?

RP: Well, we'd be able to let our listeners know that ...

CR: Sorry, but I was asking what *you* would get from that if he said yes.

[Notice how the questioner quickly redirects the content away from behaviour and justification and towards the intent of the complaint.]

RP: What would I get? I'd feel as though my ideas were at least being taken seriously for once.

CR: And if you felt your ideas were being taken seriously ... err, what purpose would that serve for you?

RP: Me? Well, I'd kinda feel as though I was making a contribution.

CR: Why is it important to you to feel you are making a contribution?

RP: I suppose I'd think I was making a contribution and was valued.

CR: So being *valued* for what you have to offer is important to you?

[Here, the questioner picks up on a high-order hot button, the word 'valued'. Notice that the exact word is used and not a variation of it, like 'valuing' or 'being valuable'.]

RP: Yes, it is, and isn't it the same with everyone?

CR: So it is. If you got to feel as though you were being valued, then however we achieve that for you is OK, isn't it?

[Note that the counsellor separates the behaviour (doing talkback) from the real intent behind the complaint (not feeling valued). Then, to avoid getting back into the 'metaphor' the complainant uses to press the complaint, the counsellor presupposes there are many ways of being valued. At this stage of the process, the questioner invited the program producer in to agree to some concrete things that would enable the presenter to feel valued.]

If you read the transcript carefully you will observe something interesting going on during the latter parts of the exchange. The counsellor elicits the highest order of criteria and begins to move away from solving the 'expression' of the conflict. He seems to be aiming for something bigger than a simple solution to a workplace spat, doesn't he?

What the counsellor was aiming for was a set of tools to help build a *relationship* between the warring parties. The surface expression of the conflict, the spat over talkback, is placed on the back burner and attention is directed towards the things *that have to be present* in order for the presenter to work cooperatively with the producer in making a radio program.

In this particular case, the counsellor made an assumption that 'being valued' would also be part of the producer's values/criteria, and later on verified the assumption by eliciting the producer's values. Being valued became one of the basic principles the presenter and producer operated from. It caused a major shift in the behaviours of both and became a building block of their professional relationship, as you will discover when you read the second part of the transcript.

If the counsellor had allowed himself to be sidetracked by the surface expression of the conflict, a solution may have been found, but it would have been quite specific to the isolated incident. The source of the disagreement, an unfulfilled value, would have remained intact. It's a sure bet that it would have 'informed' other such surface incidents in the future. Instead, the counsellor concentrated on helping the parties find common ground on which to build a better professional relationship.

The same dynamics apply to groups and, indeed, nations. If you can gain agreement on high-order beliefs, values and attitudes, or link your content to high-order sameness you can avoid many of the disruptions, objections and distractions that eat into the power of your message. You can walk along the same path as your audience and guide them towards an appreciation or acceptance of your content. The question to ask yourself is what the key values are that have to be present for you to develop a relationship with this person, group or audience.

DOING FLEXIBILITY

The mental skill that will allow you to elicit and reflect high-order sameness easily and effortlessly is called abstract/concrete flexibility. To understand how it works, let's now review the second part of the conversation between the counsellor and radio production team. You will recall that the counsellor sought to separate the surface expression of the conflict from the unfulfilled value that fanned the flames of disharmony. He recognised that harmony and agreement could best be achieved by discovering a shared value and building a relationship around it.

In the second part of the discussion, the counsellor invites both producer and presenter to have a conversation about the issues raised. He steps down the levels of abstraction until he arrives at the concrete level.

Counsellor (CR): Isn't it good when you find yourselves agreeing on the principles that count? *(Radio presenter and producer nod affirmatively.)*

CR: And I'm wondering how pleased you would be if you found yourselves agreeing on some of the things you could do to make sure that you were both being valued. What could they be, do you think?

Producer (P): I guess we could hear each other out and talk about things.

Radio presenter (RP): Hmmm ... well, as long as my contributions were taken seriously.

CR: Yeah, that's important because we agree, don't we, that being taken seriously means being valued? *(RP and P nod affirmatively.)*

CR: So, when you're hearing each other out and tossing ideas around, it would be a good thing if you used the initial idea as a starting point and then worked on making the idea good for the program, wouldn't it?

RP: So we could sort of workshop it and talk about making it work? Yeah, I would be into that.

P: But what if we disagreed? Who would decide?

CR: I'm thinking that you already agree on some principles, one of which is taking each other's ideas seriously, and you can probably imagine that being valued will guide how you work with each other, can't you? You will either know a valuable idea when you hear one, or workshop it to the point of being able to make a fair decision, right?

(RP and P nod affirmatively and RP says 'Yeah'.)

CR: So, how specifically can you make sure you are both being valued when you take an idea as a starting point, ask questions and workshop it?

P: Well, we can ask ourselves how it could work and sorta ask questions that could, umm, you know, two heads are better than one.

RP: I see what you're getting at. *(Looking at counsellor)* You're saying that we should use questions instead of arguing the toss, you mean?

CR: Would that be a way of being valued and building better ideas that can work for you both? You can see yourselves doing that, can't you? And as you look back to making that decision you may be thinking to yourselves that it was one of the best decisions you made, huh?

(RP and P laugh and nod affirmatively.)

What was happening in the conversation? Did you notice how it started at the abstract level of being valued? Then, the counsellor asks a question that steps the issue down from abstract to concrete. The first attempt evokes the old complaint of not being taken seriously, so the counsellor steps back up to the abstract layer and gains agreement again.

The next question steps down to behaviours and gains the assent of the presenter but the demurral of the producer, so he steps back up to the abstract of being valued, gaining the assent of both. You will notice that at this point the technique has resulted in the presenter and producer agreeing with each other on three occasions in a short space of time. The counsellor steps down again into specifics and slips in a concrete suggestion of asking questions. He gains the agreement of both, and for the first time in the discussion laughter erupts. Now, that's a good sign, isn't it?

In the first part of the case study you observed that the conflict was ostensibly located in the concrete realm of thought. Behaviours belong to the concrete realm, and as long as issues remain at the behavioural level they are not only very difficult to solve but can bog people down in unnecessary argument about detail. The Irish and Middle East conflicts are good examples of conflict being kept at the behavioural or surface level. A common thread that runs through the histories of both conflicts is the flawed notion of having to agree on everything before they agree on anything.

What the counsellor did was step up the discussion through the levels of abstraction until he had reached a universal principle, that of being valued. Who, apart from the most heartless of autocrats, would disagree that being valued is a worthy principle? Once having gained agreement at the values or conceptual level, the counsellor began to test the waters with concrete suggestions. Each time the discussion was in danger of derailing, the counsellor leapt back into the abstract realm and repeated the key values word to gain agreement until, finally, there was enough agreement and embedded ideas for the participants to give concrete expression to their pact.

Charismatic communicators constantly step up, down and sideways to gain agreement of listeners and audiences when they make presentations, deliver speeches and address gatherings. Value-eliciting questions, such as those posed in our case study, are asked to uncover the highest level of values. Abstract flexibility is used to the fullest extent to settle the values issue first before the concrete matters are thrashed out.

Concrete/abstract flexibility is absolutely fundamental to thinking and behaving charismatically. It allows the speaker to find the exact communication register or language level required to get a message across. In fact, it's inconceivable that an individual would be able to reach the levels of intellectual acuity and eloquence required for charismatic communication without having concrete/abstract flexibility.

Please read the following speech by President Clinton which demonstrates concrete/abstract flexibility in action. The initials SU (step up) and SD (step down) are used to denote where on the concrete/abstract ladder Clinton was heading. See if you can identify the phrases he uses to step down, and recognise when he steps up and links actions or behaviours to an abstract principle or idea:

[SD to SU] Six months ago, I convened a presidential conference on welfare at the Blair House. Democrats and Republicans from the Congress to the State houses came to Washington to forge a bipartisan agreement on welfare.

[SU] At the conference we agreed on the need for child support to be a part of any welfare reform legislation. Now, the bill passed in the House and the legislation in the Senate includes comprehensive child support reform.

[SD] Since the conference, we have agreed to drop any inclusion of orphanages in welfare reform. Since the conference, we have agreed to require teen moms to live at home and stay in school as a condition to receiving welfare. Since the conference, we have agreed that all recipients must sign a work contract as a condition upon receiving benefits.

[SU] In addition to the progress we have made on a bipartisan basis of what welfare reform legislation must include, I have signed a sweeping Executive order concerning child support collection from delinquent parents. My administration is collecting a record amount of child support, making responsibility a way of life, not an option.

[SD] This year alone I have approved a dozen welfare reform experiments. The experiments have included new proposals, among them: requiring people to work for their benefits, requiring teen moms to stay at home and in school, requiring welfare recipients to be held to a time limit, requiring delinquent parents to pay child support, and requiring people on welfare to sign a contract which would hold them accountable to finding a job. The State experiments now total 32 States reaching 7 million individuals.

[SU] It is time to put partisanship and politics aside and to get the job done. The American people deserve real welfare reform and have been kept waiting long enough. We need a bipartisan bill that ends welfare and replaces it with work. I hope the Senate will place welfare at the top of its agenda in September and take swift action.

[SD to SU] While Congress continues to debate welfare, I will proceed with the far-reaching welfare reforms I initiated with the States over the last 2 years. We will continue to move people from welfare to work. We will continue to require teen moms to stay in school and live at home as a condition of their benefits. I call on this Congress to join me in a bipartisan endeavour, with politics aside and the national interest at the centre of our efforts.

You may notice that Clinton engages in some very deft rhetorical footwork, easily and effortlessly gliding up and down the abstract/concrete scale. Notice how he links concrete actions to high-order principles that clearly reflect the aspirations or, indeed, the concerns of Middle America. He finds just the right pitch between concrete and abstract, and connects concrete events (such as 'collecting child support from delinquent parents') with high-order principles (as in 'making *responsibility* [value] a way of life, not an option').

In the following diagram you can see that values and beliefs inhabit the conceptual or abstract layer of consciousness, whereas the concrete layer deals with actions, subjects, objects and thoughts of actions, subjects and objects. The list of questions on the left will allow you to step up into the abstract. The list on the right will step you down into specifics.

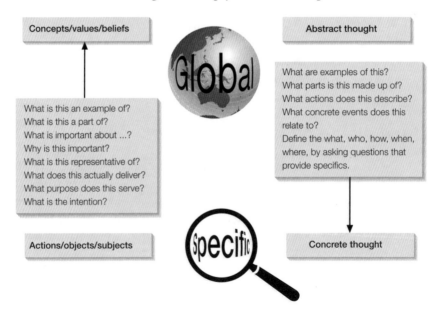

Concrete/abstract flexibility is mastered by learning to step up and down tactically. It requires a little practice before you find yourself using this invaluable mental tool in solving conflicts, in eliciting and reflecting values, and developing creative approaches to language. You may marvel at the skill of the counsellor in the case study, but it is well within your grasp. Begin to notice the differences between abstract expression and the world of concrete events and behaviour. Using the two questioning models in the diagram, practise linking concrete actions and events to values by asking questions in the left-hand box. Use the questions in the right-hand box to step down from the abstract into the world of actions and events.

Concrete events are given meaning and power by the associations you make with shared high-level beliefs, aspirations, values, needs, fears, hopes, aversions, attitudes and other universal tenets. The important thing to remember is that it is you who make the connection. It is you who exercise the mental skill of stepping up to find a legitimate and credible connection between concrete events and behaviours and the universal principles that transform them into strong and symbolic messages.

Stepping sideways

Stepping sideways is perhaps the most creative element of concrete/abstract flexibility. It encapsulates what Edward De Bono describes as lateral thinking and explains in part why charismatic leaders are generally found to be highly inventive and resourceful in their relationships with individuals and groups. Stepping sideways is quite similar to stepping down using the 'What are examples of?' question.

You have already noticed the wealth of information you gain when asking the above question, and so hold that thought, as you will revisit it. The questions you ask to step sideways are 'What is this equivalent to?' and 'What examples are similar to this?'. Let's take an example of writing a book. Imagine you are searching for a creative way of writing a chapter. In asking what the equivalent of a chapter is, you can produce the follow-ing answers:

CHAPTER	=	EPISODE, ACT, SEGMENT, SECTION, PERIOD, INSTALMENT, PASSAGE, PIECE, PACKAGE, ARTICLE, SCENE

The wonderful capacity of human beings to engage rapidly in free association opens up a treasure of choice with the blink of an eye. Take any of the equivalents mentioned above and ask yourself how they could help you draft a chapter that cleverly exploits the associations you have made. You could come up with a variety of ideas, such as writing a chapter as a television episode, complete with cliff-hangers and other dramatic devices, or using the package concept and including on-location reports written as though by a witness to an event, and so on.

There is another way of stepping sideways that generates the kind of free associations often notable in good comedians and people regarded as highly creative. It entails stepping up one level, stepping sideways and then stepping down. Let's take the chapter example again and ask a stepping up question such as 'What is a chapter a part of?'. The answer we will choose is that of a book, although you have now discovered that chapters have other interesting equivalents. The next question we ask is a stepping sideways question such as 'What are books equivalent to?' or 'What things are similar to books?'. Notice the number of options generated in the following illustration.

You may have already figured out that stepping up, sideways and down are mental processes that are at the heart of eloquence and persuasion. Some people imagine that eloquence is a characteristic of those who know a lot of words. They see them as walking dictionaries, ever ready to pull out the right words or strings of words as the occasion demands. Eloquence and persuasion, on the contrary, require no more than average vocabularies, because at the heart of eloquence are mental structures around which eloquent speakers form words.

Research shows that the more vividly data and information are expressed, the greater the probability of an audience understanding and embracing them. Where do charismatic leaders find structures to build word pictures around? You guessed it: they discover them by stepping up, down and sideways.

2 GIVING EXPRESSION TO EMOTIONS

It is not that the Englishman can't feel—it is that he is afraid to feel.

E M Forster

There are many myths circulating in Australian public life and tragic examples of misguided vocal image-building abound. Liberal Party scion Peter Costello provides an illuminating case study of an individual who has been persuaded to change his public countenance and voice to reflect misguided perceptions of how high public office bearers should come across. This attempt to take on a new public persona by creating the physical bearing, language and tone of an 'important' personage is tantamount to self-annihilation.

If you do a contrastive analysis of Costello's public performances in the earlier part of his career and those during his later role as treasurer, you will notice a significant difference in his communication and tonal structure. His later performances reveal a more compressed tonal range, less vocal colour, stilted language and changed physical composure. This is particularly noticeable when he pushes his chin closer to his neck, forcing his voice further down his throat. While it produces some throat and chest resonance, the melody of Costello's voice is lost. His tone is emotionless and lacks the colour of a voice guided by its owner's convictions. The effect of this habit is worsened by the seemingly supercilious smile he often wears.

Costello's image in the minds of many Australians is that of a glib, self-important politician who lacks heart. He seems to have suppressed the very tonal and physiognomic qualities that could make the difference between him winning or losing the hearts and minds of the electorate. His manner sometimes appears so repressed and severe that, when looking at him on television, you could be forgiven for wondering whether he was mid-way through the agony of passing a kidney stone.

Costello may well be a decent human being of high integrity but he has made the mistake of many Australian public and private figures, that of effectively cloaking the breadth and depth of his personality. He has devalued the natural and spontaneous expression of emotion and appears to have chosen to contain rather than express himself. Passion is noticeably absent from his public and media performances. He appears to be a walking mask of himself, and as a result has denied the Australian public access to the elements of his personality that would allow many of us to trust and/or like him more.

If Peter Costello permitted himself the luxury of tonal, facial and bodily expression within the reasonable constraints of his position, he might increase his chances of garnering enough personal charisma to lead his party successfully. He may like to consider giving himself permission to express openly in his voice, face and body a range of appropriate emotions, like enthusiasm, concern, empathy, delight, gravity, triumph, compassion, curiosity, humour, approachability, balance and so on.

Peter Costello is far from the worst example of self-containment resulting from misguided advice on how to behave in certain public and private roles. He is simply one of the more visible cases. The self-important doctor with the bedside manner of a demigod; the social climber who is more snobbish than a poverty-stricken peer of the realm; the stuffed-shirt judge who manifests the convictions of an Ayatollah: all are much closer and more comical archetypes of people who assume status-related personae.

An important point to understand is that *all behaviour is communication.* You cannot *not* communicate, even when you are silent. The way you do your public persona speaks volumes. Your handling of your face, voice and body sends a constant stream of information to those who are listening and observing. As much as 95 per cent of the information you send out is processed unconsciously by your audience. People may not consciously deconstruct what they see and hear of you, but they can sense something's amiss, have a feeling about you and come to potentially severe judgments within a short time of meeting you.

People will choose to like and listen to you between the first few seconds and four minutes of the encounter. During that initial contact, physiognomy, tonality and the structure of your message account for over 90 per cent of the internal assessment they make of you. So, if you have constructed an idealised, albeit misguided, image of yourself, and in so doing have contained some of the more natural and appealing elements of your personality, your audience will register it and may not like what it sees and hears. In a way, the contents of your message will be greeted with the contempt and disapproval they deserve.

Charismatic communicators are acutely aware of the pitfalls of falsely projecting status tonality and physiology. They have come to recognise, as you can, that status, credibility, authority or any other value you care to mention is contained in the structure and content of their speeches and presentations. They know that the job of delivery is simply to give body, life and voice to the structure and content they have created.

THE MODERN VACUUM-PACKED PERSONALITY

Your body movements; the way you use your eyes and face; your changing skin tone; your physical posture; your voice tonality, pace and pitch; and even your level and positioning of breath give clues to other people about who and what you are. In our distant evolutionary past, the accurate sending and receiving of those clues could mean the difference between grunts of approval and acceptance, or assault and battery with a crude weapon.

Today, we invest a large part of our early lives learning how not to show what we're thinking, perfecting how not to reveal our feelings and practising how not to be read or understood by others. We learn to manage the impressions others have of us during an uncompromising indoctrination into polite society in our formative years. We create public and often private facades to hide behind, to put people off the scent. We have been conditioned to send out false cues, to project as someone other than who we really are. As our culture has allegedly become more sophisticated, it seems that one of the greatest fears to emerge is that of being discovered to be completely and wondrously human.

We have developed a range of defences to prevent people from dis-covering that we are as human as the next person. We are taught to devalue the honest expression of our emotions. We learn, usually in collusion with significant others such as parents and teachers, to suppress spontaneous reactions and expressions of true sentiment. By the time we reach our mid-twenties, many of us have become so good at self-containment that even those closest to us rarely get a glimpse of our true selves. The tyranny of compliance and socialisation exact a high price.

So, when we do containment, what does it look and sound like to others? Most self-containment acts are very amateurish indeed. To excel at self-containment you need to focus on two things simultaneously: hiding your feelings, opinions and responses, and creating a credible mask to replace them. It's very difficult to think and hit the ball at the same time, and most of us simply don't have the expertise and flexibility to do that. The best we can usually come up with is some neutral or dissociated state that can at times be interpreted as even-tempered. With time and practice it can come to represent our so-called nature, and at worst we may mirror the disposition and energy of that deliberately expressionless comedian, Elliot Goblett. How come we laugh at him when so many of us are like him?

Even temperament is a favoured disguise in our culture. The carefully modulated voice, the narrow tonal range, controlled facial mask, purposeful and limited body movement, and neutral postures are occasionally interpreted as signs of stability and emotional control. But, do those so-called qualities win hearts and minds, build corporate cultures, convince people to support your ideas or stop an ugly development from blighting your suburb? For that you need to give voice, body and passion to your convictions.

RENOVATING YOUR PUBLIC PERSONALITY

Your ability to express a range of emotions, your capacity to let energy flow and your ability to let your voice and body mirror the 'emotional fingerprint' of your content is an extremely important part of charisma and influence. In public speaking, if you deny people access to legitimate emotion associated with your sentiments, you may send them tonal and physiological signals that undermine or neutralise your content.

In some studies conducted on the range of emotions that respondents consistently found themselves experiencing, it was discovered that the majority went through life aware of four or five enduring states. Such was the success of their personal self-containment strategies that the respondents had repudiated or forgotten literally hundreds of other states of mind available to them.

A thought that may not have occurred to you until now is that the greater number of emotional states you can access, the more flexibility you will have in dealing with life's daily challenges. It follows that the more flexibility you have, the greater number of behavioural options you will have available to you. The more options you have, the better your chances of being able to control and influence your environment.

Take an average family of young children and adults and notice who's really in control of their environment. Seemingly the adults, but we all know it's the youngest child. Young children, thank goodness, generally haven't learned to deny themselves permission to express their message fully. Normal children have the widest range of behaviours and personal flexibility of any demographic category. They just do emotion and behaviour, and they do it with purpose and passion, much to our delight and, occasionally, chagrin. When younger children do behaviour, notice how their body movements, tones of voice, energy levels and facial and eye expressions are in total harmony. Sadly, they have something that we once had before we learned how to contain ourselves.

Of course, you need to monitor yourself in a variety of situations. It isn't commonsense to give way to your 'inner child' during a company function and throw food at the guest of honour. You wouldn't go to the funeral of a wealthy benefactor in board shorts and sing 'I'm in the money!' during the service, even if you felt that way. You may even think twice about revealing your unqualified disappointment at your partner returning home with a hairstyle that makes them look like an articulated toilet brush. You can, however, respond and react within the boundaries of commonsense and reasonable behaviour. In choosing to do so, you can congratulate yourself for having taken a major step towards building a more charismatic public profile.

In yielding to the enormous pressures of socialisation, many people seem to have thrown the baby out with the bath water. What you may choose to consider is bringing back the bits of the baby that had the capacity to align its voice, body and heart to the expression of its message. On page 40 is a list of emotional states that represent a small sample of the range of human feelings or states of mind. You may come across one or two that you find yourself continually experiencing and expressing at the expense of a broader range of states synchronous with your sentiments and environment. You may notice you are programmed into a few 'meta' states that seem to rapidly override other emotions just as you begin to feel them.

Make a note of the states of mind you rarely, if ever, experience. Try a few of them out. Go back to a time in your life and notice how surprising and delightful it can be to remember the physical and emotional sensations attached to those states. How did your body 'speak' those emotions? What physical movement and countenance was involved, and how did you voice them? And as you find yourself reviewing your memory of long-gone expressions of emotion, begin to appreciate the fact that all you need to do is get in touch with them to bring them into the present.

When you bring forgotten states of mind into the present, practise them. Think of future issues, ideas and experiences you may encounter, get in touch with the associated emotions and give voice and body to them. Revisiting the honest and legitimate expression of emotion and giving your body and voice the freedom to express it can lead you to greater self-assuredness and competence in public speaking. It can also radiate into other areas of your life and deliver rewards beyond your

EMOTIONAL STATES CHECKLIST

fascination	oneness	joy
eagerness	affection	dynamism
even-temperedness	patience	wellness
graciousness	gladness	jollity
assertiveness	wonderment	amazement
contemplation	calmness	deep relaxation
boldness	confidence	rationality
surprise	triumph	good-heartedness
empathy	friendliness	heightened awareness
warmth	bliss	delight
happiness	exuberance	anticipation
excitement	determination	flexibility
apathy	flirtatiousness	zestfulness
perseverance	protectiveness	anger
pessimism	real curiosity	deep rapport
depression	vigilance	cheerfulness
cheekiness	openness	frustration
fear	anxiety	dread
loathing	sadness	resignation
competitiveness	longing	defensiveness

imagination. As you reveal a truer picture of your broader self, you may begin to find people being drawn to you in a way you haven't experienced before.

EMOTIONAL AEROBICS

If you want to be able to express your emotions easily and congruously you have to practise them. Emotional fitness is not dissimilar to cardiovascular fitness. You need to give your emotions regular workouts until you achieve the desired flexibility and tone. The first thing a non-fit person notices when beginning an aerobics regime is that their body will not necessarily respond to the commands they give it. The same thing applies with the expression of emotions.

When you initially take an aerobics class, endurance becomes a real issue. You may find yourself feeling extremely fatigued and well and truly out of your comfort zone. You may even consider giving up as it all seems too hard, but you know that perseverance will produce the rewards you're seeking and so you continue with the struggle. And it's also OK to struggle with emotional aerobics before you successfully extend the range and intensity of emotions to which you give body and voice.

The warm-up phase of emotional aerobics is important. In physical aerobics, if your muscles are not stretched and warm, you can either do yourself an injury or make the task harder. Warming up your emotions makes the task easier too, and here's what you do.

Verbal stretching is best done with a partner, although it can be done alone with an imaginary partner. It can be a fun family exercise: kids love it and it's an excellent way of releasing family tensions. Pick a partner, stand about a metre away and directly opposite them, and find something to shout about. Choose any emotion that has to be expressed loudly. For sixty seconds both people loudly ejaculate a string of sentences at the other. Don't listen to what the other person says, simply focus on being as loud and noisy as you can. Make sure your statements are not personally directed towards the other individual.

Verbal stretching is a particularly good exercise for people who are afraid to accept attention. Shouting certainly invites that and gives you the experience of giving yourself permission to be at the centre of attention. It also prepares you for the following tape exercise.

Take the list of emotions as your starting point. Consider using a cassette recorder to record your practice sessions. Negative emotions such as sadness and anger are probably the easiest to do, so begin with a selection of positive emotions. Take about half a dozen at a time and select a piece of senseless prose like 'Green onions gaze lazily into sweet dreams of Betty's blancmange'. Say the first emotion into the microphone, so that during playback you can listen specifically for it, and voice the emotion aloud as you recite the senseless prose. Tick off the emotions you can voice easily and try some harder ones. You may find that emotions that require more energy and volume are the most difficult to intone. Pay particular attention to these. Practise them regularly, pushing the envelope a little more each time.

An important thing to remember is that you need to feel the emotion before you express it. You can, during practice sessions, use your imagination to experience a forgotten emotion but, if you try to fake it during a public address, it will sound unconvincing. You've experienced people faking emotional expression so you know what it sounds like and how you react when you encounter such insincerity. Draw on your experiences of real emotion by accessing your memories and prior knowledge.

THE CRADLE OF TONAL EXPRESSION

The tones you use in your voice to express emotion are known as paralinguistic cues. They are significant in that people pay a lot of unconscious attention to them when a mismatch occurs between the words you utter and the tone in which you deliver them. People also listen to them as a kind of guide or map to the way you are really feeling.

The paralinguistic cues that really count in communication are those associated with the expression of important emotions. The essence of congruous verbal communication is to match tone with the 'emotional fingerprint' contained in your content and to do it with the appropriate energy. Every issue, event, encounter, idea, thought and action has an emotion attached to it. In fact, it can be said that everything in the world has an emotional value positioned somewhere along the index represented in the following diagram.

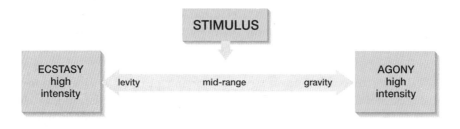

Agony and ecstasy, the two extremes of human emotion, have roughly the same degree of intensity. There is as much power in heart-wrenching grief and some forms of fear and rage as there is in jubilation, exuberance and unbridled joy. As a rule, levity has more energy than gravity. Loudness, pace, pitch and physical expression are more pronounced in levity. When expressing gravity you tend to speak more slowly, more softly, at a lower pitch and with subdued physical expression.

There is a relationship between the intensity of feelings and the emotional distance that separates you from the person, event or object. This is particularly the case with negative emotions like grief, fear, anger and guilt. You may laugh at a report of a British pensioner being maimed by a flying cauliflower, but if it happened to your partner, parent, friend or child it would become a terrible tragedy. The dearer something is to your heart, the more emotion you can permit yourself to release through expression.

The intensity of positive emotions also has a connection to how close or far the subject matter is to you. You may feel as much elation and triumph when an Australian wins at Wimbledon as you do when you win your own game at the local tennis club. Yet, an Australian test cricket win can leave you cold and uninterested if you're not close to cricket.

Distance/closeness is a good general rule of thumb to apply in public speaking, with some exceptions. The exceptions relate to public expectations, and this is where empathy plays a significant role. For instance, if during a question and answer session a member of your audience relates a tragic story, there will be a high audience expectation of an appropriate emotional response to it. You may not know the person or care that her husband left her, her children ran amok and her cat defecated on her bed, but your audience may well expect that you care.

Often speakers seek to hide their apparent discomfort at people revealing their inner secrets by distancing themselves from the emotions the stories evoke. Variations of 'Yes, err, well, we all have our problems in life' and 'Have you tried this solution?' can be heard by people unskilled in the art of empathy. This can have a profound effect on your credibility. If you adopt a detached position to something that is said or happens, your voice will take on evenness in pitch, pace, emphasis and loudness, and your physiology will reflect the neutrality or distance of your emotions, and your audience will probably interpret your response as dispassionate, cold-hearted or emotionally repressed.

The only way to physically and tonally express empathy is to *feel* it. Empathy is not difficult to feel, but you may need to make the choice to feel it. It's one of three basic perceptual positions you can take when confronted by an event, person or thing. Your options are shown in the following diagram.

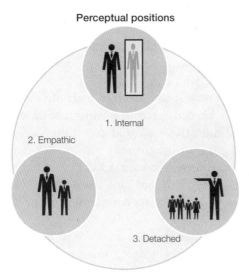

Perceptual positions

Think back to a time when you felt self-conscious in your surroundings. The governing perceptual position of self-consciousness is internal, as shown at position 1 in the diagram. The locus of your attention is directed inward. When doing self-consciousness, you constantly refer to your inner feelings, often hear a clear inner com-mentary and see through your eyes how your body is reacting to the situation. Your voice, body and behaviour will mirror your self-reflection with more intense demonstrations of emotion. In terms of closeness and distance, the internal perceptual position is about as close as you can get.

It's very useful to move in and out of the internal perceptual position to check how you feel, personally, about things. If you are locked into other perceptual positions and rarely visit the internal position, it's extremely difficult to experience a heartfelt attachment to what you're saying. Eschewing perceptual position 1 is the equivalent of depriving your inner being of the right to express itself. This position is the one you choose when you need to articulate how you really feel about things. However, if you spend too much time visiting this perceptual position at the expense of the others, people will begin to observe that you are too irrational and emotional, perhaps a bit of a mush-ball, and maybe too into yourself.

When was the last time you decided to stand back and take a good look at yourself, or gave someone else that instruction? As you stand back and look at your behaviour in particular situations, you enter a detached perceptual position illustrated by position 3. It is characterised by a very low intensity of feeling and expression. The detached state is the favoured state of academia and the scientific method. It makes sense to be able to take a reasonable, logical, so-called objective perceptual position when you're in 'thinking' mode. When you are confronted with crises and need a cool head, when you're hijacked by your emotions or when you need to make some serious decisions, it's a very good idea to stand back and look at the situation, including your part in it.

Tragically, some people spend much of their lifetime stuck in perceptual position 3. They often come across as automatons, unfeeling, too cool-headed and unresponsive to people and events that occur around them. Are you beginning to gain an insight into one of the favoured positions of those who are experts in self-containment? Perceptual position 3 cuts you off from expressing deep feelings. This has a subtle numbing effect over time and impedes your ability to communicate openly and tenderly to people.

The empathic perceptual position is shown in position 2. How regularly do you put yourself in other people's shoes to gain an understanding of how they may feel in a particular situation? We often demand that significant others 'walk a mile in our moccasins' because of our need to be understood and validated. It's natural that very significant others, namely your audience or people you need to persuade, will demand similar attention.

When we step into the shoes of other people, we can gain a rough-to-reasonable understanding of what it's like to be them. The emotions experienced are similarly rough-to-reasonable. Depending on whether they are positive or negative emotions, the pitch, emphasis, pace and loudness of your expression will register between the middle to upper, or the middle to lower, range of intensity. People who stay too long in perceptual position 2 are more likely to become doormats.

It makes sense to develop the flexibility to visit the three perceptual positions by choice, doesn't it? It makes even better sense to become a frequent and purposeful visitor to all three when you need a broad fix on an issue. It can deliver multiple perspectives on the one issue, which is far better than having only one perspective.

Empathy can only be felt and expressed when you visit perceptual position 2. Take a recent situation in which you had a disagreement, and as you go back in time, imagine looking at yourself and the other party having the disagreement while noticing how you felt. Now, please go back to it again, imagining the same scene and begin to enter the other party's experience of the event. Then, enter their body and see yourself as they would see you during the disagreement. Notice what feelings they would have as they engaged in the process of relating to you. Do you notice any difference in intensity of feeling? Finally, go back to the scene and see yourself through their eyes. Move out of their body and into your own and experience the disagreement through your eyes, hearing what you heard and feeling what you felt. If you followed the procedure exactly you would have travelled through the three perceptual positions and noticed feelings of differing intensity along the way.

Charismatic communicators have been observed to go into perceptual position 2 (either instinctively or through learning) as a natural course when people recount good and bad news. They picture or imagine themselves in the event described, and you can notice their physiology change as they begin to imagine being there. This experience furnishes them with some knowledge upon which they can give an honest and congruous response. The following example illustrates the point.

Margaret, I'm understanding what it must be like to be deserted by one's partner just as the children are reaching an uncontrollable age, and then, among it all, having to deal with an incontinent cat. I can hear in your voice the anguish of your predicament [empathic response with congruous tone and physiology]. And I know this may be the hardest thing you have ever had to accept, deal with and draw on your inner strengths to overcome [change of tonal and physiological expression to reflect hope, accompanied by a positive suggestion].

The same empathic process can be undertaken to join others in their triumphs and positive experiences. This willingness to enter the experiences of others is one of the hallmarks of influential speakers. It sends the signal 'I am a real person like you and I have taken the time to test your experiences on myself'— a powerful reminder of sameness.

To sum up, it's important to reflect all perceptual positions when you speak in front of an audience. If you jump in and out of all three as part of your regular communication cycle, you can achieve two significant effects. The first is that you will be matching the preferred perceptual positions of all of your audience some of the time. The second is that you will achieve tonal and physiological light and shade in your presentation, giving voice, body, heart and soul to your content. You may find the following general rules of thumb useful.

POSITION 1: INTERNAL

When you want to recount personal stories or want people to join a real or imaginary experience, be in the experience and talk about it. Go back in time and live the experience again. Talk about it as you do, describing what you see, hear and feel. Let your voice and body have their way.

POSITION 2: EMPATHIC

When you want to respond to the experiences of others, join the experience and talk about it. Imagine being that person, notice what it would be like and describe how you would think and feel.

POSITION 3: DETACHED

When you want to take stock, stand back to look at situations and describe them. This position is ideal when you want to talk about concepts, reason something out, use logic as a persuasion tool or take a non-subjective viewpoint.

In our professional lives we may like to operate under the illusion that reason is the basis of most of our major decisions. Why is it that, in survey after survey of business leaders and executives, the vast majority of respondents report that they make their major decisions mainly on hunches and 'gut feel'? Under the veneer of reason you will inevitably discover emotions at play. This is why the expression and reading of emotions are so important in the persuasion process.

Charismatic communicators are mindful that emotions play a primary role in people's choices to act or not to act on their ideas and suggestions. They understand two important aspects of emotional exchange. First, they pay attention to their audience's collective state of mind and constantly monitor for changes in the emotional state of their listeners. They calibrate responses and fashion the form and content of their messages so as to pace and lead their audience to more receptive emotional states.

The second important factor about those who act and behave charismatically is that they give themselves permission to show the degree of emotional commitment they have in their own ideas and visions. They reveal that the origins of their ideas are not only from their heads but also from their hearts. From a whisper to a roar, the appeal of their message mirrors the emotional fingerprint of the content.

THE EXECUTIVE WHO RAGED

Mastery of emotions means giving yourself permission to express appropriate emotion and *withdrawing permission* on occasions when the expression of negative emotion might damage your status and credibility. Most of us at some time will confront situations that trigger rage, anxiety and fear. This little trio has the potential to obliterate hard-earned reputations. It often requires a long recovery period before prior status and respect is earned again. The corporate and political worlds, in particular, are contaminated with leaders who, after having learned as children how to stamp their feet and turn red with rage, carry those behaviours into their adult lives.

An interesting sideline to executive rage is the often-reported calm after an outburst. Once the storm has died down, the offender frequently behaves as if nothing happened. This can be seen as a fairly accurate reflection of an adult bringing their childhood experiences to work, because it epitomises what happened when they were children. The rage was quickly extinguished because the child got what it wanted and life went on.

Understanding the reasons for executive rage is one thing, tolerating it is another. Most mature adults find outbursts of rage to be very poor form and are generally disposed to interpret them as accurate reflections of another's 'true' character. During a temper tantrum offenders often hurl bitter, sarcastic or cruel accusations at those they see as being the cause of their bad feelings—another indication of infantile behaviour brought into adulthood. Once again, it has been found that those on the receiving end of the onslaught will decipher what is said as being closer to the truth than when the perpetrator's guard is up.

Consider the story of former CEO Daniel and you will begin to appreciate how infantile outbursts of rage can damage personal reputations and the corporate bottom line. During the first six months of Daniel's tenure he embarked on a vigorous learning exercise, visiting the length and breadth of the country to understand the business of his company. He met hundreds of people and impressed them with the quality of his questions, the depth of his knowledge, the sharpness of his mind and the eloquence of his speech.

After this information-gathering quest and a subsequent shake-up of the lines of command, Daniel floated a detailed business and corporate plan designed to better position his company in the highly competitive environment in which it was operating. So far so good, but then things began to go awry.

The test of Daniel's leadership and charismatic qualities had just begun. As it should be, his emotional commitment to the vision he had outlined was high. His personal reputation and the support of his board were riding on his ability to translate vision and plan into practice.

Daniel thought that his position as CEO, his ability to hire and fire, and the authority he thought he had were enough to carry his plan to fruition. He never once thought to get people on board by incorporating their organisational hopes and visions in his blueprint, preferring to view many incumbent executives and staff as enemies to be overcome.

The tantrums began with minor eruptions of temper when deadlines for the implementation of his plan loomed. Firings became more frequent and the head office foyer was renamed the Departure Lounge by some executives desperately trying to hang on to their senses of humour. Daniel began to centralise more and more of the company's operations, and reports of his ranting and raving at members of his senior team became more frequent. A climate of fear began to permeate the executive floors of his company, inflamed by his declaration that 'I want my executives to know that if they fail then they may not have a job to come to the next day'.

The impact of Daniel's behaviour had some reasonably predictable effects. Some things got done because of fear of the consequences. A combination of fear for their jobs and fear of the prospect of being humiliated in front of their executive colleagues ensured that senior management toed the line up to a point. An atmosphere of malevolent compliance prevailed in the upper echelons of the company as executives began to submit only those ideas and proposals they knew would not precipitate eruptions of rage and scorn. The unwillingness of senior managers to float creative solutions and to discuss objectively the merits and weaknesses of Daniel's business propositions soon transformed the company into a one-man band.

The financial press got wind of the turmoil at the top and began to make oblique references to 'ructions in the ranks', former and existing senior managers began talking with journalists, and reports of management problems began to appear more frequently. As you would imagine, it was only a matter of time before the company's share price began to suffer. The board suddenly took notice and sought to counsel its hitherto considered 'champion of change'. As the two-year anniversary of his tenure was approaching, Daniel jumped ship, but not before telling the board it 'had no balls' and that its reprehensible lack of support had 'made' him look elsewhere.

The company was left with an almighty mess to clear up: a plan half-implemented; an executive team in disarray, robbed of some of its most experienced performers who had either been fired or left in disgust; a hostile workforce who felt betrayed; and a weakened position in the marketplace.

The story of Daniel exemplifies how an inability to control the expression of a range of negative emotions and impulses nearly wrecked an organisation, but you can't help considering how effective a leader he might have been, if he had learned how to permit himself to express appropriate emotion and withdraw permission when he sensed he was going to blow his top or act on destructive impulses.

If Daniel ever decides to search for an antidote to his binges of self-destruction, he could learn how to step into perceptual positions 2 and 3 'cleanly'. He might discover that self-destructive emotions are replaced with a range of other, more useful emotions. The insights gained from the experience might allow him to reconstruct, over time, his tattered reputation.

3 FINDING YOUR BEST VOICE

Spoken language is normally suffused with 'tone', embedded in an expressiveness which transcends the verbal.
Oliver Sacks

The voice best used in public speaking is your *best* voice, the one that actually belongs to you. Your best voice is far better than any other voice you may be able to copy, fake or cultivate. Your best voice is your natural voice, with balanced resonance and full use of tonal range. In the previous chapter you explored how giving voice and body to your emotions offers your audience greater accessibility to the deeper and broader aspects of your personality. This chapter is devoted to transforming your voice into a finely honed instrument of communication.

When we speak of 'voice', we refer to the quality and diversity of sound produced by your vocal system. While elocution is linked to the way you use your vocal system, it is a separate matter. Generally, an 'educated' form of Australian pronunciation and elocution will open the most doors. If you speak with the nasality and recklessness of a Northern Territory roustabout, you can expect to lose some credibility points. People who flatten their vowels to sound earthier, and those who affect the verbal countenance of Vaucluse dowagers, are likely to be ridiculed in some quarters.

It's both comical and sad that people 'put on' voices. In a misguided attempt to sound more authoritative, credible, persuasive, friendly, more manly, mature and the like, they do hatchet jobs on their credibility. If you put on a voice, there's a high probability that your listener/s will detect some inconsistency between your physical countenance and the expressive and tonal quality of your delivery. They may not be quite able to isolate the anomaly, but rest assured they'll notice and act upon it.

Five important variables govern the quality of your verbal delivery. By learning and practising five sets of simple techniques you can move towards fully realising your vocal potential. By improving one or two, you, and others, will notice a significant difference in how you sound. You have the built-in potential to sound richer, more authoritative, more colourful and more melodic. Who could resist the temptation to realise more of that potential?

PITCH

Pitch is a description we will use to refer to an arbitrary 'centre' of the voice. Imagine starting out from some central point and intoning notes that are higher or lower than that point. The ups and downs from the central point are known as 'range', or the musical notes we use in our voice to give it life. This is why the voice is often referred to as an instrument.

A good musician could actually produce a score of those up and down notes we use in our speech. Lamentably, the musician's notational skills would not be taxed by the typical Australian speaker, who uses between three and five different notes on average in everyday communication. A very limited song indeed, if it were put to music.

In day-to-day communication, it's generally acceptable to communicate with a limited range and a stable pitch. The people we talk to are usually known to us and they have at least a notion of who and what we are. Nevertheless, colourful speakers who give appropriate tone and body to their expressions present more of themselves to be liked by peers, friends and intimates.

As soon as your communication goes beyond an intimate discussion, however, your energy levels need to increase. A toneless performance at a staff meeting, for example, is very close to people's memories of the boring teacher or lecturer who made tedium their main message. If, for instance, you're talking about a threat from a competitor or want to convince staff to give their whole-hearted support to a new system of reporting, you need to reflect your convictions in both the pitch and range of your voice. Not to do so is to devalue your message and invite it to be misunderstood.

The exercises in the previous chapter, dealing with the expression of emotion, relate to both pitch and range. If you have completed the exercises, you may have noticed that your pitch (centre) changes and conforms to the emotion you express. Unbridled expressions of joy will come from a higher centre than expressions of sorrow. It's useful in public speaking to discover your centre, as it will allow you to return to a resting point or optimal pitch from which to colour your voice.

Many speakers automatically raise the pitch of their voice when they confront a microphone or begin speaking in front of an audience. This habit is often ingrained and may be caused by a combination of fear (stage fright) and the mistaken belief that the voice must be raised when you speak to an audience. If you begin speaking at a higher pitch, where are you going to go when you need to emphasise, or colour, your words—further upward into falsetto? Modern microphones make it unnecessary to sound as if you're conducting a trans-Tasman conversation entirely without the aid of technology.

Other speakers drop their pitch and speak from the bottom end of their range in the mistaken belief that they will deliver multiple 'eargasms' to their audiences. Males are particular offenders in forcing the voice deeper into the throat and chest. Some image advisers counsel their clients to drop their voice to a lower pitch. This is not the answer to adding authority to the voice. It is dangerous advice and can cause pathological problems.

Contrary to some beliefs, faked deep voices do not necessarily advertise high sperm counts, sexual prowess or greater authority. If anything, they communicate sexual insecurity or gender ambivalence. *The key to finding your best voice is to make the pitch compatible with the emotion being expressed and to use tonal range to colour the words that need to be stressed.*

Most of us, most of the time, will experience and express emotion in the middle range of the levity-gravity scale shown in the previous chapter, and so it can make sense to have an idea of your resting or optimum pitch. The way to discover it is simple: intone the highest and lowest notes you can without your voice breaking up. Halfway between should approxi-mate your centre or resting pitch. If you can intone more high notes and fewer low notes from the central point then your voice is pitched too low; if you can intone more low notes and fewer high notes then your voice is pitched too high. Do this exercise with the aid of a cassette or mini disk recorder. Once having found your centre, or resting pitch, you can carry on to the next stage of developing your best voice.

RESONANCE

Resonance is the means by which you open up the full potential of your voice. To achieve full resonance, you need to balance your resonators. Balanced resonance reflects the best voice an individual can produce. It's the vocal equivalent of preventative medicine, because it produces a healthy voice by spreading the resonance load and placing fewer stresses on the mechanical parts of the voice.

Resonance occurs when the source of vibration (the vocal folds or chords) set up vibrations in other parts of your body. Your primary resonating structures (the parts of your body where sound waves directly or indirectly cause vibration) are your teeth, hard palate, nasal bone, cheekbones, sinuses, forehead and cranium. If you resonate efficiently, the vibrations can continue to other parts of your body, such as the rib cage and the spinal vertebrae. Speakers with well-trained voices 'feel' their voices all over their bodies.

Few of us use our full powers of resonance, thereby rarely ever reaching our potential of producing rich, beautiful, balanced and uninhibited sound. In fact, most speakers with untrained voices use about half or fewer of their resonating areas. Voices that don't achieve full resonance potential, or that centre on a couple of resonators, usually sound a little chesty, tinny, thin or nasal.

If you're eager to realise your natural vocal potential to enhance the impact of what you say, work with the following series of exercises, designed to give you a bigger and more natural voice.

The head hum

Hum into your head, making sure your breathing is deep and your throat is open and unstressed. Imagine the sound vibrating at the top of your head: feel it, make it tingle. Visualise the sound rising from your vocal chords and exiting from the top of your head. Visualise your throat being completely open with no stress; feel it.

Once you have experienced the sensation of sound resonating through the top of your head, start speaking: say anything, keep the breath deep and supportive, and continue to speak out of the top of your head until you are able to 'install' the feeling and associated mechanics. Do this exercise in the morning when you wake up, and whenever you have a few spare, private moments.

The nose hum

Begin again with as natural a hum as you can produce. Repeat the same sequence as for the head hum. Hum and then begin speaking gibberish if you like. Make sure your throat is clear of stress and your larynx feels unconstricted. Imagine/visualise the sound freely rising from your throat and resonating in your nasal chamber. Feel the sensation it makes. Make the area around your nose vibrate or tingle.

Keep your breath deep and allow your abdomen to expand as you fill your lower lungs with fuel for your voice. Install the feeling; remember well how it feels.

The face hum

Think of what a 'reedy' sound would sound like. With this exercise you will imagine that the sound is coming through the pores of your facial mask. Once again, make sure your throat feels relaxed.

Start with the hum. Now visualise or imagine the sound rising from your throat effortlessly. Speak through your *face*. Feel the tingle in your cheeks, mouth and lips.

The throat and chest hum

The throat and chest are called the 'universal resonators' and are the easiest to activate. Make sure when you begin your humming and speaking exercises you don't lock or put a cap on the sound being produced. Go through the visualising/imagining process. Make sure you can feel the resonance. Ensure you make a distinction between throat and chest resonance by trying each individually.

As you complete the exercises take note of the sensory experiences created by them. If these sensory experiences are new or feel alien, you have a very good indicator of the resonance potential you have not been explor-ing or developing. Give the new resonance experience your attention and get the resonators working for you. Your voice will change and become bigger, more natural and more mellifluous as a result.

The balancing act

Finally, to achieve resonator balance and to equalise your resonance, do the following: keep your breathing fluid and make sure you are supporting appropriately. Hum and ensure your voice is well forward: imagine the sound is being formed into words a couple of centimetres out from your lips. Start speaking, keeping the imaginary word formation that few centimetres out from your lips.

Now, hum a little higher than you normally do and then speak at this higher tone, again making the sound form into words a few centimetres out from your lips. Let your voice naturally drop into place.

If you have completed the exercises successfully, you will begin to experience the fully resonant voice, with all resonators working together. Enjoy the experience, install it in your memory, feel how easy and comfortable it sounds! Continue with the exercises until you notice a significant improvement in how your voice sounds and feels.

EMPHASIS

Emphasis describes, for our purposes, the colour we apply to words to convey meaning. By stressing or accenting words, we draw our listeners' attention to them. In ordinary, extemporaneous speech, the stress values you place on words are 100 per cent accurate. You filter your stream of words in accordance with the intellectual value you place on their meaning in a conversation.

The natural filtering processes can go awry when we speak in front of gatherings of people. The emotion we feel in response to facing an audience sometimes overwhelms the emotion we would normally express through emphasis. We fall into silly vocal patterns such as using an upward inflection at the end of each sentence, we punctuate our phrases with patterned 'um's and 'err's, we inhibit the vitality in our voice with restrictive breathing patterns, and so on. The result is a vocal performance that can be duller than dull.

Two crucial elements of emphasis are range and energy. If you have a limited range, as most Australians do, most people will interpret your voice as being flat. The typical response from people with a limited range when their voices are recorded and played back is 'My voice sounds so boring!', and so it does. If you have a limited range, your voice may not sound boring on the inside because you can feel as well as hear its energy. But, the voice you hear on tape is the voice everyone else hears, and it can put people to sleep better than any proprietary medicine if it reflects a limited range.

A broader range gives you more flexibility and greater latitude of expression. The best professional speakers have a range of at least two octaves. Good actors will usually have around three octaves at their disposal. That's a lot of notes, and if you really want to become a virtuoso public speaker, you'll need every one of them.

Professional speakers and actors use their range to help their audiences grasp the import and meaning of what they say. They colour their words to manage the emotional state of their audiences from minute to minute, heightening and lowering emotions as their content demands. It goes without saying that stretching your range will give you more ability to keep your audience in the palms of your hands.

The emotional aerobics exercises in the previous chapter can be used either as a starting point to extend your tonal range or as a super-workout after you have succeeded in stretching your range well beyond three to five notes. Do the following exercises until your range matches that of at least twelve white keys on a piano.

GIVE YOURSELF THE PROPER SUPPORT
Release any tension in your jaw and neck. Imagine your spine is a jet of water coming out of a large hose, fluid but supportive. Imagine your head is like a ping-pong ball riding on the top of the jet of water. Draw deep breaths.

RUN A TAPE RECORDER
Speak at the highest and lowest notes you can muster. Listen back so you remember the range. Then play a tape of you having a conversation. Notice the difference.

STRETCH YOUR RANGE
Take a piece of newspaper copy. Read aloud one word at your highest note and the following word at your lowest note. Make sure you are in 'support' mode, as described above, and try and bring your voice as forward into your mouth as you can. Read a few dozen words, and then relax.

FIND YOUR 'BUM' NOTES
Take up the newspaper copy again and, starting from your lowest note, go up the scales with each word to your highest note. Do this three or four times. Notice any notes that are strange or unfamiliar to you. Begin to notice how your body supports different notes.

TUNE YOUR 'BUM' NOTES
Practise the notes that feel alien to you until you can intone them easily and effortlessly. Speak sentences using only your bum notes.

BE TONALLY WANTON AND RECKLESS
Take up your newspaper copy again. Start reading it the way actors and actresses sound in BBC period dramas. Lengthen the vowels and speak aaaaaawwwfully naiiiiiiiiiicely. Become more and more dramatic, stretching words so that there is almost a song in each longer word you utter.

As you begin to enjoy playing with the words, give them more energy and give yourself freedom to become more and more outrageous. When you have finished enjoying being outrageous, read normally and notice how your tonal range has become more flexible and available.

The above sequence, combined with emotional aerobics, can give you an experience of both range and energy. With time and practice, you can build a broader and more energetic speaking voice as part of your habitual system of expression.

DYNAMIC RANGE: LOUDNESS

Loudness is a key issue in public speaking because of the myths that have corrupted our understanding of effective voice projection. Most people, when told to project, raise their voice in pitch (constricting the larynx) and elevate their volume. They proceed to speak from the higher pitch and volume throughout their presentation. This misapplied technique is the vocal equivalent of aggravated assault, both on your audience and your vocal chords.

You've discovered that speaking at a higher pitch will necessarily limit your range and ability to direct the emotions of your audience. Shrieking at your audience because you need to cover the distance between them and you is the most primitive of solutions. The answer is to speak with balanced resonators and increase your volume to fill the required space. This allows you to maintain control over your tonal range and reserve your energy for expressing the meaning of your content.

It is a very good idea to learn how to balance your resonators before you experiment with volume control. Assuming you have, practise the following sequence:

1. Start in the toilet. Begin speaking and in the course of your first sentence, balance your resonators. Tell yourself a story, any story, and as you do imagine you have a remote volume control in your hand. As you hear yourself relating the story, fill the toilet up with sound and begin tweaking it down until it is at a comfortable level, only as loud as is necessary for every word to be heard. Keep doing this until you can do it effortlessly.

2. Go to the laundry. Find a room about the size of an average laundry and repeat the process. Fill the space with sound and tweak it down until every word can be heard in any corner of the room.

3. Pick larger and larger rooms and repeat the process. In larger rooms, pay particular attention to maintaining balanced resonance. Just increase your volume to fill the room, ensuring that your pitch remains constant. Avoid any rises in pitch as you increase your loudness. Use your remote control to adjust the volume so your words can be heard at any point in the room.

Continue this process until you are able to speak at a central, or resting, pitch with balanced resonance in very large spaces.

Your dalliance with loudness, or dynamic range, has so far concerned the exposure of the projection myth and how you can develop control over loudness and softness. There is another critical dimension to loudness and it is directly connected to human emotion.

In doing emotional aerobics and stretching your range, you may have noticed that emotions with greater intensity demand greater volume. If you do not give true voice and body to emotion, the volume will not match what is demanded. The volume prescribed for elation, for example, is much louder than that required for mild amusement.

A 'trick' of those who are deeply into self-containment is to cap loud emotions as a trouble-shooter would cap an oil well. The general rule is that the greater the agony or ecstasy, the louder the volume required to express or discharge it. Self-containment junkies have found that they can repress a 'big' emotion by imprisoning the sound it's supposed to make in their bodies. This capping behaviour can have significant psychological consequences over time, and if not corrected can lead to a fully an-aesthetised personality.

In public speaking, it's necessary to match volume with the intensity of the emotion being expressed. Yes, you can keep emotions in check, as your journey along the path of maturity has shown. You can choose how to feel about a range of stimuli, but once you have chosen to feel and express emotion you have little option other than to voice it. You need to give it the loudness it deserves. To do otherwise is to deprive your audience of access to you. Is that what you want?

Choose to be multi-dynamic. Recognise that the loudness you employ in the everyday expression of emotion varies in accordance with the intensity of the feeling. Avoid at all costs being monodynamic. A boring speaker who sends an audience into involuntary catatonia is more likely to be monodynamic (one loudness) rather than monotonic (one pitch) So, be louder and softer as the circumstances demand.

PACE

Try this experiment. Tune into a five-minute radio news bulletin delivered by one of the ABC's few remaining 'golden voices'. Just listen: don't force yourself to absorb the content but just indulge in the experience of listening as you do every day when listening to news.

What will you discover? Chances are you will find yourself enjoying the sensory experience of beautiful, resonant sound, sound delivered with an amazing constancy— evenly paced, evenly loud, evenly pitched. It's enough to prod your auditory G-spot. What you will also notice is that you have lower comprehension of the news stories and difficulty in recalling the content. There's a very simple reason for this. The delicious uniformity of the delivery may well have sent you into a different brainwave state, most likely the state of daydreaming! This is what happens when people produce a maddening consistency of pace, pitch and loudness.

The human brain soon tires of sameness in stimulus, as opposed to sameness mentioned in Chapter 1. You will either drift into the alpha (daydreaming) state or go off in search of something more stimulating. Arguably, the 'golden voice' with its beautiful, mellifluous tones and polished regularity is a wonderful adjunct to meditation and hypnosis but, sadly, there is not much use for it in public speaking. Build the following into your delivery:

VARY YOUR PACE
Pace variation plays a significant role in maintaining the attention of your listeners.

QUICKEN YOUR PACE
When you throw away (drop your tonal range to a flatter or more even tonality) unimportant or repetitive information, speed up your rate of words.
Slow down. When you want to emphasise important information, linger for a while on the word or speak it in a measured way.

REFLECT THE EMOTIONAL CONTENT OF YOUR MATERIAL
Make sure your pace is commensurate with the emotional fingerprint of what you are saying (e.g. slow your pace when talking about important feelings and use a fast pace when excited).

ARREST YOUR PACE. STOP!
A pause effectively used can be of immense dramatic value. See how long you can pause before your alarm system is triggered, and then pause a little longer. The rules of pause are easy to integrate into your presentation or speech patterns. Here are four types of pause:
- Mini pause (about a half second in duration). These allow you to break your sentences into chunks or pieces of meaning. They help your audience absorb different ideas contained in your sentences or content.
- Segment pause (around one to two seconds). You hear newsreaders use segment pauses between stories to indicate a break between one story and

the next. Segment pauses prevent your listeners confusing one idea with another.

- Unit pause (between two and four seconds). This allows your listeners time to let an important idea sink in and flags to them that something significant or momentous has been said.
- Dramatic pause (from a second to about five seconds). This form of pause can be used before or after important words or phrases. It can also be used to get your audience to fill in a word before you have said it.

GO THE RACES!

Walk, trot, canter and gallop. Speak rapidly, slow down to a crawl, up the pace, and so on as your content demands. Develop your sense of timing and use it for dramatic effect.

DEVELOP YOUR INNER SENSE OF PACE

Practise and listen to those who use pace masterfully. Listen to your inner sense and it will signal you when to increase or decrease pace.

Longfellow wrote: 'How wonderful is the human voice! It is indeed the organ of the soul'. A good voice with balanced resonance has a special 'timbre', a superior quality of tone, colour and body, and a richness and warmth that can touch the souls of others. A voice alive with contrasting emotions and loudness, with pace and pause that match the moment, is a powerful instrument of persuasion. You don't need to envy a good voice because all of the resources you need are within you. Your task can be to invest some time and practice in releasing them.

CHAPTER 4

IDENTITY ENGINEERING: BUILDING A SUSTAINABLE PUBLIC IMAGE

He who determines the end, provides the means.
Benedetto Varchi

Just who do you think you are?

When you speak or imagine speaking in front of a group, who is the person doing the performance? Is it someone you like and recognise and who would be liked and recognised by your friends, intimates and colleagues? Are you a natural, or plastic and unnatural? How do you behave when you're speaking in front of a group, and does that behaviour convey unique and valued personality and character traits? Is your public or work persona consistent, or are you all over the place depending on mood and circumstance? These important questions go to the heart of your identity and the image you communicate to others.

Some people are walking repositories of technique. They appear to know every trick in the book. They communicate with superb artistry, and yet you can detect a missing dimension that you're unable to finger. You admire them for their dexterity but you sense something hidden, something not quite right, a Svengali-like quality that leaves you feeling suspicious and uneasy. Chances are these individuals have built their public personae from the *bottom up* as a means of moving away from a previous, undesired public self.

A healthier and more practical approach to building a public identity is to envision a worthwhile self-concept and work towards becoming it. This self, or identity, is the thing that defines who you are, and it's a very good idea to have an intimate understanding of who and what is speaking in your name. A way of building a sustainable public identity is to work from the *top down*, to identify a cluster of meaningful definitions that can guide and inform your public behaviour.

The first function of an identity is that of an intra-personal tool. Having a well-defined public identity will allow you to make the many large and small adjustments, decisions and choices required to keep the public self in order and in alignment with your interpersonal goals. Most, if not all, high visibility individuals have devoted time, energy and angst to the creation and maintenance of their public identities. In meeting some famous personalities over the next few pages you will begin to notice how rewarding and useful building a top-down identity can be.

THE GOLD COINAGE OF CONSISTENCY

A major factor in durable and attractive public identities is consistency. This is not to say that successful public figures freeze their identities in time and remain exactly the same over decades. Rather, they display in their public lives a cluster of fixed characteristics that distinguish them from their more changeable and erratic contemporaries.

One of the most enduring examples of consistency in Australian public life is Justice Michael Kirby. Kirby has remained one of the mass media's favourite commentators in his specialist areas of law and law reform. The hallmark characteristics that made Kirby a charming and distinctive commentator have never changed. He has represented the human, merciful and intelligent face of the legal aristocracy with great distinction for more than twenty years.

Judge Kirby could not have achieved his unique place in the hearts and minds of thinking Australians without having a profound sense of consistency and continuity. The qualities that made him distinctively competent are as much a part of the Kirby persona now as they were in the early 1980s. He built his public identity on values of fair-mindedness, public service as opposed to self-service, intelligent inquiry, empathy and integrity. This contrasts with the yappy, brow-beating and pompous voices of much of the legal profession today. It gives Kirby as much public currency now as ever.

In many ways, consistency of identity equates with shelf life, but why is consistency such an important commodity? People need and expect both physical and psychological consistency in their lives. We want and expect the sun to come up in the morning, the train to be on time and our jobs to be still there when we get to work. We also expect our relationships with people to be much the same today as they were yesterday. Consistency is said to be the adhesive that gums the various parts of our model of the world together. It helps us make sense of what goes on in the world and allows us to have a comfortable set of expectations.

When something unexpected happens, when we encounter inconsistency, a state of 'dissonance' occurs. If the train doesn't arrive, if a friend is suddenly unfriendly, if a colleague acts out of character, our first response is one of puzzlement and a sense of discontinuity. Have you ever had the experience of walking past an object, getting caught on it and suddenly being hauled back in its direction? The 'What happened there?' feeling you experience immediately after the event is fairly close to the feeling you have when inconsistency occurs. The initial shock of inconsistency is followed by other feelings of uneasiness, anxiety and, often, anger.

Dissonance isn't a nice feeling to have, and the human brain-body has evolved some neat tricks for releasing it and returning to a state of consistency. All of the tricks involve a change of perception in some way. We come to see the person, object or event in a way that removes the unpleasant internal sensation of dissonance. There are numerous ways we do this, ranging from denial (it didn't happen) and justification (it's out of character) to changing expectations (everyone screws up sometimes) and re-evaluating (she's a fraud).

You can imagine the potential damage to your public identity and prospects if you don't conform to the consistency principle. The lesson is that if you build a persona based on values such as integrity, openness and fairness, for example, you must continually align your actions and behaviour with your claims. The corporate, political and public graveyards are filled with the corpses of those who thought they were inoculated against the consistency principle. However, those who understand the need for consistency and who are given to healthy introspection can create public identities that appear to defy the use-by rule.

MAKING A BLUEPRINT

For the purposes of identity engineering, there are some important considerations you should notice and incorporate into your design. The first is that whatever public identity you create needs to be an expression of your larger self. In the course of your everyday life, you assume various identities: parent, manager, friend, spouse, entertainer, a person prone to urinary infections, enemy, teacher, facilitator, home renovator, dab hand at the ukulele, and so on. Those multiple identities are loosely held together by a super-self that, for the most part, will align them with bigger conceptions of potentiality, beliefs, values and attitudes.

If your individual identities are compatible with your super-self, surroundings and context, you will achieve reasonable personal outcomes and results. If they're not, you may find yourself working against your self. For example, there's no point in designing a persona that needs to exhibit inclusiveness and consensus if you're an incorrigible egotist who thinks people are sheep in need of a strong shepherd. Conflicting identities can sometimes cause problems, so it makes sense to draw from the strengths you already know you possess. This will allow you to have a comfortable foundation on which to build your public identity.

The second factor relates to starting the process of identity engineering with what you are. Every individual on the planet is unique in some ways. Do you have unique qualities that, if developed and amplified, could allow you to stand apart from your contemporaries? Which bits of you and your personality produce positive responses in your friends, your colleagues and those who meet you? Which bits of your personality do you notice working against you? What personal idiosyncrasies lend individuality and charm to your personality?

Answers to the above questions allow you to develop what is known as distinctive competence. If you were an imperfect double of an admired speaker or personal hero, how would you stand out as a unique individual who brings a special quality to your encounters with other people?

The third consideration centres on what you can *become* as opposed to what you are. You can select qualities that you would like to have and work at gaining them. You can develop a self-guide that contrasts the undesired self with the desired self. Knowing both the undesired and desired self can provide a powerful kick of motivation in developing a durable and marketable identity. This mirrors what you have been doing in other parts of your life and you will be entering familiar territory as you go about engineering your public identity.

Phase 1

Let's begin with the first of the three main elements of identity engineering, your inherent qualities and strengths. It's in your interests to approach this task with as much objectivity as you can. Aim for clarity and avoid self-deception. So, take a look at yourself, get a feel for how you register with other people, imagine you are an independent observer of your behaviour, and sound out the qualities that demonstrate your better self.

Context has a strong bearing on which qualities you bring to particular circumstances and events. What are your overriding qualities and strengths that you bring to bear in most situations? An example of an overriding quality would be, say, optimism. If in most contexts you approach life with a positive spin that infects and motivates others, write it down.

Identify about six or seven overriding qualities that lubricate and enhance your interpersonal relationships.

Draw up a table with two columns and head them as shown in the following example. List your six or seven overriding qualities in the first column.

My meta qualities	How best I show them

Think deeply about the qualities you have identified and consider the values placed on them by others. What would happen if you amplified or modified them? How best would you demonstrate them? You may like to consider asking the opinions of those who are generally considered fair and unbiased towards you. Get a mix of opinions from significant others and respected outsiders. Fill out the second column in your table. When you have developed a clear idea of your major qualities and know how they can be best expressed, you can move confidently on to Phase 2.

Phase 2

In this phase your primary purpose is to identify the qualities, attributes, behaviours and personal history that make you stand out as a unique individual. The qualities you can look for are those that help define your differences and the effects your differences have on those around you.

Understanding the effects of your behaviour is a prime element of good people-ecology. We all scan people for reactions to our behaviour, but few of us take the time and effort to list which behaviours consistently work and which behaviours work against us. We often fail to consider context and notice that when contexts change behaviours and approaches may need to change. We may blame those on the receiving end of our behaviours for taking us the 'wrong way', instead of investigating the circumstances and asking ourselves how we could have achieved more pleasing outcomes. People-ecology centres on doing ethically whatever it takes to achieve mutually desirable responses, so notice when you hit the mark and when you don't.

A useful way to determine your distinctive competencies is to spend a week observing how you positively and negatively influence and affect others. You may like to entertain the idea of observing yourself in perceptual positions 2 and 3 (see p. 43). Stand back, notice how the distinctive parts of you engage others and produce agreeable outcomes. See yourself through the eyes of those with whom you interact and register the occasions when you strike a responsive chord. Imagine how intrigued and pleased you will be to become aware of those behaviours that amuse, entertain, challenge, attract, tempt, please and ennoble others.

Spend as much time as it takes to identify what makes you a distinctive individual, and write down the results in a table, paying particular attention to the context in which they work best. Some areas you may wish to consider are:

- humour and its expression
- ways of looking at the world
- how you express your energy
- your people skills and their impacts
- distinctive intellectual approaches
- your way of connecting with people
- interesting physical characteristics
- values and how you personify them
- character traits people admire
- your personal history and insights
- behaviour quirks that delight others
- turns of phrase and their effects
- how/when you trigger intense curiosity
- special ways of exalting or dignifying others

Again, draw up a table with two columns as in the following example, and fill them in.

My distinctive qualities	Where they work best and why

Phase 3

Phases 1 and 2 of the process can help you improve your self-knowledge and identify the bits of you that work best. These bits can form a meaningful part of your self-guide as a public speaker and performer. They may also be useful in many of the professional and personal relationships you have and will forge. Phase 3 attends to any clefts and deficiencies you uncovered during your self-search and supports your endeavours to become the person you want to become when interacting with audiences and groups.

In this phase, as in Phase 1, you're invited to survey what others think of you in order to test your ideas about yourself. This can help offset some of the more excessive effects of your natural tendency towards self-deception. You can easily arrive at the conclusion that it's prudent to approach this exercise with some objectivity when you consider how self-deception can prevent you from identifying both strengths and weaknesses. If, heaven forbid, you view yourself as a spectacular flop, then the following exercise will resemble a personal testament to failure. If, on the contrary, you feel that you are the quintessential charismatic needing to become nothing more than what you are, an appraisal of your talents by your enemies and friends alike may be just the tonic you need.

In engineering your ideal public identity it's important to place a little more weight on how others evaluate you than you would in your personal relationships. Be cautious about taking individual opinions at face value. Look for trends. If one person says you come across like a belligerent Amazon suffering from PMT, seek impressions from a range of other people before you access the suicide how-to pages on the Internet.

Current attributes

Try to take feedback as just feedback and avoid interpreting it as a personal attack. Ask questions if you are given negative feedback. If, for example, someone says you come across as 'too calculating', ask them neutral questions to gain an understanding of what they meant. Press your 'curiosity' button and invite them to cooperatively explore what it is you do that allows them to choose that particular interpretation of your behaviour. Then ask what concrete actions you would need to take to overcome the interpretation.

There's no point in soliciting feedback unless you are left with things to do or change. Abstract responses like 'you need to be warmer', 'you lack energy' or 'you're inconsistent' are not actionable. You may need to know how to show warmth, how to exude more energy and how to render consistency if the feedback is to be of benefit. Ask the feedback giver to show you how you could be warmer or have more energy.

Draw up a table with two columns as in the following example.

| Current attributes | Desired attributes |

This table will help you identify those elements of your public self that may need modification or development. It will come to represent your self-development guide in public performance, a series of goals you can measure yourself against and make adjustments to as you go along. Fill out the left-hand column first. Some examples of areas that may need modification are:

- reflection of key values (such as integrity, truth, empathy)
- ability to engage others
- listening ability
- keeping promises
- level of consistency
- sense of humour
- understanding of human differences
- level of humility
- dogmatism quotient
- self management and control
- level of straightforwardness
- empathy skills
- emotional flexibility
- degree of adaptability
- self-importance levels
- sense of fair play
- personal warmth
- degree of curiosity
- level of generosity

The suggestions listed for your self-search are universal components of likeability, and to some extent everyone will at some time fail to meet such standards. Write down the ones you consider need amplifying or developing. There may be other traits identified during your information gathering activities that are more relevant to you and how you appear to others. Ensure they are at the top of your list. As you continue reading this book you may consider adding other attributes you want to improve. When you have completed your list, select the six or seven most important traits you want to expand or improve on and follow the second half of the Phase 3 process.

Desired attributes

When you have selected the most important of the current traits you want to change, turn your attention to the right-hand column. Select the first attribute you want to change and ask yourself what attribute or trait you would like to have in its place. What quality can you congruently replace the undesired attribute with? What personal label can you give it? Fill out the opposite column with the name you have given it. For example, if you have chosen 'low sense of humour' as the undesirable attribute and 'appropriate light-heartedness' as its replacement, write 'appropriate light-heartedness' in the second column opposite 'low sense of humour'.

The attribute represents a *means* to achieve certain *ends*. To flesh out what the ends will be for you, you must go there and discover what happens when you actually do the trait. Here's how you do it.

Imagine being, say, appropriately light-hearted in a future situation. Jump into your body and notice how it feels, observe the audience response, hear how your voice sounds, notice how your body moves and sense how you go about naturally being light-hearted.

Now step out of your body and see how it all comes together. Look at yourself, as you would if you were watching yourself on wide-screen television. See yourself standing in front of a group or audience and being appropriately light-hearted. How are you doing light-heartedness? How are you responding to your audience? How much is too much and too little? Notice how you personify the things you saw, heard and felt when you were doing light-heartedness inside your body. What things do you notice appropriate light-heartedness achieving for you? Write them down under the heading you have written. You will now have something that looks like this:

Low sense of humour	Appropriate light-heartedness
	helps me overcome tense situations
	shows people my lighter side
	gives me more flexibility
	allows me to laugh along with others
	lets me better connect with people

Continue with this process of imagining that you are doing each desired trait until you have completed the list. You may be wondering why you need to undergo the above process. The answer is simple. People who have an intensely clear representation of the traits they want to amplify or develop are much more likely to achieve them. The more you visit the idealised trait or attribute (as in imagining what it is like) the more probable it becomes that you will generate the behaviours required to achieve it.

So let's take stock. You have produced three pages of valuable information with the following details:

1. Your meta-qualities: the qualities that work for you in your interpersonal relationships across many contexts. Your meta-qualities may not be distinctive, but they are the personal attributes that allow you to function as a social being. They could be optimism, integrity, curiosity, self-awareness, generosity, empathy and other attributes that you have developed to a fairly high level. They are characterised by statements such as 'Catherine is a very open and honest person' and 'John is so good-hearted'.

2. Your distinctive qualities: special and unique personal attributes that make you stand out in a positive light. These qualities effectively define who you are as a public personality. They represent your uniqueness or distinctive competence. They are qualities that evoke interest, curiosity, amity, novelty and the like. They are characterised by statements such as 'she has such a way with words' and 'he has this incredible knack of taking humour to an absolutely hilarious level'.

3. Your current attributes contrasted with your desired qualities: the qualities and attributes that you desire to have and the means and ends associated with them. Desired qualities represent the things you need to add to your self to more successfully operate in your business, speaking or other persuasion contexts. They are qualities that are broadly valued and much in demand.

IDENTITY MODEL

Michael Parkinson of 'Parkinson' fame has been celebrated for the last three decades as the Genial Inquisitor. When Parkinson is in front of the cameras, he assumes the totality of his professional identity: *how he sees himself*. He doesn't simply see himself as a journalist or interviewer but as the embodiment of his chosen identity. This allows him to take on all the attributes, skills and behaviour of his incredibly durable professional persona. Parkinson's identity of the Genial Inquisitor has ensured him a regular spot on prime-time television for three decades.

Parkinson's Genial Inquisitor identity allows him 360 degree penetration. It is as much an identity for the audience as it is for the interviewees. For example, lavish curiosity is an attribute that Parkinson has built into his professional identity and he had a very good reason for developing it. He is aware that the tonality of curiosity in his voice produces signal responses in both his guests and wider television audience that compel his guests to answer his questions and his audience to wait and listen for the answer. So, how does his sense of identity line up a raft of

Levels of change

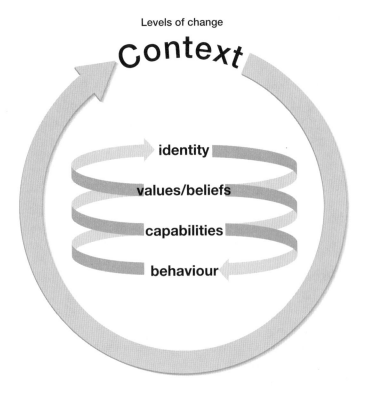

attributes and capabilities that generate charismatic behaviour and audience appeal? The model above illustrates how the process works.

The model is a representation of the complex processes involved in the development of a self-guide in a particular context. You can notice how the model illustrates the recursive nature of identity engineering. The spiral represents how each level can influence the levels above and below and, indeed, influence itself.

For example, say you have an identity as Irena the Indomitable, an identity that exemplifies a rock-hard belief in your invincibility. What kinds of behaviours would you engage in? If you were a true embodiment of invincibility you would do all kinds of behaviours that reflected it, like walking confidently into a hail of bullets with the sure knowledge of survival. What if one of those bullets scored a hit? Can you see an identity crisis coming on? Suddenly, at the level of behaviour you meet the consequences of your actions and it travels right up the levels to how you see yourself.

The trauma of the discovery will almost certainly send shock waves all the way up to the identity level. It will cause you to re-evaluate your behaviours and capabilities, it will directly challenge the beliefs you had about yourself and will cause you to make some serious adjustments to your identity. Irena the Indomitable may well transform into Irena the Clueless. Your own experience may tell you that when a belief is exploded it can leave a distressing void in its place, particularly when it relates to your self. Conversely, if you do certain things proficiently it can have the effect of reinforcing or elevating beliefs about your capabilities and will feed into your identity or self-image.

Events may occur at any level on the levels of change scale and impact on levels above or below. However, it is at the identity level that all other levels are aggregated into a meta self-schema. If you were to develop a series of charismatic capabilities without attending to the higher levels of the scale, the result would not be dissimilar to a robot who could perform a range of clever manoeuvres without ever knowing why and for what purpose.

The walking repositories of technique mentioned at the beginning of this chapter refer to individuals who fit the robot definition. They have learned a series of behaviours without consolidating them into a bigger system of supporting beliefs, values and strategies. They are performers without a mission, which is why you sense something is missing. Building an identity from the bottom up gives you little organisation and mastery over placing your public persona on the right platform for success. To build and direct charismatic behaviours and thinking patterns you need to start at the top and work down, as Parkinson does.

1. Identity: who you are

Parkinson assumes an identity: he thinks of himself as a Genial Inquisitor. He has consciously and unconsciously searched for a *useful label* to define his identity and build a self-guide. In choosing the identity he would have tried it on to see if it fitted. He would have consciously and unconsciously explored the attributes of his identity by asking himself questions like 'What image or persona must I embrace to present as a compelling and entertaining television personality?' and 'Who precisely am I and can I be when I walk onto a television set?'.

On arriving at the definition of Genial Inquisitor he would have begun to explore how a Genial Inquisitor thinks and the values his persona would need to reflect to come across as believable, entertaining and trustworthy. Over time he would have arrived at a solid set of attributes around which his identity was built. This is reflected by his values, beliefs and attitudes.

2. Values, beliefs and attitudes

Values, beliefs and attitudes are the things that determine *why* a Genial Inquisitor behaves the way he does. They govern purpose and intent, and sustain or undermine the skills and behaviours that flow from the identity a person takes on. There are two kinds of values: *means values* and *end values*. For example, you might eat vegetarian food (means value) because you want to live a long and healthy life (end value). Let's put values to the imagined Parkinson test. At some level of his consciousness Parkinson has built clusters of values, such as the following:

- I establish rapport with my subjects because this establishes their trust and enables me to ask deeply personal questions.
- I research my subjects comprehensively as this conveys to them a real interest in them as people, which, in turn, encourages them to be more revealing.
- I listen carefully to my subject's responses because this prevents me missing important lines of inquiry.
- I ask my tough questions when rapport is at its deepest because this takes the 'threat' away from the question, and usually I'll get a revealing answer.
- I treat people with respect because my audience will like me less if I am aggressive.

You may notice that the above values are consistent with the identity of Genial Inquisitor. Parkinson has a reservoir of values that support his professional identity.

Beliefs, on the other hand, are one of the larger frameworks for behaviour. When you believe something, your capabilities and behaviours will be directed and informed by your belief. If, for example, you believe that people in the workplace are generally lazy and untrustworthy, and close the front door on their scruples when they leave home for work in the morning, the strategies and behaviours you apply as a manager will reflect that particular slant on the world. It will be reflected in the daily decisions you make about people and also in your non-verbal behaviour: the tone of your voice, your facial expressions and your physical positioning when communicating with colleagues and staff.

Your beliefs about the cause and meaning of things, and your beliefs about yourself, structure your perception of reality. Anything that doesn't conform to your framework of beliefs and values, which includes your beliefs about what is possible, will at some level of your consciousness be rejected. Conversely, anything that supports your beliefs will be affirmed and will act to reinforce those beliefs.

Beliefs aren't necessarily true, even when you think they are. They are more like deeply embedded opinions of the world than matters of fact. What appears to be true is that they regulate the way you behave, until a new mental or physical experience, or set of experiences, sweeps an old belief away and replaces it with a new belief.

So what kinds of beliefs about himself and others does Parkinson have to have to behave consistently as a Genial Inquisitor? Review the following:

- People are more likely to reveal themselves when they are not fighting for survival or feeling defensive.
- Interviewers must question without fear or favour if they want to have maximum credibility with both subjects and audiences.
- It is easy to be a 'fair' person.
- I like people warming to me when they see me as a real person who is intensely curious about them.
- My sense of humour and ability to enjoy the lighter side of life works for me as an interviewer and gives my audiences experiences of light and shade.
- Credibility and integrity are important for me to retain the respect of my guests and audience.

The above incomplete set of beliefs has been modelled from Parkinson's behaviours and significantly determines the approach he takes to his job. Furthermore, because Parkinson has endured as an icon of the British interviewing genre, you can rest assured he would have constantly evaluated the potency and usefulness of his values and beliefs to ensure they kept up with public expectations and trends in the media. Values and beliefs support and, at times, inhibit the motivation for what are termed capabilities.

3. Capabilities

Some people see capabilities as skill and knowledge, but it is useful to focus not only on those elements but also on how knowledge is utilised and how behaviour (skill) is applied to achieve specific outcomes. These are called 'distinctions'.

The distinctions a person makes influence every outcome. For example, say you cut a child's hair. Chances are you do not have the same identity as a professional hairdresser. Your goal may be simply to produce a short, neat result. Hairdressers, on the other hand, would make many distinctions, based on their identity as a professional. A hairdresser would make distinctions such as layering, contour, working with the direction the hair grows, shaping to match facial contours, thinning and sculpting to produce height and so on. Distinctions, as you can see, are very important.

To continue with the Parkinson exercise, the distinctions he makes as a Genial Inquisitor would vary from interview to interview. He would match criteria (distinctions) to the feedback he was getting while conducting each interview to indicate how near he was to achieving his outcomes.

Behavioural flexibility is the key to the relationship between capabilities and results, or outcomes. To keep his interviews on track and produce informative, entertaining television, Parkinson engages in a continuous process of comparing his capabilities (how he puts his skills and knowledge to work) with the results he is achieving in the interview. He generally establishes very clear goals for each interview he conducts, thus providing a yardstick to measure his outcomes against.

Anyone who watches a Parkinson show on ABC television closely would notice subtle shifts in Parkinson's behaviour and technique. Those shifts match the context of the interview he is conducting: an interview with a brassy celebrity produces different distinctions and behaviours than an interview with a minor member of the royal family. Parkinson's identity remains that of the Genial Inquisitor, but his behaviour shifts to accommodate the particular context of the interview: the content, the personality involved, the sensitivity of the subject material, how the topic sits in the public domain, and so on.

The key to making distinctions is to gather as much feedback as possible during the activity you are engaging in, and to experiment with different techniques and behaviours until you produce the outcome you desire.

The value of distinctions is that they promote flexibility of behaviour.

4. Behaviour

Behaviour is how you *act* in a given context. A virtuoso interviewer like Parkinson instinctively 'reads' an interviewee and modifies his own behaviour in accordance with the signals he receives from his subjects. He demonstrates awareness that his subjects will unconsciously interpret his behaviour. He creates tonal and physiological patterns that are positively charged and designed to place his interviewees in a relaxed and cooperative state of mind. Parkinson's behaviours are directly linked to the values, beliefs and attitudes that support his identity. The high level of capability he demonstrates is in complete alignment with his chosen public persona.

Appropriate and flexible behaviour will allow you to effectively operate in your chosen context.

5. Context

In many ways your professional identity will determine the contexts in which you are able to operate competently. For example, say you have chosen the identity of 'manager' as opposed to 'leader'. What sets of beliefs and values would support your identity? If you're like many people who identify with the label 'manager', your supporting beliefs and values will centre on processes, means, practicalities, facts and usefulness to tasks at hand. Your values and beliefs will produce capabilities and behaviours that reflect the principal dictates of a 'manager'.

What if your position demanded the attributes, capabilities and behaviours of a leader? Instead of managing processes, leaders frequently disrupt processes with the question 'why?'. Rather than the 'strict parent' model of management, leaders more often employ what is termed the 'nurturing parent' model. Leaders are focused on the future, managers on the present; leaders regularly dwell on what is possible, whereas managers pay attention to the actual and so on. How well would you as a 'manager' operate in the new context?

Let's imagine that you had the foresight to adopt a broader, more flexible, professional identity at the beginning of your career as a corporate executive. Let's say you saw yourself as a leader/enabler. Think about the kinds of values and beliefs you would need to embrace to support such an identity, and think about the capabilities you would generate as a result. It's fair to assume that if you adopted the professional identity of leader/enabler, you would be able to operate more effectively in contexts that demand flexibility as well as pure managerial ability.

In developing a self-guide to support the identity of leader/enabler you may have come to appreciate the importance of understanding human differences and of the need to fit ideas, processes and change into a broader framework, which includes the aspirations and needs of those who will carry out the work. You may have recognised that a common mission is an important motivating force, that having integrity and generating trust are preconditions for people walking over hot coals for you, and that strong rhetorical skills will enable you to create powerful word pictures that motivate and inspire.

Sure, you may be able to manage your time and processes, but the identity of leader/enabler would bring with it a set of capabilities and behaviours that would give you greater flexibility and marketability in today's competitive environment. In designing your identity, pay attention to existing and possible contexts of the future.

Having explored the five levels of change, you will notice how they influence each other. If you change at one level, chances are that all levels *below* that will also change because that level organises what happens at the lower levels. Note that the levels *above* the changes you make will often not change, so if you do not consider exploring your career at the identity level you may be *short*-changing yourself.

A final word on Parkinson: the Genial Inquisitor identity allows him to operate in a broad variety of environments. The beliefs, values, capabilities and behaviours of a Genial Inquisitor are centred on 'finding out' and eliciting high-value information. High-value information gathering can be fashioned to fit numerous genres from television anchor/interviewer to documentary maker, columnist, author and beyond.

So, who do you really want to be?

CONSUMMATION

As a result of following Parkinson's journey through the levels of change process, have you discovered other qualities and attributes you want to add to the three lists you have already completed? If so, add them now before you create a name or label for your new professional identity.

Think of a title or name that encapsulates all the attributes and qualities you have assembled. For example, as a CEO of a company or organisation you could choose the title 'Grand Poo Bah', if that was the way you saw yourself operating charismatically in your field of endeavour. You may have known mothers of young families take on the identity of 'The Rock' because that's the way they saw themselves in the context of rearing a husband and young family. The name you choose can be personal and private, and it can be a descriptive or abstract term that has great meaning for you.

Choosing the right name for your identity is critical because it informs what you are, what you do, or what you hope to do and become. It represents a 'hot button' that instantly switches on the self-schema you have designed and built. Think about the perfect name for your identity. Identify a name that allows you to operate in as broad a context as possible.

My professional identity is that of a ...

No matter what career or vocation you're in, your capabilities and behaviours will be limited or expanded by the label you choose and the beliefs, values and attitudes that support it. Be generous with your definition and notice how it offers you the freedom to expand your role beyond that of conservative definitions. Having done so, give yourself another pat on the back for doing what charismatic personalities do.

Your final task in building a strong and consistent identity is to refer back to your self-guide, pay attention to the list of desired attributes, and create a series of strong beliefs to support the qualities you want to embody.

Beliefs are the cornerstone of your personal outcomes. Beliefs about yourself, others and the world in general can limit, confirm or expand opportunities for self-development. In building a more charismatic identity you are directing your attention to beliefs about what is possible, and creating a series of benchmarks that you can believe in. You may be helped in this process by the information provided in this book, which allows you to follow the sequences of those who have successfully improved their charisma quotients.

Beliefs have a remarkable tendency to become self-fulfilling prophecies. Beliefs and non-beliefs about your personal capacities and potential can be seen as roadmaps that lead you to particular destinations. Think about some of the limiting beliefs or 'can'ts' you have about yourself. Say you had a limiting belief about swimming and regularly told yourself and others when invited to the beach or pool parties, 'I can't swim'. Deconstructed, that means that you *can* do the process of *not* swimming, doesn't it? So, if you were thrown into a deep pool, what would happen? You would either dump the belief as not useful in the circumstances and start splashing about and paddling to safety, or you would go about not swimming, uniting all your behaviours in an effort to fulfil the prophecy— all the way down to the bottom.

Not surprisingly, many people spend a lot of their lives doing the processes of 'not', rarely ever choosing to jump in at the deep end, let alone learn to swim. In doing so, they deny themselves the opportunity to discover the personal resources that are available to them to survive and flourish. This is especially the case when there are no physical or environmental factors preventing them from succeeding. You are a wise person indeed to have learned to do the process of not flying off tall buildings, but where is the wisdom in learning how to do the process of not flying into a mood of self-confidence, not doing good social skills, not giving yourself permission to express your emotions, not being empathic, not using the power of ethical persuasion, and so on?

Self-fulfilling prophecies are also at work when you have empowering beliefs. Empowering beliefs in situations you haven't encountered before are characterised by 'I can do that' impulses. If you believe you will succeed in a particular goal, the odds are well and truly in your favour as long as your goals are specific, measurable, achievable and realistic, and have a timeline placed on them.

The rules for self-improvement are not all that complicated. The cardinal rule is that if you want to change or develop, then start doing something! In starting to do something, the best place to begin is at the end, which is what the entire identity engineering process is all about. By focusing on ends (in this case your ultimate identity, and the thinking and behaviours that embody it) you have set up a destination, a space where you will want to be. In other words, you have created a prophecy to fulfil.

In reviewing your self-development guide, think about the beliefs you *will* have when you have fulfilled your identity prophecy. It's important that you create and adopt empowering beliefs. Choose not to allow limiting beliefs to tarnish the process. You may be surprised and delighted to learn that you don't have to limit yourself because many of the key thinking patterns and behaviours of charismatic performance are well within your limits. You can demonstrate to yourself, as others have done, that you don't have to be superwoman or superman to succeed as a person who thinks and communicates charismatically.

Studies have shown that people with a strong sense of purpose in life, an ability to self-monitor and manage expressive behaviour, empathy, good ethical grounding, good delivery skills and average intelligence can be as good at leading as those with higher intelligence. High IQ is no guarantee of success in life. In one longitudinal study over a thirty-five year period of 268 men, it was found that those who scored the highest in IQ tests and university entrance exams fared no better than their lower scoring contemporaries. High scorers achieved no greater results in life satisfaction; happiness with family, friends or significant others; or productivity, salary and status in their chosen field.

In a profiling exercise of American CEOs, Daniel Goleman (author of *Emotional Intelligence*) and his colleagues found that those who reached the top had insignificant analytical and conceptual superiority (IQ) over those who had been overlooked. What they did have was:

1. twice as much competency in self-confidence;
2. seven times more self-control;
3. double the achievement orientation;
4. three times as much competency in empathy and teamwork skills.

You don't need to be a prodigy to learn those behaviours, do you?

Use the example on page 74 as a model to construct a series of empowering beliefs that will add impetus and support to your mission of building a more desirable public identity. See yourself *doing* the desired attributes and begin to observe and record the kinds of beliefs that have allowed you to master it. For example, if you have nominated self-confidence as a desired attribute, put your self in the position of being self-confident. Here you are doing self-confidence and what are you thinking about as you do it? What are the things that permit you to exude self-confidence? Which limitations have melted away? What new insights and beliefs do you have as a result of being able to do self-confidence? Note your observations down in the form of beliefs. Use the following guide to build beliefs for all your desired attributes.

Desired attributes	*Supporting beliefs*
Self-confidence	When I look at my list of personal achievements I believe that I have a lot to be confident about.
	I have a right to be heard because I have a good contribution to make.
	It's delightful to make other people feel committed and enthusiastic when I do self-confidence.
	I notice that people are more easily convinced when I present an idea confidently.
	Self-confidence is a state of mind I can access at will.
	The more I'm self-confident the easier it is to do, and the easier it is to do the more self-confident I become.

Let's consolidate what you have learned and achieved in this final phase of the identity engineering process:

1. You have built a self-guide detailing your present attributes and contrasting them with desired attributes you need to develop to have a more charismatic personality.
2. You have created a set of means and ends values that give purpose to the desired attributes you want to personify.
3. You have invented a name or phrase that encapsulates your new identity and represents a mental rallying point.
4. You have attached a cluster of useful beliefs around each of your desired attributes.

Review your handiwork only as often as it takes to install a powerful internal symbolic representation of your chosen identity, and the qualities, attributes and capabilities it portrays. Revisit your notes knowing that the more often you visualise yourself *being* the new identity, the closer you will become to personifying it. It's perfectly in order to make changes and modifications to your identity model before you arrive at an ideal prototype that fits your circumstances like a glove.

Identity engineering is a process many successful CEOs, personalities, leaders, politicians and other individuals carry out instinctively and without much awareness of what they're doing. You can appreciate that what you have explored is a model that demystifies a series of seemingly cryptic actions and thoughts. Identity engineering is do-able and it requires some initial effort, but a lot less effort than is necessary for those who engineer an identity without having the benefits of a plan to follow and a powerful prototype to give it human form.

HOW PERSONAL VISION DRIVES CHARISMATIC COMMUNICATION

5

The people's prayer, the glad diviner's theme, the young
men's vision, and the old men's dream!
John Dryden

It's 1931 and you wander onto the site of the unfinished Sydney Harbour
Bridge and ask a metalworker, 'What's your part in the scheme of this
bridge?'. He says, 'I'm making sections that will be bolted onto the arch to
give the bridge support. It's how I earn my living.' You might say to
yourself, 'There's a bloke who knows his job and his place in the whole
scheme of things. He's got a goal and he'll meet that goal over and again
on numerous construction sites during his working life.' This fellow is like
many of us. He's in survival mode, choosing an occupation that will earn
him enough money to buy the material comforts he needs.

You drift over to another metalworker and ask him the same question,
and he says, 'I'd work here for nothing, you know. I'm making one of the
finest structures the world has known. This bridge is going to rival the
Eiffel Tower as one of the marvels of the world. People will look at it and
be astonished by its beauty and majesty. I'll be able to tell my
grandchildren that I was here, that I was a part of engineering history in
this country.'

How does one worker transform the day-to-day drudgery of earning a
living into something that united his whole being behind the building of a
great structure? What qualities characterise his attitude and approach to
working on the Sydney Harbour Bridge project? The answer is obvious,
isn't it? He isn't doing a job, he's living a dream and has set his heart upon
fulfilling a fundamental purpose in his life. He is doing what he loves, and
loving what he does.

And the other worker? What prevents him from taking pride in his part
in the making of engineering history? In essence, he's doing as many of us

do: separating our working lives from the rest of our existence, hating Mondays and loving Fridays, and doing what we do as opposed to doing what we love. Work represents a means to some other end, our heart isn't in it, and we often long to be somewhere else.

You may have experienced some of the unintended consequences of the division of work and play. You may have felt the void of not having a passion for what you do, you may know the frustration and sense of defeat in being in a job you don't enjoy, and you can wonder what it takes to lift yourself out of such a meaningless mire. We spend a large part of our lives in the workplace. If we can't somehow find a purpose to it all, other than as a means to material comfort, then how do we differ from the androids of science fiction or the 'army of grey, faceless men in suits'?

It takes vision and the integration of work and play to propel yourself out of survival mode and into personal revival mode. Vision and personal mission are like inseparable Siamese twins. Vision is about defining what matters to you, what really excites your passion, what feeds your imagination and what directs your life from within. Personal mission relates to how you go about fulfilling your vision: how you actualise it through work and deeds and the linkages you make in life to give it expression.

In the case of the second bridge worker, something from within fuels his enthusiasm and love of his work. To understand its origins we may have to go back a couple of decades to see a child enchanted by his Meccano set, to watch him engrossed in a world of working models and dreams of transforming them into real-life structures.

It may come as no surprise to you that our second bridge worker took up an occupation that totally aligned his childhood vision with his adult mission. If we were to peer into his psyche, we would find a child-like fascination with architectural wonders made out of steel and a love of them that probably bordered on obsession. Our bridge worker has discovered a niche in life that brings him contentment, satisfaction and the happiness that ensues from doing what he loves.

Vision is one of the most predictive factors for both success and personal satisfaction in life. Meaning-driven vision, as opposed to wealth, power and status-driven vision is essential in the evolution of charismatic leadership and communication. It makes sense that when people have a compelling vision for their lives, and refer to their life's vision to make critical personal decisions, they will be happier and their lives will be more balanced. Meaning-driven vision is the stuff that comes from within and rarely has a dollar sign attached to it.

People who possess internally directed vision develop finely tuned senses of personal mission. Strong values and ideology strengthen their faith in the righteousness of their personal missions and guide their actions. It's a logical step to conclude that a leader who is driven by a powerful inner vision and personal mission is more likely to provide meaning and purpose to followers than a hollow super-salesperson driven by visions of fame and fortune. Socially sensitive leaders fulfil a basic tenet of influence theory in that people are more likely to become supporters and followers of those who act beyond self-interest.

The common theme that runs through the lives and times of many contemporary charismatic communicators is that of being driven by something, someone, other than themselves. Just as our second bridge worker is driven by a personal mission to be part of the creation of an engineering marvel, today's charismatic leaders are motivated by things other than wealth, power and status.

CNN's Ted Turner is a classic model of a man motivated by a vision that has little to do with material dividends. In his early years, Turner was heavily influenced by his father to strive for material success. He worked in his father's business and one day learned that his father was going to sell out. A blistering argument ensued in which Turner hurled his father's favourite truisms back in his face. Not long after the altercation, Turner's father turned a pistol on himself and died by his own hand.

During the period of grief, reflection and self-examination that followed, Turner came to realise that his father's values were not the values he wanted to carry with him through life. 'I spent a lot of time trying to figure out what it was that he did wrong. He put too much emphasis on material success. I can tell you it's fool's gold.'

Turner went on to create the world's largest news and information network. His personal tragedies led him to re-evaluate what was important in life for him, as often happens when trauma and loss knock on our doors. He sensed he had energy and great potential, he knew what he cared deeply about and he wanted to 'change things, do things, and go places'. He likens his quest to that of Columbus: 'When you do something that's never been done before, sail on uncharted waters, and don't know where you're going, you're not sure what you're going to find when you get there but at least you're going somewhere'. Going somewhere new figures largely in the scheme of Turner's life, as does a grand vision of endless potentiality.

As is often the case with people who sort out their life's priorities and know what they love and care about, an opportunity happens by, a need presents itself and suddenly it becomes a personal mission. Gestalt therapy calls this the 'Aha!' experience, a blinding flash of lucidity in which everything becomes clear and your purpose appears to be set out before you.

Turner is alert for new opportunities and new places to go and continues to be passionately involved in numerous causes, from AIDS to world peace.

The essence of personal vision is that you have to care deeply about some things. You don't have to care as profoundly as those who want to eradicate world poverty, but you need to care enough to be able to find the inspiration that unites your actions, values, sense of purpose and the person you feel you are behind a quest or personal mission. Discovering your inner vision begins with unearthing the things that matter to you, that can, or do, give meaning to your life.

Many people live their lives without vision purely because they haven't invented or learned a process to take them to the heart of their passions. You may want to invest some time in completing the following exercises, knowing that the time invested could make an amazing difference to the rest of your life. They are designed to help you explore what matters to you, what you care about, and what excites your desires and wishes. Remember to focus on meaning-driven vision, as you've already discovered that more than often wealth and fame are by-products of vision.

Make sure that your vision is not dependent on the approval or actions of other people. Other people will undoubtedly be involved in your vision somewhere, but it's extremely important for you to let your vision come forth without being impeded by circumstance and the heavy expectations of others. Finding your vision is an exercise requiring no permission from anyone but you, because you need to tap into your deepest and most personal dreams and principles.

DISCOVERING YOUR LIFE'S PASSIONS

You already possess the necessary resources to discover the things that can really set you on fire: a memory and a limitless imagination. All you need to do is put them to work. Memory and imagination work better when you allow your conscious mind to take a tea break and permit your unconscious mind to guide you on a journey through your past, present and future.

One way to give your conscious mind a rest is to go into a relaxed state by spending a few minutes in a peaceful environment, breathing in and out, and gently placing your full focus on your breath. This simple exercise can produce the same state of mind as your daydreaming state. Close your eyes, inhale and exhale, and let any other thoughts drift away easily and effortlessly as you pay full attention to your breath. Before you go any further, try this relaxation technique and notice how it has a healthy and calming effect.

When you have tried and succeeded in achieving a calm state, do it again, and as you reach a state of relaxation ask yourself this precise question: 'I wonder how delighted and amazed I'll be to discover the things in my past and present that really inspire and energise me'. Just allow your thoughts to drift, see the pictures in your mind's eye, hear the sounds that go with them, notice the feelings and tastes and smells that come and go. Come out of the state of relaxation and note any discoveries you feel are important. Keep your notebook handy and repeat this exercise at intervals, gradually asking yourself more of the following questions, always beginning with variations of 'I wonder how delighted, amazed, grateful, chuffed, inspired, I would be to discover':

- what I love so much that I'd actually pay to do it;
- the things that fired my imagination during my childhood;
- the elements of life that I'm really interested in: people, objects, situations, environments, challenges, activities;
- the times that I really felt a surge of interest and energy and felt propelled into action;
- the people who encourage and motivate me to be like them;
- my past and present dreams, both conscious and when I'm asleep;
- the things I could do that would make my life rich and meaningful.

You may find that after you've done the exercise a few times it will enter your awareness during those moments where you give yourself a short daydreaming spell. Let your quest to discover the meaningful things in your life visit you regularly, and become aware of the melange of images, sounds and feelings you are building up as a consequence. Experience the pleasure and delight of immersing yourself in your deepest dreams and passions, and begin to observe how you remember them so clearly.

Continue bringing back the assemblage of images, sounds and feelings until just thinking about them can trigger their return in an instant. Your next step is to go into your daydreaming state and wonder how enchanting it would be to take some of your individual passions and the things you love into the future. Imagine making a video of your future, see yourself cast in the central role doing the things that make your life rich and meaningful. You can almost taste the sweetness of living out your deepest desires. And it beats the hell out of playing a minor role in someone else's soap opera, doesn't it?

Persist with the exercise only as long as it takes for your personal portfolio of life's passions to become like an invisible companion, accessible whenever you desire it to enter your consciousness. Carry it with you wherever you go, and when times are trying, invite it to join you for a few seconds as a revival tonic.

WHAT COUNTS?

The second element in developing a strong vision is to determine a cluster of values that, for you, can make the difference between an ordinary, somewhat ambiguous existence and an energised and purposeful life. You have already gained some experience in determining values during the identity engineering exercise. Now you have the opportunity to uncover your core values and discover how to approach your missions in life with self-assurance and conviction. You can choose to remember that values do not remain constant. They change as *context* changes. The context in which you will complete the values elicitation exercise is cross-contextual: across your whole life as opposed to one particular part of it.

Your core values are the things that really count in your life. Core values provide the purpose for your choices and behaviour. They also serve as criteria for after-the-fact evaluation of events. They are the filters by which you judge your own and others' behaviour and they serve as benchmarks for determining 'good' from 'bad', so-called right from wrong, proper from improper, useful from useless, and so on. Values are often listed as criteria. For example, a person may list such things as security, satisfaction, freedom, people contact and recognition as the things they need to have in order to be happy in a particular environment.

Generally, you give little thought to any level of values unless they are violated or fulfilled in some exceptional way. If something angers, upsets or throws you off balance, there are values infringements or issues somewhere in the picture. Take the simple example of someone stealing your parking spot as you were about to reverse into it. Your ensuing rage could be attributed to the violation of a number of different values: the values of courtesy, first-in-first-served and fairness, to name three. Conversely, if you were waiting in a side street to get onto a main road during peak hour and someone gave way to you, the nice feeling you gained from the experience could be ascribed to the satisfaction of values such as courtesy, respect and generosity.

When you feel upset, or for that matter exhilarated, it's doubtful you'll hear an inner voice that cries, 'Warning, warning, a values violation!' or 'We have lift-off, positive value ignition!'. It doesn't happen that way, because your deepest and most important values are generally not available to you as readily identifiable or conscious concepts. Rather, you experience positive or negative emotions that signal something has either satisfied or disturbed you. Your heart's desires and core values, however, become more powerful when they become part of your conscious existence.

Charismatic communicators are conspicuous by their understanding and expression of their deepest desires and most important values. Unlike many, they have an extremely keen awareness of what counts to them and what doesn't in the grand scheme of things. But, there is another crucial element in the way charismatic leaders live and breathe their deepest desires and values. They rarely ever experience the confusion of conflicting personal values. This is a major reason why they present as strong, confident and compelling personalities.

To understand how personal-value conflicts inhibit and, indeed, derail your sense of purpose and mission, and therefore your confidence, consider a time when a part of you wanted to do one thing and another part of you wanted to do something else. Say, for example, you really wanted to take an overseas holiday at some idyllic spot, and yet another part of you demanded your savings be spent on reducing your mortgage because of a need for security. Suddenly, you find yourself right in the middle of a values conflict.

Your desire for a holiday may be informed by values of novelty, fun, adventure and relaxation, whereas those pestering thoughts about the mortgage could be sustained by values of security/insecurity, thrift/extravagance and, possibly, caution. If you neglected to resolve the values conflict and your quandary remained that of a struggle between holiday and mortgage, you would continue in a state of indecision until you made a choice. It's impossible to equivocate and have confidence and certitude at the same time, isn't it?

Now, say you made a choice without attending to the deeper values conflict. What would happen? If you chose the holiday, you can almost be assured that the luxury of tanning on some sun-drenched tropical beach would be interrupted with nagging doubts about the wisdom of the decision you made. Do you think you would do your holiday with absolute confidence and leap into the experience with single-minded hedonism? Of course not: your doubts would take away some of your enjoyment and weaken your commitment to having the time of your life. And, imagine your misery if you gave in to your needs for security and ploughed your savings into the mortgage. How much drive, energy and confidence would you invest in the task of transferring your savings to your mortgage account?

Are you beginning to understand a key difference between those who think and behave charismatically and those who don't? One of the secrets behind the drive and energy charismatic leaders give to their missions in life is an absence of values conflicts. Can you imagine our second bridge worker experiencing a values conflict in the context of his mission in life? Can you imagine Ted Turner being torn with indecision over competing values? Not likely, because both have undergone experiences that have given them the opportunity to identify what counts in their lives.

Their core values are part of their conscious existence and they clearly understand which values are more important than others. The quandary of holiday versus mortgage wouldn't occur to them, because their decisions would be based on a personal ranking of values. You probably wouldn't lose your money if you wagered on them both taking the holiday.

The following exercise is designed to help you discover your core values and rank them in order of importance. Have a notepad handy to write down your discoveries.

STEP 1

1. Recall four or five of the most meaningful events in your life so far. They can be positive or negative experiences as long as they are the most significant experiences you have had to date. Write them down.

2. Work through the list of events, starting with the first experience. If it is a positive event, go into your memory and see things through your own eyes. Notice the things that made the experience important and particularly meaningful. Ask yourself, 'What was really important to me about the experience?'. Write down words or phrases that represent the significant things that you got from the experience, for example, words like fun, enthusiasm, independence, perseverance, justice, harmony, love and happiness. If it is a negative event that may cause you distress, view the experience as you would a movie, see yourself and write down the most important things you see yourself gaining from the incident.

3. Continue with the exercise until you have worked through your four or five most significant or meaningful events. You will have four or five separate lists of key words or phrases.

STEP 2

1. Look through the words and phrases and identify those that keep repeating through your lists and were really important about the events.

2. Select a batch of about six if you can. These words and phrases represent your core values, the things that really count in your life.

3. Write them out separately. They could be the most important words and phrases you have ever constructed. Now take the final step of prioritising your values.

STEP 3

1. Look at the six core values you have identified and ask yourself this question: 'If I had to give one of them up, which one would it be?'. Rather than engaging your logical processes, use your intuition and choose the one that you feel right about giving up. When you have decided, write the number six alongside it.

2. Go through the above process, asking yourself which one of the remaining values you would be prepared to give up. As you eliminate a value, write a number beside it until you are left with two values.

3. Now, look at the two values and understand what they mean to you. Then ask yourself, 'Which of these two values do I absolutely have to have if I want to feel most fulfilled in my life?'. If need be, put one value in the palm of one hand and the other value in the palm of your other hand and ask yourself the question. Notice the hand that feels more potent or possessive. Mark the value you absolutely have to have with the number one and the other with the number two.

You have now created an important decision-making tool, a tool that charismatic communicators conscientiously use when making significant decisions, evaluating evidence and making judgments. With a set of prioritised core values at your disposal, you can make better informed decisions across different contexts in your life. Many people, after having undertaken this exercise, choose to translate the information they have gathered into an elegant one-page document. It begs to be framed and placed in a prominent place as a constant reminder of the things that really count in your life.

CREATING YOUR VISION

When you combine your heart's desires with your core values, you create a chemical reaction that produces an integrated sense of purpose and potential. This powerful union gives you the 'shove' to begin your life's mission in earnest. Your mission may not represent a singular quest requiring a lifetime of devotion, although many charismatic communicators walk down that path. It can manifest itself in a series of quests that satisfy a greater, grander vision.

Dick Smith is one of Australia's best known charismatic personalities. As an adventurer, explorer, businessman, philanthropist and, more recently, controversial chairman of the Civil Aviation Safety Authority, Smith can be seen as a man who has given expression to his grand vision through numerous quests.

Smith and his wife built a $610 company into an empire of fifty stores, turning over $50 million a year when it was sold to Woolworths in 1982. He founded *Australian Geographic* in 1985, another success story, with the aim of encouraging a love of Australia's unique flora and fauna. Passion and not dollars fuel his latest business venture, Dick Smith Foods. 'I'm not greedy, I have adequate money,' he says. 'This is something I really want to do because I'd like to bring $100 million worth of sales back to Australian ownership.'

Dick Smith has taken on the overseas giants of the food industry in a personal mission to encourage Australians to support locally produced and manufactured foods. He put up $5 million of his money to build alliances with existing small manufacturers to produce a range of locally owned and home-grown products. Defying the status quo is very much part of his values system.

In the early part of 2000, Dick Smith embarked on another triumphant adventure: the first trans-Tasman balloon flight from New Zealand to Australia. He explained on a nationally televised interview during the flight that a major reason for this latest quest to enter the record books was that 'it had not been done before'. 'It's a symbolic flight for bringing ownership back to Australia,' he added. He said that a prime motivation for his adventures was that of 'extending my boundaries'. Smith is a great optimist, and like many charismatic personalities longs to do things that haven't been done before. He puts himself 'on the line' in almost every venture he undertakes.

Flying against the generally prevailing winds is something Dick Smith is comfortable with. Whether it's a trans-Tasman balloon flight, being the first person to fly around the world via the poles, flying around the world solo in a helicopter or working towards change in a lumbering bureaucracy such as the Civil Aviation Safety Authority, Smith has converted his 'love of flying' into a series of adventures or missions.

Adventure figures largely in Dick Smith's dreams. But where did this sense of adventure and ability to inspire others to support his exploits come from? To build an organisation such as Dick Smith Electronics he required the help of many other people. To transform a love of the Australian bush into a publishing and retailing success he required the active and enthusiastic support of numerous individuals and groups, from staffers to subscribers. Smith's business and personal adventures necessarily require others to take on his vision and help make it a reality. Without devoted followers, Smith would not be able to rapidly get things done.

The roots of Smith's persuasive abilities and vision can be found in the experiences of a lonely eight-year-old boy who joined the scouting movement. 'I began as a Cub at eight and went right through to Rovers at age twenty-three. I was very much a loner and Scouting gave me mateship, taught me organisation and how to motivate people. That's why I was able to be the success I am.' Dick Smith feels a great debt to Scouting and attributes his ability to get on with people to his early experiences in the scouting movement. 'It had to be the most fantastic influence on my life.'

Smith's attitude towards risk is a textbook example of how charismatic leaders view it. 'Scouting taught me responsible risk-taking', he says. Risk is relished and seen as something that can be managed. Risk-assessment, however, features heavily during Smith's planning phase. When setting out on a new venture, he forms a clear concept of the risks he's taking and the pitfalls he needs to avoid. As with many charismatic leaders, Smith has a romantic relationship with risk. It is linked to his concept of courage, sense of confidence built up from previous risk-taking ventures and the challenge of creating new pathways and establishing new standards.

Dick Smith's core values and passions merge to form a grand vision of his purpose in life. This 'wholeness' pattern is incredibly consistent throughout his adult life, as his activities and exploits demonstrate. Smith loves flying, he loves nature and the bush, he loves gadgetry, he loves testing and pushing himself, he loves the thrill of taking risks and, as is the case with most charismatic personalities, he loves doing things that haven't been done before. His life's passions drive every major project he engages in, and his core values are reflected in the means he employs to reach the goals he sets.

Smith, our second bridge worker, Ted Turner and countless other charismatic personalities and leaders truly love what they do and do what they love. The vitality, enthusiasm and enormous energy they invest in their projects and missions come from a grand vision of their purpose in life. They have asked the tougher questions: they know what their passions are, they know what counts and they know the kind of person they have become. They may have one great mission in life or a series of missions in which they totally align themselves.

The examples of Turner, Smith and our second bridge worker can offer a model of how to integrate your values and deepest passions into one grand vision. Take some time to review the notes you have made in the previous exercises. Begin to think about how your passions and values can come together to form a whole far greater than the sum of its parts. When you have reviewed your work in identifying your life's passions and core values, transform them into a grand vision by following the process below.

If you have a capacity to get lost in your dreams and become oblivious to your surroundings as many charismatic personalities do, you could conceivably complete the following exercise in the busiest and noisiest of surroundings. However, if you haven't reached the stage of being able to lose yourself in thought at will, you may like to consider completing this exercise in a place that offers solitude and quietness.

Your mission is to determine how your life's passions and core values interlace to create your vision. Find your quiet spot and begin to enter the state of relaxation you experienced in earlier exercises.

Creating your grand vision

1. Begin daydreaming about how your core values, your passions and any secret or unspoken dreams and goals could materialise into one large whole. Ask yourself how they could form together to give you a clearer sense of your purpose in life. Your purpose in life may begin to show itself by some feeling of attraction or 'pull'. Allow yourself to be drawn towards the source of the attraction. If you were able to see yourself at the centre of the gravitational point, on centre stage of life, what would you see yourself doing?

2. Knowing what you really love to do, how would you see yourself doing it? In what settings can you sense yourself doing what you love and how are your core values being satisfied in these scenes? Begin to take some still shots of your activities and place them in an imaginary album. Begin to look through the album and remove any images that you sense are not really you, leaving only the most important ones in your album. When the sorting process is complete, look through the album, notice how effortlessly you remember the photographs and begin to realise how your dreams and values are reflected in the scenes.

3. Come out of your relaxed state and begin to flip through your mental album, pausing on any images that really create strong feelings of satisfaction and joy.

4. Think about some people who live their lives the way you want to live your life. See yourself engaging in activities that produce the same feelings in you as you have when you imagine your role models. Begin to notice yourself doing the things that really count to you and take some more photographs. Add the photographs to your imaginary photo album. Sort them, discarding any of the new shots that don't fit in.

5. Come out of your relaxed state and again begin to flip through your album, allowing each image to indelibly etch itself in your memory. Feel the strong feelings you have when you begin to think of the album filling up with your snapshots and notice what it's like to know how the photographs begin to show a strong pattern.

6. Sense the pattern that is forming and become the producer of your own video. Give your setting bright lighting, add colour, turn up the sound and see

yourself being in real-life situations that reflect the pattern that has formed with the photographs you have taken.

7. Direct different scenes of your future life. Place yourself in various well-lit settings and begin to see how great you feel in those scenes. With each scene, take a note of which of your core values are being satisfied, paying attention to their priority. Pan out, zoom in and begin to see many different camera angles of yourself in your personal video. Engage in the pure pleasure of making selected still shots come to life in your video, always seeing yourself as the main character.

8. As you look at your video in various settings and scenes, just allow the part of you that contains and preserves all the major lessons in your life to incorporate what you have experienced. Let it take you out into the future and show you how you will be with a unified vision, living your life with passion and vigour.

When you have completed the exercise, write it down as a story, giving only as much detail as required for your snapshots and videos to come alive as you re-read the words. Invest some time reviewing and refining the process until you could write your life story in a few short sentences.

Often when people do this exercise once, they come out of it with a vivid sense of their vision and purpose in life. With others it can take two or three reviews of the complete exercise before they experience that inner sense of something significant having changed in their lives.

Your vision of your purpose in life reflects at the deepest level who you are. It incorporates the values that count to you and it defines how you will go about giving expression to your deepest desires. The exercise you have undertaken may seem strikingly similar to experiences, no matter how fleeting, you have had in the past. You may have been taking a shower, sitting on the toilet, relaxing in a garden or just staring into blank space when suddenly thoughts and pictures begin to form about future possibilities or past hopes and dreams. You may not have made much sense of these images and feelings surfacing from your unconscious mind and may not have seen a pattern. The above exercise is designed purely to give some form and direction to something you already do, often without paying much attention to it.

A major difference between charismatic communicators and others is the tendency to give their unconscious mind a bit of slack and allow it to take them as observers into a future world of personal potential and possibilities. They're often mistakenly labelled as dreamers, whereas they're doing one of the more intelligent things a human being can do— allowing the power of their imagination to help in the process of creating a better future for themselves and others.

HOW IT'S SAID:

CONTENT DESIGN AND STRUCTURE

6 START WITH A PURPOSE

If you don't know where you're going, any path will take you there.

Sioux proverb

If you decided to take a journey without having a clear idea of where you were going, how would you know if and when you actually got there? Strange as it may seem, many communicators take audiences on expeditions with little thought of itinerary or destination. They fail to set their hearts upon a communication goal and seldom map the route they'll take to make the excursion interesting, comfortable and memorable.

Purposeless presentations and conversations are like trips to nowhere. Just as people without clearly defined goals and visions wander haphazardly through life, seldom reaching their potential, speakers without a mission often meander purposelessly through presentations, failing to capitalise on the opportunities a presentation, speech or conversation offers. They rarely have an impact on audiences because they don't support their presentations with determination.

Determination can be seen as the mental and physical energy a person invests in a task, goal or purpose. In other words, determination is linked to an end-result. Without an outcome or result in mind, determination weakens and resolve dissipates. Establishing a reason, a goal or outcome for your message is a simple process that begins with you recognising that persuasion involves your audience understanding and valuing:

- you
- a service
- a behaviour
- someone else
- an idea
- your expertise
- a product
- a proposal
- your division or organisation

In persuading an individual or group to understand and value something, you must first determine if there is a need to be fulfilled and an end to achieve. If there isn't an apparent need, you can choose to discover one.

MEANS AND ENDS

Remember your inquiry into means values and ends values in the chapter on identity engineering? Let's revisit one of the examples given and make some further and important distinctions. The following statement implies a shift from somewhere to somewhere else, doesn't it? So, where was the starting point?

I am eating vegetarian food [means value] because I want to live a long and healthy life [end value].

Let's assume that the person making the shift had thought about their present state of health and didn't like what they saw. Imagine they contemplated issues such as fitness and existing physical complaints, and reflected on the conventional view that our Western diet is causing a number of conditions that become threatening later in life. The 'somewhere' the person shifted away from was their former eating habits and the negative associations attached to those habits. The 'somewhere else' was a shift towards a future long and healthy life and the positive associations attached to that vision. The means of attaining the objective was eating vegetarian food. The process can be represented visually in the following diagram.

This model has three essential components:

1. your point of departure (the present state of affairs);
2. your mode of transport (the means of getting to your destination);
3. a clearly defined destination so you know where you are going (your purpose or desired state of affairs).

Embarking on a journey without a destination in mind will result in an aimless presentation or message, but identifying a point of departure is equally as significant in persuasion and influence as it is in real life. Say you choose to visit Hobart and decide on air travel as the means of getting there. You're going to look pretty stupid if you haven't identified the airport you're leaving from, and yet many speakers fail to consider departure *and* destination when crafting their messages.

Where you want to take an audience from is an important factor in the process of changing their attitudes. A critical part of persuading people to take on new ideas, change attitudes or shift positions is to replace one set of beliefs, values and attitudes about an existing state of affairs with a new set of values, beliefs and attitudes. In the vegetarian food example, the old values inherent in maintaining a conventional Western diet were replaced with a new set that supported the purpose of having a long and healthy life.

THE PURPOSE SET

A significant step in the sequence of attitude change is unpacking the status quo and presenting it as something to move away from. To argue against the status quo you need to have investigated the disadvantages and drawbacks of the present state of affairs in some detail. Contrasting the shortcomings of the status quo with the benefits of the desired state of affairs appears to be a key rhetorical tool of those who think and behave charismatically.

Charismatic communicators become less charismatic and influential the closer their positions get to conventional wisdom. Charismatic leadership is, at its core, contrary to the status quo. It is, more often than not, about challenging conventions and offering a better vision for the future. Investing time in understanding an existing state of affairs and visualising a more compelling or desirable state of affairs is at the heart of both charisma and innovation.

Defining a problem, need, purpose or challenge cannot be achieved accurately unless you compare the specifics of now with the specifics of where you want to be (the desired state of affairs). The issue or question actually becomes clear when a comparison is made between 'present state' and 'desired state'. The difference between the two states represents the point at issue, the challenge or the means you suggest to transport your audience from the now to a brighter destination.

In determining a purpose for your presentation, speech or persuasion process, use the steps in the following purpose set.

1. DETERMINE THE ELEMENTS THAT MAKE THE STATUS QUO UNDESIRABLE (WHERE ARE WE NOW?)

- What is the current state of play? What are the limitations, the effects, the benefits and the drawbacks? In other words, 'where' do I want my audience/group to shift from?
- What effects does the status quo have on people, productivity, the bottom line, and so on?
- What can people not do/have under the present state of affairs?
- What do you want people to *feel* about the current situation?
- What other things do you want people to know about the status quo?

2. DECIDE ON A HIGHLY DESIRABLE ALTERNATIVE (WHERE WOULD WE LIKE TO BE?)

- What is the most desirable and attainable state of affairs?
- What will it actually be like to have achieved a more desirable state of affairs?
- How (establish criteria) will I know I have reached the desired state?
- What specific effects will it produce?
- What additional advantages and benefits will be available?
- What *feelings* do you want people to have about this future state?

3. WHAT ARE THE BEST MEANS TO EMPLOY TO GET THERE?

- What solutions do you offer?
- How will those solutions achieve the effects you desire?
- What do you want your audience to say *yes* to, so as to cause a shift from the current state of play?
- What do you want people to *do* in order to achieve the desired state of affairs?
- How do you want your audience to *feel* as they are employing the means you offer?

The purpose set mirrors an argument strategy used extensively by charismatic communicators to gain support for their proposals and ideas. Completing the purpose set before designing your message or speech furnishes you with a wealth of information that can be incorporated into your message. It helps you define the form and content of your message and gives strong clues on how to organise yourself, your structure and your evidence. It establishes a clear departure point, it sets a purpose or destination, it identifies the gap between the present and desired states and helps you design the means to satisfy the needs you have outlined.

FEELINGS

You will notice all three of the purpose set questions invite you to consider what you want your listeners to 'feel' about the various aspects raised. It's estimated that around 90 per cent of the decisions we make in life are based on emotion. Feelings are what compel people to take action; logic is applied after the fact to justify our actions.

Charismatic communicators customarily design their presentation structures around a series of intense emotional anchors. They know that people are going to have feelings during a speech or presentation, and for their messages to strike the right chords, they need to be able to guide their listeners into emotional states that support the vision and mission they're proclaiming. They embrace the simple but powerful principle that people are intuitive and emotional *first*, and objective and rational *second*.

In thinking about your purpose and the feelings you may need to evoke to help arouse emotional commitment, consider emotions that will empower your audience to make an easy transition from the present state to a more desirable state of affairs. Use concrete words to evoke and reflect those emotions. Draw from the reservoir of human emotions: from indignation at injustice, tenderness at a story that illustrates a point, enthusiasm for the task at hand, curiosity about what is possible, confidence in your audience's ability to achieve your mutual goals, and so on.

Crafting your message around high points of emotion more accurately reflects how most human beings go about interacting with the world around them. As Nobel Laureate Gerald Edelman says, 'The mind arises from the body and its development. It is embodied and therefore part of nature.' Feelings are felt in the body, and charismatic communicators inherently know that if they win over the hearts of their listeners their minds will follow.

MEGA-FRAMING YOUR PURPOSE

A mega-frame is like the ornate framing that surrounds a picture or painting. It encloses and defines information. Amateur and professional artists deeply appreciate the value of framing: the right frames will enhance their pictures, the wrong frames will devalue them. Many an artist has created works that have not become truly expressive or beautiful until they have been enclosed in the right frame.

Framing has a long and rich history. The Sophists in ancient Greece were masterful framers and re-framers. Aristotle coined the word *atechnoi* to describe it. One of ancient Rome's greatest orators, Cicero, elevated frames (*statis*) to an art form. His speeches are still studied by students of influence and rhetoric.

Mega-framing describes strategic or psychological framing and underpins the art of managing perception. It takes in the 'big picture' rather than detail. It may be an overarching theme that enjoins or describes the detail in your presentation, or it may link all your points to a lesson, a purpose or a moral. Mega-frames are powerful because they allow you to enclose your message within a framework of higher intentions, virtues or a big-picture concept generally understood or held to be true by most people. This is termed frame alignment, and it refers to the linkage of a message to a set of common interests, values or beliefs, so as to position a speaker and audience as one. In selecting a mega-frame, your aim can be to link your total presentation to one major idea, high principle or key value.

Every society is rooted in deep sets or clusters of ideals. In Australia, for example, we 'believe' in democracy. From that belief comes a raft of 'virtues', represented by abstracts such as Freedom of Speech, the Right to Choose, Respect for Individual Rights, Freedom of Movement, Equity in Society (in some quarters), and so on. The key is to establish a legitimate association between your idea/message/proposal/action and a universal virtue or value. Examine the following words and see if you can detect a 'virtue' in them. Put them into a sentence, internalise them and notice the emotional responses they bring about.

goodness	health	love
peace	choice	dream
happiness	fairness	liberty
vision	truth	justice
rights	honesty	opportunity
ethics	safeguard	success
strength	prosperity	freedom
righteousness	self-control	family
safety	purity	empowerment
compassion	protection	relief
science	respect	

The above words represent values embraced by most people in Australia. They are anchors for the aspirations of our community, and few individuals would venture to challenge them. Each person will have their own personal interpretation of what they mean but, in all but a few cases, the feelings people associate with the words will be positive ones.

Virtue frames induce unconscious acceptance of the content in which they are wrapped. They add immense power to your presentation because most people embrace them as self-evident truths. Review the following sentences and notice how a strong virtue frame helps the speaker evoke powerful emotional responses to support the case.

This is not an issue about governments resuming private land to subdivide and on-sell. This is an issue about freedom. Freedom from the greedy intentions of bureaucrats who want to fund their grandiose projects by robbing you of your birthright; freedom to live your life on a piece of rural Australia without fear that the land of your hard labour can be snatched from you; freedom from the whims of fat-cats who live hundreds of miles away, never having experienced life in a close rural community.

I know that, as small landowners, you value freedom above all else. Why else would you have chosen to build your life here, free from all the contamination of big-city life? Now is the time to fight for the justice of your cause; to fight for your freedom; to send an unequivocal message to those who would destroy your community forever.

And know that your calls will be heard by many decent-minded country Australians. They will help you in your fight, because they know that you must never, never, never, give in to big city bully boys who, like common thieves, would take your freedom from you. They know that the price of giving in would be their freedom too.

In everyday life, you unconsciously assess information through the filters of your values, beliefs, decisions and attitudes. Emotions, or feelings, erupt from the filtering process and drive action. It's a natural process, and stepping up to virtue frames taps into that process. It allows you to filter your message through the core values, beliefs and embraced virtues of your audience.

While virtue frames link your message with positively charged emotions, another type of frame has the opposite effect. Base frames focus on behaviours, words and actions that can be viewed as contemptible, immoral and unwholesome. Virtue frames appeal to our sense of morality; base frames trigger our outrage. Let's look at some examples. Below is a partial list of negatively charged words that candidates of the Republican Party were instructed to frame around their arguments when referring to the Democrats in the 1992 and 1996 United States presidential and congressional elections:

abandon	'compassion' is not enough
anti- (issue) flag, family, child, jobs	betrayal
coercion	collapse
corruption	crisis
decay	destroy
devour	endanger
failure	greed
hypocrisy	ideological
impose	insecurity
lie	permissive
radical	shallow
sick	they/them
threaten	traitors

Pick a word, put it into a sentence, go inside yourself for a moment and sense how that word makes you feel. Get the picture? While the Republicans didn't win the presidency, they did gain historic control of Congress. The above word-weaponry was created by former House Speaker Newt Gingrich and formed part of the dirty tricks campaign waged by Republicans from the day Bill Clinton announced his intention to run for the presidency. This campaign was designed to evoke revulsion in the hearts of conservative and vacillating American voters.

Charismatic communicators usually come across as people of generosity, empathy and fair-mindedness. They routinely make clear distinctions between the behaviours, ideas and actions of people and the people themselves. They are much more likely to say 'The minister behaved in an underhanded way' than 'The minister is underhanded and dishonest'.

Base frames are best used in argument as part of your exploration of the pitfalls and dangers inherent in the proposals, opinions and actions of your opponents, or when unpacking the present state of affairs as part of the process of encouraging audiences to move to a more desirable state of affairs. Virtue frames can form part of a passionate search for, and unearthing of, solutions. As you will discover, the use of base frames in frontal attacks on opponents and their supporters is likely to reinforce their arguments in their own minds and make them more fanatical in their attitudes.

When you design your mega-frame, find a plausible, sustainable and *legitimate* connection between it and the message you want to deliver to your listener/s. Ask yourself and answer all or some of the following questions:

1. What higher value or belief can I link my message to?
2. What is really important here?
3. If I placed clusters of points under one or two categories what would the names of the categories be?
4. What is my message an example of?
5. What virtue or base values can I link my mega-frame/s to?

Dramatic frames

Apart from virtue frames, base frames and big picture frames, there exist what are termed dramatic frames. Dramatic frames are structures that connect points, lessons or morals to people's story archives. From childhood we encounter many story lines or structures that give stories particular forms. While we may not consciously detect the structures of stories when we hear them, repetition ensures we build a library of them at the unconscious level.

People rarely gain insight in a vacuum. In order to learn something new it's far more likely that listener/s will seek to link new information to some generalisation that they have already made. When you choose a familiar story line or structure for your speech or presentation, you make the job of understanding your content easier. It's rather like taking people on a journey they have made many times and directing their attention to points of interest they may have overlooked. This enhances the power of your presentation by providing a comfort zone in which your audience can more easily accommodate and integrate your content.

Below are some examples of dramatic frames:

- the little battler who takes on authority
- the stranger/fiend who tempts and corrupts the weak
- a lone voice in the wilderness
- victims and martyrs of an unjust system
- overcoming a major obstacle on Life's highways
- the man/woman before his/her time
- the ugly duckling who grows into a beautiful swan
- what comes around goes around
- justice will prevail
- love conquers all
- the grand struggle for principle
- the chickens come home to roost
- life is a journey
- one bad apple

- the prodigal son or daughter
- the bad boy/girl who became transformed by a single, powerful experience
- the grand second chance at life

Recall the stories you were told as a child and look beyond the prose to the structure or story line. View news or current affairs programs and notice the recurring story lines, most of which a first year theatre arts student would have little difficulty in identifying. Notice the basic structure of stories in movies, soaps and contemporary novels. They are rich sources for dramatic frames in presentations.

Using framing for key arguments

People frame all the time without knowing they're doing it. For example, if you describe a fine, sunny day as a 'beautiful' day, you are looking at it from a certain perspective, in this case fine + sunny = beautiful. Now, imagine what a fine, sunny day would represent to farmers waiting desperately on finishing rains for their crops. They would probably wrap a very different frame around the same information: fine + sunny = bad (possible damage to or lower yield from crops).

The above is an example of a meaning frame. Some event, idea or behaviour occurs and people naturally align it to a viewpoint that in no small way expresses their personal world view or map of the world.

Framing can be used in ways that are more purposeful. In advertising and marketing, in politics, in debate and in the pursuit of, and escape from, justice you encounter the deliberate framing of ideas, products, events and behaviours. In everyday situations when people attempt to influence others they will frame and re-frame all the time. So, it can be said that deliberate and unconscious framing of content is a behaviour we all engage in.

There are many specific ways of framing, but for simplification's sake we will explore two general categories: meaning frames and context frames. Review the following examples and begin to notice how framing can make some things important while other considerations disappear.

Meaning frames

A meaning frame is described by the equation $X = Y$. It works like this:

1. People take some external or internal stimulus (idea, event, feeling, thought, proposition, behaviour).

2. They run it through their perceptual filters.

3. They come up with a meaning.

Review the following meaning frames and notice how the meaning changes as a different frame is wrapped around the content.

Example 1

I hate this. It's so frustrating when I can't grasp the idea of framing and re-framing.

This can be converted to:

It's good to struggle with something like this because that feeling of frustration is your body's way of telling you that you're actually out of your comfort zone and learning something new. And, it's great to learn new things, isn't it?

In the above example, frustration with the concept was redefined by wrapping a new frame around the content. Frustration becomes a 'good' thing linked to learning. Consequently, the meaning of the experience the speaker is having changes. Let's now apply the meaning re-frame technique step by step and change the meaning of the following statement.

Example 2

The minister's support for mandatory sentencing after three strikes is nothing more than a cheap ploy to capture the law-and-order vote.

In this statement by an opposition spokesperson, we observe that the minister's support means a cheap ploy, the subtext of which is an accusation of low political cunning. Now, let's ask ourselves this question: 'Is there any larger or different picture in which his action could have a different meaning?'. Can you think of one?

In the example below, a different picture was chosen. In response to the accusation, the minister chooses a powerful and concrete frame to wrap around the mandatory sentencing issue. She finds a frame that drives home what she views as the consequences of going soft on repeat offenders. The meaning changes from that of political posturing (cheap ploy) to that of helping to save people from the real human consequences of crime against property.

I ask the shadow minister to answer honestly the following question. What if a break-in at your home resulted in the fourth arrest of a repeat offender. How would that alter your perspective on the three strikes rule? And what do you have to say to those many other victims who also just happened to be fourth in line?

The above re-frame can be read as suggesting that the minister's support for mandatory sentencing *means* stopping 'me' from being number four on the list, and so equals concern for the potential victims of crime. Notice also that the re-frame has been structured as a series of questions that audiences are likely to answer for themselves.

Context frames

It is a fundamental principle of communication theory that a stimulus or signal only has meaning in terms of the frame or context in which it appears. Change the context and you change the meaning. The following example demonstrates a complex series of re-frames. See if you can determine where contexts have been changed.

John is a door-to-door mobile phone salesman and through experience has learned to convert cold calls into sales. He is talking to a couple and is about half way through his sales pitch. He has learned that the couple has two teenage daughters who are beginning to socialise at various hangouts.

He raises the topic of payment plans with his prospective clients. He presents them with an expensive, but comprehensive, plan. They demur over the expense and he launches into his 're-frame' pitch:

If you look at the total dollars it may seem expensive at first but, as you begin to think about what it costs per day to protect your daughters' security, you will notice that it costs less than the price of a Big Mac. You'd say that your daughters' security and your freedom from anxiety about where they are is worth at least a Big Mac a day, wouldn't you?

Not having perceived the issue in that particular way, the parents agree to sign up for the expensive plan, without ever having asked about other plans.

John's artful and self-serving use of framing diverted the parents' attention away from the issue of price and affordability. He re-contextualised the price ('that's too expensive'), making it as inconsequential as a Big Mac and contrasting it with peace of mind and security. Wouldn't you sign on the dotted line if you had two teenage daughters and wanted to be able to sleep when they were out?

The following example of a context re-frame demonstrates how context changes can also be used in a positive and ethical way. Here, the re-frame encourages the speaker to view a behaviour that causes him and his marriage stress in a light that could cause him a great deal of self-satisfaction:

I just hate going shopping with my wife. She's so bloody hard to please. She spends an absolute eternity making comparisons, asking questions, getting everyone's opinion and testing things out before she'll agree to fork over her money and buy anything!

The above statement represents what is called a comparative generalisation. Comparative generalisations work like this: Spending time making comparisons and so on (behaviour) *compares with* being hard to please (generalisation). Therefore, the wife is hard to please.

The speaker associates being 'bloody hard to please' and all the emotional baggage that goes along with that condition with his wife. Now, see if you can think of a context where the behaviour of the wife would have some use or value. If the shopping context were removed and replaced with a more positive context, what would that context be?

So she is a very prudent and careful decision-maker, isn't she? You must feel so flattered that out of all the fish at the market, she chose you!

In the example above, the context has been changed to that of the wife's choice of husband. By changing the contextual framework of the behaviour from shopping to choosing a mate, the meaning changes completely.

Re-framing and framing allow you to have more control over how people perceive certain things. A frame, by its nature, directs the attention of the listener to a particular perspective. For example, by using the frame 'reform of the labour market' the Howard government created a perspective on its industrial relations policies that obscured other perspectives, to the extent that the mass media adopted it as a favourite phrase and used it without question. The word 'reform' offered a very flattering description indeed of the dramatic change in the nature of the relationship between workers and management.

The second important element of framing is that it directs attention to what is inside the frame and obscures what is outside the frame. It makes some things more conspicuous and others less conspicuous. For example, a frame separates a picture from the wall it adorns. Go back to your experiences of looking at pictures. How often do you look at the wall and explore it in detail? How often do you see others at art galleries carefully examining the hanging space in between pictures? Their eyes are glued to what is captured within the series of frames occupying the hanging space, aren't they? Frames obscure all that is outside their boundaries, which is why your response to the framing of Ellen DeGeneris as a lesbian was different from your response to her framing as a blond television star with a hit series.

Third, frames inform and direct understanding and judgment. There's a famous story of an art aficionado from Florence who went to Leonardo da Vinci with a magnificent frame in hand and requested da Vinci paint a picture to fit within its borders. While da Vinci may have been outraged at such a proposition, the Florentine art collector had a good point in asking the artist to create his magic within the boundaries of a frame. He may well have known that the frame would have imposed a new discipline on da Vinci, that of creating artistic meaning within an already established context. All of da Vinci's efforts were directed towards creating a picture in harmony with its surrounds. That's what frames do.

MAKING YOUR MESSAGE FULLY AVAILABLE TO YOUR AUDIENCE

7

> We are drowning in information but starved for knowledge.
> *John Naisbitt*

It's estimated that the volume of information in the world doubles every seven years. Recent projections have information volume doubling every twenty months within the next decade. Today we are engulfed by information. From mass media and the world-wide-web to in-house newsletters and emails, more information rains down on us in one day than a sixteenth century citizen had to cope with in handfuls of years.

Today time is valuable because we have so little of it to spare, but information is plentiful. So, rather than having to invest a lot of time in the search for information, the issue that many people confront today is how to survive the flood: how to salvage some practical, useful knowledge from an almost infinite number of sources. There aren't enough hours in a day to withstand the deluge and make sense of it all.

Knowledge is still power, and what renders it precious and yet so often beyond our reach is that it's caught in a great swirl of data. Having access to a colossal flood of information is a world away from knowing what is significant and what is irrelevant. Information consumes the attention of its recipients and a flood of information creates an excessive demand on attention and the need to allocate that attention more productively. This could represent an opportunity for you to carve a valuable niche in the communication marketplace. It stands to reason that those who can offer ordered information, and who can explain what is worth knowing and why, will have a significant advantage over those who don't.

A major side-effect of the information explosion is that it has produced a social craving for simplification, a popular demand for translating simplicity into action, a tendency to confuse ends with means and seldom a questioning of the larger purpose of the action proposed. This popular need for clarity has resulted in a clamour for political correctness and a narrowing of options at a time when more, rather than fewer, options may need to be explored to help solve many of our most pressing issues.

The dogged application of preconceived beliefs and analytical wowser-ism are two features of our struggle to make sense out of the ever-increasing flow of information, and this is where you may find a highly rewarding market niche. If you want to corner a decent share of the information market in your area of operation, choose to become known as someone who makes new-sense, rather than nonsense, out of high-volume information. Choose to be someone who offers the 'third way', someone who seeks to expand people's models of the world rather than narrow them, and someone who offers pre-analysed options and information in digestible chunks.

Hugh McKay, Paul Clitheroe, Norman Swan, Robin Williams, Robert Gottliebson, Karl Kruszelnicki and Adam Spencer are among a small group of Australian virtuosi making a very tidy living out of interpreting and explaining complex specialist information. In this chapter you will encounter a downstream processing inventory that can help you choose to become an information tour guide and join the ranks of this small but influential cohort. If you establish a reputation as someone who chunks down the complexities of life into clear, relevant, interesting and grounded definitions, you will be a sought-after commodity indeed.

Individuals with a high degree of flexibility of form (how they structure and communicate content) are by far the more effective persuaders. To have and do flexibility, you need to have options available to you and in this section you will canvass many options of form.

THE DOWNSTREAM PROCESS

How do you downstream-process information and empower audiences to efficiently consume information in the context of interpersonal communications and public speaking? You may never achieve it by remaining a bona fide member of the public speaking pack. You probably won't achieve it by remaining a player in the phoney war of words that occurs in many public forums, and you may register little success if you stick with conventional ways of imparting information, analysis and ideas.

The above practices add to the information explosion rather than help impose some structure or order on it, because of their bias towards process, confrontation and massive streams of data. They have a low market value in the sense that they don't guide people towards order or closure. Order and closure, as you may realise, are major elements of the brokerage of high-value information.

It's possible that a solution is staring you in the face when you switch on your computer and occasionally when you turn on your television. A hot property in the information industry is the search engine. Entities such as Yahoo! Lycos and Google have become multi-million dollar operations almost overnight because they provide pathways to more time-efficient consumption of information. Newer search engines like Findarticles.com, Ebsco and NorthernLights.com have refined the process even further. Movie reviews on television are a somewhat overused and clichéd example of downstream processing, but they save people the time and effort of having to wade through countless movies to find one that suits them.

Chunk, contrast, close

Paul Clitheroe's 'Money' program on television is an excellent example of downstream processing because it adds value by providing a framework for choice. Clitheroe commonly takes raw financial and investment information, chunks it into categories and matches it against universal benchmarks (frames) of prudence, thrift, wealth creation, investment return, security, and so on. His approach is entirely different from that of many other stodgy business programs that leave viewers awash in data on stocks, shares, gold price, fiscal information and statistics.

There are some common rules evident in Clitheroe's approach. You can form them into a three-part process, which, for convenience, you can remember as 'chunk, contrast, close'.

Chunk

Information is 'chunked' into categories or frames. Example: Interest-bearing investments for fixed periods are categorised as 'term deposits'.

Contrast

- Categories are placed alongside other categories for comparison. Example: Term deposits are placed alongside other fixed period investments, such as debentures, management funds and mortgages.
- Contrastive analysis is offered to guide viewers' understanding of the distinctions Clitheroe chooses to make. This is a powerful form of framing and has been covered in the previous chapter. Example: Debentures are contrasted with bank fixed deposits. Clitheroe may choose to frame the analysis as a risk versus return contrast. In such a case, he effectively manages his viewers'

impressions through the benchmarks he offers to interpret and evaluate the raw information.

- Concrete examples are given to add relevance to the analysis he offers. Example: He will tell a short story or hypothetical in which a character is faced with a choice. The story leads the viewer by example to a predetermined destination.

Close

Viewers are led towards making a conclusion. Contrastive analysis gives audiences clear choices as the data is interpreted for them in a particular manner. Clitheroe often ranks choices against universal benchmarks. Example: 'If you're looking for low risk, fixed-term investments with returns well above inflation, then A, B and C are the better products to consider.'

The above rules can be applied in almost any field of information, be it company reports, research presentations, promotional appearances, politics, international affairs, economics, social issues or most of the so-called softer issues.

INFORMATION LOOPS

Intelligent downstream processing of information gives you an edge over your competitors. Your role as a communicator can be that of offering a pathway or guided tour of the individual and preferred choices available to people. Information and facts become meaningful when they are used to make a point or draw an audience towards a conclusion. A series of disconnected or badly arranged facts, no matter how interesting, will not allow your listeners to arrive at the conclusions you want them to consider and adopt. You must first decide on the conclusion or behaviour you want your audience to embrace, and then:

1. open a 'loop' by finding a powerful starting point;
2. build your argument, preferably using the path of least resistance;
3. close the loop by leading your audience to the objective you initially set.

Your information loops, as the Clitheroe example demonstrates, must be completed, or 'closed', before you move on to the next point or idea. Closing an information loop is essential if you want your audience to retain information and support your overall arguments and theme.

Information loops as represented in the diagram below can form a significant part of your influencing structure.

Information loops are remarkably seductive when they contain clusters of three. Three facts, three arguments or three points appear to be the ideal number in the transfer of information from working (short-term) memory to long-term memory. Our culture is littered with symbols incorporating what is termed the 'rule of threes': slip, slap, slop; stop, look and listen; the holy trinity; the three Rs; the three tiers of government; democracy of the people, for the people, by the people. These are but a few of the three-part clusters that pervade our experience of life and learning.

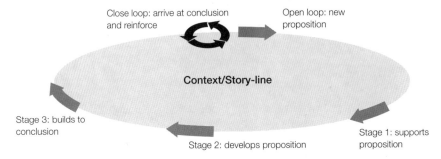

When building your arguments, design information loops using the above model. Begin with a powerful appeal, proposition, statement or set question. Cluster a maximum of three facts, points or arguments around it. Make sure you close the loop by ending with a strong conclusion, preferably in alignment with a major theme.

The Rule of Three is a supreme communication tool. The following Rule of Three models are custom-designed for particular downstream processing objectives and purposes. They incorporate clusters of three in various ways to add power, purpose and precision to your information loops. Charismatic communicators are usually familiar with two or three of these models or mental guides. When called upon to speak, they select the most effective model for the context in which they're speaking. The models have usually been learned over time and are often the result of trial and error. Through learning and repetition, they become second nature to the speaker.

Learn two or three of the models and practise them to the point of being able to automatically draw on them when you need them. You'll have at your immediate disposal a set of tools to call on when you are planning a communication campaign or you need to speak extemporaneously.

Hook, heart, how to

This model is designed to move people *towards* a product, point, service or idea. It incorporates an additional three-cluster in the middle of the loop.

Hook

■ Say something that arrests attention.
■ Find something that presses an emotional hot button.
■ Link decisively into a highly desirable event or objective.

For example: 'If you want your team to top your company's sales figures every month, here's a step-by-step plan that can mean bigger dollars, more commission and the recognition you deserve.'

Heart

Do a FAB statement:

Features: notable characteristics of the product, idea or point
Advantages: what is gained by having such features
Benefits: what the idea, point or product actually delivers

For example: 'This plan starts with a Power Greeting [feature]. Power Greetings are designed to overcome initial buyer resistance to sales approaches by using "open-ended" questions [advantage]. Using the open-ended questions contained in a Power Greeting will enable you to (1) set edgy customers at ease, (2) give you information you can act on and (3) allow you to create early rapport [benefit].'

How to

Explain what the audience needs to do to gain or achieve what is offered. For example: 'Here's what you can do to achieve and exceed your retail sales targets. Train each team in the CCF program, which turns Power Greetings into sales, train managers in follow-up and intervention, reinforce it through area manager visits and incentive programs, and watch the dollars roll in.'

The above model can be used to go through the main features of the product, point or idea. You can see that in each complete loop there is weighting in favour of what people can gain. People tend to be more receptive to ideas if they are linked to personal gain and benefit. On occasions, particularly when you want to mention several features in succession, you may find it useful to leave the 'How to' until after your final FAB statement is delivered.

Impact, reason, action

This model is designed to appeal to people who are motivated by what they don't like, rather than what they do like (see Chapter 14 on motivation filters). It is structured to evoke what is called an 'aversion response'. Variations of this model are frequently used in political advertising and public information campaigns on drugs, smoking, alcohol and road safety.

When you are considering using this model it's important that you think about the ethics of scaring the pants off people. The advertising industry is notorious in its unethical use of this model to anchor the relief of fear with particular products and services, so choose to be selective with its use. The question you may need to answer before using this model is, 'Will the outcome be mutually desirable?'. In other words, if your audience is influenced to say yes to the proposition you embed in this model, will they benefit appropriately from their acquiescence?

You can use both 'away-from' and 'toward' language techniques to broaden the impact of your message if you choose. 'Toward' and 'away-from' language techniques appear in Chapter 14, page 268. Both techniques are used below and are in italics. Can you tell the difference?

Impact

King-hit the audience with a piece of information that produces an 'aversion' response.

For example: 'Sixteen people will die at our beaches this Christmas. Do you want to escape that fate and *stay alive?*'

Reason

Give the reasons behind the statement. Make sure you offer no more than three.

For example: 'If you don't want to be one of those *statistics, embrace* these simple life saving hints. (1) *Avoid* losing sight of the safety flags; *stay within them.* (2) *Quell* any urge to swim alone; *keep with the crowd.* And (3) *stop any panic so you have a clear head* if you get into trouble.'

Action

Provide a solution to enable the listeners to 'avoid' the impact of the king-hit.

For example: '*To avoid being one of the statistics and enjoy the beach to its fullest,* all you need to do is invest one hour in a free Safety at the Beach demonstration being held throughout the weekend at Manly, or check out our web-site on www.swimsafe.com.au.'

The above model fulfils the conditions of a successful 'aversion' appeal, as detailed below:

1. It must really instil fear or aversion.
2. The content must contain specific recommendations of how to avoid a negative outcome (away-from) and how to overcome the threat (toward).
3. People must believe the stated action will work and that the action can be easily carried out.

Generally, if one of the conditions is left out, the aversion appeal will not work.

Concept, model, application

The concept, model, application structure has been used to explain this model.

Concept

The idea behind this model is that people assimilate material in different ways. Everyone has a preferred mode and sequence in the absorption of material. Some people prefer concepts, others find structure and models appealing, while some will prefer to know about uses and practical applications (global versus specific expression; see the diagram on page 32).

Generally speaking, if you want people to act on what you say, you must give them a complete picture: they must understand the idea, grasp what you are saying about the practical uses of the idea and have a clear notion of how everything fits together.

Some speakers exclusively use their preferred mode to explain complex ideas. For example, they may wax lyrically on the philosophy or concept behind an idea and leave out the structure of the model and the applications of the idea.

As with all communication models in this book, this one has three principal components that act to open and close an information 'loop'. A loop is incomplete if you leave out one of the components. The point is that information gaps cause confusion in the minds of audiences. Close the loop and you eliminate confusion and accelerate people's understanding.

Model

CONCEPT

This is the abstract: the philosophy, theory and thinking behind the idea; the theories behind the models.

MODEL

This is how everything connects or works: the structure or organisation of the material (the models), how the pieces fit together. Maps and diagrams are useful.

APPLICATION

This gives the applications and benefits of the idea: what the material is good for, what practical applications the material has and how it can be put to work, the benefits of using or applying the models or concepts. If application is left out, your idea will be nice and structured but impractical to those listening.

Application

This model of information delivery is broadly useful if you want to ensure that a normally diverse group of people can grasp the information you are presenting and stay interested.

It is particularly apt when dealing with complex ideas or submissions, such as funding requests, project proposals, new plans and strategies, or new policies.

By including each component of the model, you will satisfy the diverse ways people prefer to take in information. They will be less confused and will probably 'get it' first time, which makes your job of communicating that little bit easier.

The charismatic model

In Part 1 of this book you learned that a speaker's vision and thematic approach to speaking is paramount in the advocacy of change. Strong vision and mission provide the oomph and energy charismatic speakers need to give body and soul to their performances. Below is a model that many charismatic communicators use when seeking to persuade or manage the impressions of an audience. There are particular elements in this model that, when brought together in a charismatic performance, are particularly potent in convincing followers to follow. The strong missions in life and sustaining belief structures of charismatic communicators provide high motivation for them to promote vigorously their visions of a better future. In a nutshell, passion + eloquence + structure/form = high-level persuasion results and attributions of charisma. The following is a do-able model of a charismatic performance.

1. NEGATE THE STATUS QUO

■ Point out the inadequacies and flaws of the existing state of affairs.

■ Deconstruct the present using rhetorical devices to transact an agreement with the audience on the need to overcome or move away from the current negative state of affairs.

■ Elucidate how the present state of affairs prevents followers from realising their higher intentions.

2. ARTICULATE THE VISION

■ Transact agreement with the audience on how the vision will remedy the existing unsatisfactory state of affairs.

■ Demonstrate how the vision will better fulfil followers' needs.

■ Paint a better and brighter future detailing the benefits and advantages of the vision.

3. PROVIDE THE PLAN

■ Provide a plausible strategy for achieving the vision.

■ Detail and describe how the plan will fulfil the vision.

■ Show the audience what they specifically need to do to succeed with the plan.

■ Vest true faith in the ability of the audience to carry out the plan.

■ Future-pace: paint a compelling vision for the future. Invite the audience to imagine (vivid pictures, sounds, smells, feelings and even tastes) a future where the vision has been fulfilled.

In these days of short attention spans, busy lives and media conditioning, the optimum number of chunks, or 'loops', is best set at between three and five. In structuring your presentation or speech, try to limit your points to three big loops or chunks which, in turn, have a maximum of three smaller chunks, facts or arguments contained within them. You may, on occasions, need to extend the number of chunks, but you are courageous indeed if you extend them beyond five.

PERSUASION PLANNING

There are many fine publications on communication planning and effective preparation of speeches, so we will dwell only briefly on incorporating the principles of downstream processing into a simple but powerful planning process.

Step 1

Start at the conclusion. Imagine having delivered a successful presentation or having successfully persuaded an individual or group to take on a specific idea. Having done so, how do you think you went about successfully persuading your audience to embrace your message? A good idea is to draw on the information you generate during the purpose set outlined in Chapter 6. In the model below the challenge was to convince a neighbourhood meeting to establish a security collective.

Your analysis might go like this:

At the end of this presentation I have:
■ persuaded
■ demonstrated
■ taught
■ informed
■ entertained
my audience to embrace the following mega-frame: Solidarity is the key to personal security.
It serves the following purposes:
1. Achieve a shared understanding and definition of the neighbourhood crime problem.
2. Gain affirmation to work together.
3. Establish a security collective and committee.

Step 2

From your outcomes, design your arguments to support your message goals. Observe the 'less is more' principle and include only as many information loops as necessary to deliver a succinct and persuasive message. Charismatic communicators rely on a few of the most cogent and convincing arguments. This helps them avoid saturating their messages with unnecessary side issues and superfluous information. It gives them the space and time to build better arguments and give their listeners closure. Map out your evidence procedure and create information or argument loops that appeal to both the heads and hearts of your audience.

LOOP 1: IMPACT, REASON, ACTION LOOP
■ Pace/detail local crime and its impact.
■ Propose main solution.
■ Show that plan is workable, efficacious and easy to implement, and encourage audience to visualise a better future.
Bridging statement

LOOP 2: SUPPORTING STORIES
Other neighbourhoods that have successfully implemented security collectives and cut down on crime.
Bridging statement

LOOP 3: DESIRED OUTCOME: CONCEPT, MODEL, APPLICATION LOOP
- Detail ideas behind collective security.
- Show the components of the plan.
- Demonstrate how it will work in the neighbourhood, and emphasise benefits and advantages by giving the example of the success of the St Kilda project.
Bridging statement

The speaker has chosen three information/persuasion loops through which to communicate the message. The salient information of each loop is detailed so as to jolt the speaker's memory during the composing and rehearsing stage. At the end of each loop room is left to construct a bridging statement that will allow smooth transition from one loop to the next.

Step 3

Once you have designed your persuasion/information loops, develop your closing statement. Your closing statement needs to touch on your mega-frame to bring everything together and reinforce the major themes you have introduced in your loops. Short closing statements are generally better than long closing statements. Your closing statement should in most cases include a call to action. Review the following and note how it fulfils the outcomes/purposes the speaker set for the message:

The key to us feeling safe in our houses at night and going to work secure in the knowledge that our homes are protected is solidarity—for us to work together. Can we not do what the police have failed to do? They have turned their backs on us, saying crime against property isn't a priority.

Is it not up to us to *make* it a priority? Together, we have the power and the means to be the eyes and ears of our neighbourhood. Together, we can protect what is ours and defend our rights to live in peace without the ever-present threat of home burglary and, increasingly, home invasion.

Together, we can drive out the thugs, the thieves and the addicts. And, together, we can make our neighbourhood safe again. This small investment of our time and resources can give us the things you have said that you value most of all: security and peace of mind. Let's *do it now* [embedded command] and begin the struggle to reclaim our neighbourhood.

Many of the most potent closing statements call on an audience to act, to take up a struggle, to do something that will mark the beginning of a commitment to a course of action. Your closing statement represents your last word on the subject matter. It's your final opportunity to make a difference. Your last minutes and seconds in front of your listeners should represent a determining moment for them, a turning point, a point where your message should culminate in a fusion of impressions that leads to action and reflects the ultimate purpose of your message.

Step 4

The most important component of many, if not all, persuasion attempts is the opening statement, and that is why you leave it until last. You have much to do in the initial stages of delivering your message and it's imperative that it helps rapidly to establish three things:

1. the full attention of your audience;
2. your credibility;
3. the tangible benefits your listeners will gain by listening to you.

You have reached an important tenet of charismatic communication that challenges you to link your message to common ground and shared benefits. Many parents will tell you that the quickest way to exact a child's cooperation on a trip to the supermarket is to explain that there are heaps of lollies right near the checkout. While some people may claim such a practice is manipulative, they may not have considered that it can be seen merely as a convincing way of pointing out the advantages of cooperation. So, how could the lollies-at-the-till principle be applied to the neighbourhood security example you have been reviewing? How would you offer a quid pro quo to your audience in return for its attention? Perhaps, it could be something along the following lines.

I know you have come here for a purpose, that your concern about crime in the neighbourhood is in the forefront of your mind, and that you are looking for solutions. As we spend the next fifteen minutes together you will encounter a three-point plan of action that offers you easy, workable solutions and that will make your journey here tonight not only worthwhile, but one that will give you hope for the future.

The above statement can be seen to have established common ground and illuminated the benefits of giving full attention to the speaker. How so? Examine the first of the two sentences, placing yourself in the position of someone who has gone along to the meeting. The first sentence contains three statements, and as you look at them carefully you will notice that there is nothing in them you could disagree with. In fact, it's reasonable to assume that, if you heard those statements being uttered, you would be nodding or saying yes internally:

■ Yes, I have come here for a purpose. (Notice the purpose is not stated.)
■ Yes, I am concerned about neighbourhood crime.
■ Yes, I'm looking for solutions.

The speaker began the opening statement with what is termed a 'triple pace' and chose three different pieces of information to set up a three-step pattern of internal agreement for the audience. If an audience finds itself agreeing with you three times, particularly in the opening stages of a presentation, you can assume that you've established a common bond in the first few seconds of your presentation. Agreement reflects the audience's experience of feeling positive towards you and your presentation. You will discover more about how to pace, along with other powerful agreement techniques, in Chapter 11.

Now, examine the second sentence in the example. The second sentence offers a solution to the problems raised in the first sentence and promises a benefit in exchange for an investment of fifteen minutes of the audience's time. This statement may not be rhetorically attractive but, linguistically speaking, it's almost irresistible. In sixty-three words, or less than thirty seconds of talk, the speaker has created a powerful relationship with the audience:

■ The speaker gained rapport and credibility by pacing the audience's experience, evoking three expressions of positive will in less than thirty seconds.
■ The speaker sent the signal 'I know your concerns and I'm like you because I want to find a solution' to the audience.
■ The speaker promised compelling benefits in return for the audience's attention.

Charismatic speakers are notable for their attention to questions of commonality and audience benefit in the opening stages of their communications. They are adept at embedding their ideas and positions within the ambit of their audience's needs, experiences and concerns. They take the time to learn about their audiences and potential followers.

They enter the reality of their audiences and focus on shared benefits, as opposed to less resourceful speakers who just can't wait to impose their reality on anyone who will listen.

You have approximately four minutes to establish an initial relationship with your listeners. These first few valuable minutes of the encounter will determine the degree of attention people are willing to invest and whether they choose to actively process what you have to say. If your opening statement is clumsy and inept, expect many in your audience to label you as such and to process what they hear through those filters. People rarely separate speakers from their behaviour in such instances. If your statement is confused, woolly, silly or uncertain, don't be surprised when you notice that a fair number of your listeners have turned their cognitive lights out.

You can easily begin to appreciate the significance of strong, direct, cogent and audience-focused opening statements when you recall your experiences of the opposite. Ask yourself how you respond to muddled and uncertain opening statements. Ask yourself where your mind goes when you encounter speakers who are unprepared or inept at conveying first impressions with vigour and purpose.

It is always possible to arrest the attention of your listeners at a later stage. In fact your entire message needs to be punctuated with events that change the pace of your communication and rededicate your audience's attention. If, however, you've initially let them down, gaining deeper attention and commitment is not an easy task.

8 MAKING LISTENING EASY

He who will not reason, is a bigot; he who cannot is a fool;
and he who dares not is a slave.
William Drummond

The meaning and value of your message can only be determined by the response you achieve. Now, that turns things upside-down, doesn't it? It suggests that you are responsible for what your listeners *do* with what you say. It places the onus on you to create structures and forms of delivery that make the job easy for your listeners to get meaning and gain understanding. If they don't get it, then your responsibility can be to view their negative responses as simple feedback: valuable information that allows you to modify, improve and make a difference as you go along.

Putting easy-listening techniques into practice can spark the beginning of a new and wondrous relationship with audiences. Imagine your message hitting the mark with beautifully crafted form and structure. Savour the surge of positive energy coming from an audience or group that is with you all the way. Having experienced being in complete synchronicity with your listeners, would you ever want to do it any other way?

The easy-listening approach to communication can produce an immensely empowering experience for both speakers and audiences. The remaining chapters in this section flesh out techniques and behaviours that allow you to share your communication space with your listeners and make it easier for them to embrace your messages.

The first lesson of easy listening involves ordering your evidence into easy-to-follow chunks that lead people towards clear choices. Most people like order. If you don't provide order your listeners may do it for you, and perhaps not to your liking. The communication models in the previous chapter, for example, are a way of providing high order by structuring content in particular clusters. It is also important to have order within the clusters that you build. This allows you to produce sharp, direct and poignant argument. Following is a series of pointers that will help you enhance the clarity and power of your delivery. You will discover methods that allow you to present your evidence in structures and forms that make for truly easy listening.

QUOTE FROM THE BEST SOURCES

Quote the most plausible authorities, use data collected from the most reputable sources and ensure that the research methodology behind the data has high credibility. Intersperse and reinforce your own conclusions with highly credible 'names'. Be careful about making too many 'I' statements. For example, instead of saying:

I believe that you have to talk the language of the people you want to change.

find a quote from a reputable source and attribute it:

International management guru Peter Drucker says that the key to managing change is to couch it in the language of those you want to change.

When you quote from expert sources, be sure to establish their credentials, as shown in the example above. Research consistently shows that the use of expert sources actually leads to stronger perceptions of a speaker's credibility.

USE STATISTICS CAREFULLY

Statistics alone are not very persuasive, particularly if they are presented in bulk. It is far better to link statistics with specific examples or case studies.

- Humanise your statistics by linking them with concrete examples of human behaviour.
- Tell a story and align it to the data you offer.

Be intelligent in your presentation of statistics. For example, if you were a manager of a radio station it would be better to say 'The station's ratings have fallen two percentage points', if ratings had dropped from 12 to 10 per cent. Gains can be presented as pure percentages, such as 'The station's ratings have increased 33 per cent over the last two survey periods' if ratings improved from 9 to 12 per cent. Be careful with your data and ensure that you place them in unassailable contexts.

Bombarding your listener/s with statistics will often produce sensory overload. Observe the 'less is more' rule and choose the most compelling data, leaving supporting information to back up your argument during question and answer periods.

GIVE POWERFUL EXAMPLES

Take any generalisation or inference drawn from a fact and chances are some people will take issue with the conclusion you have drawn. It pays to locate your facts and conclusions within an example, because examples allow people to link abstract information like statistics with a concrete reality you have portrayed. By offering an example, the attention of your audience will be focused on your story, your context or your interpretation. Strong examples can help you stop people placing their spin on your statistics. Take the example below, which involves research indicating that the management style of top male managers in US business is based on the football metaphor:

We agonise over the glass ceiling and wonder why we can't break through. Could it be our mothers' fault and the games they forbade us to play?

Could it be no accident that 80 per cent of the businessmen who comprise today's chief executive officers told *Fortune* magazine that football was their favourite spectator sport?

Top management clearly feels an intense affinity to the head coach of a football team; their problems seem to them almost identical. Sports metaphors abound in business talk ... back-up team or bench strength ... coach and coaching ... disqualified player ... end run ... huddle ... jock ... tackle the job ... good quarterback ... the list goes on.

Their knowledge of the game, the rules, the hard play and the subtleties run as a major pattern in corporate America. Is it little wonder then that over 70 per cent of middle ranking female executives reported to the Harvard Corporate Cultures Study that they had little social rapport with their senior executives, and that networking with senior males was an extremely difficult task?

Watch football, girls! Learn the rules! Understand the plays! And make sure your daughters are sitting there with you.

The above example takes two seemingly separate statistics and builds a story around them. Humour is used to support the key inference, and anecdotal evidence in the form of football terminology is used to gain acceptance of the initial statistic.

GET TO THE CORE OF YOUR POINT QUICKLY

When opening a new information loop, introduce your proposition quickly. Make your introductory statement compelling and direct.

Bricks and mortar never ask why. Capital equipment never asks for an explanation. But people do, and they will keep on asking why until they get answers. If we close down this plant, our answers will need to convince the remaining workforce that the company would have bled to death without such drastic surgery.

The above statement raises a poignant issue and lays down a direct challenge for which the speaker has crafted an argument. Often the best openings are the most direct and simple. When fashioning your opening lines, think of the most compact and salient means of conveying the essence of your loop, idea or argument.

USE CONTRAST FRAMES FOR INCREDIBLE CLARITY

While, in reality, there are usually many more than two sides of an argument, it can be advantageous to use opposite values when structuring the points you make in information loops. The human brain finds it easy to process information that is couched in opposite values such as:

- different/same
- novel/familiar
- cause/effect
- problem/solution
- this/that
- safe/dangerous
- positive/negative

Two-value argument provides contrariety and limited choice. The following two-value statements take the idea of positive and negative contrast one step further. They demonstrate how limited choice enhances the probability of audiences embracing and remembering your implicit message:

- You can't create experience—you must undergo it.
- The innovator is not an opponent of the old—he is a proponent of the new.
- It is commitment, not authority, that produces results.
- To teach is to learn twice.
- To live like a Republican you have to vote Democrat.

If you want to make your communication more memorable and powerful, consider using two-value rhetoric to encapsulate or sum up your main points. The key to making simple contrasting statements is to think opposites. Take the following statement as an example:

Strength, not in the forearm—but in the forehead.

You will notice that a negative is counterbalanced with a positive. This technique has produced many memorable quotes. Observe how writers produce a natural rhythm to their quotable phrases by also balancing the number of words. The following statement by Voltaire takes two extremes to produce a powerful literary image:

The truths of religion are never so well understood—as by those who have lost the power of reasoning.

Voltaire creates a complicated tension between a positive and a negative, using a pause before the word 'as' as the rhetorical pivot. His words are simple and his meaning burns through with the intensity of a flame-thrower. Think of this technique as the verbal equivalent of a set of scales:

Method

- Think of what it is you want your audience to do and roughly sketch it out.
- Now think of the opposite, the negative case or point, and write it out as simply as you can.

- Ensure you use concrete language and short, sharp words.
- Play with the negative script until you find words that can be reversed.
- Make the balancing statement positive or the opposite of the first statement.
- Try to take key words from the first statement and use or twist them to build your positive statement: plays on words can add power and novelty to the statement.
- Balance the sentiments, the beat and time it takes to utter the words on both sides of the scale.

Communication guru Professor Ronald Carpenter has identified a top-shelf form of contrast framing he describes as AB-BA reversal. Carpenter is a specialist in the analysis of American political rhetoric. In a critique of the speeches of John F. Kennedy he identifies some of the last century's most memorable and potent examples of AB-BA reversal.

Ask not what your *country* can do for *you*—ask what *you* can do for your *country*.
        A   *B*   *B*   *A*

The key to this impressive rhetorical device is first to select the most important words in the first sequence and then to construct a meaning that is either the reverse or different in the second sequence and use it to create a contrasting statement. In the above quote, Kennedy's speechwriter, Edward Sorenson, chose to begin with negation (a negative statement using the word 'not') and counterbalanced it with a positive suggestion. You can start with a positive and end with a negative if you choose, but generally your statement will have more impact if you end with a positive. Take the following Kennedy statement and identify the AB-BA reversal sequence:

Let us never negotiate out of fear, but let us never fear to negotiate.

Once again the quote ends with a positive. Notice how the statement would lose some of its elegance and power if it were to read 'Let us never fear to negotiate, but let us never negotiate out of fear'.

You may have to struggle a little with contrast framing before you begin to easily incorporate it into your speeches. Having invested some time in learning to do the sequence and noticing the impact you are having on people, you'll look back to your decision to master it as one of the best choices you ever made.

PROOF POSITIVE

In the more controversial areas of public debate, the battleground is one where few prisoners are taken. Meaning frames are a favourite method of discrediting rivals. In these instances, your ability to identify the structure of damaging accusations and create an effective counter-frame may be critical to staying in the game. Observe the following benchmarks when constructing counter-arguments.

Often rivals will attempt to neutralise or damage your position with negative labelling. Negative labels have a habit of sticking unless they're dealt with quickly and effectively. It is wise to respond to such accusations and neutralise them in the initial part of your speech or address. For example:

Charles X says you're racist.

Review the following response and notice how the speaker re-frames it:

It's so easy to throw labels around. Well, I have some labels that we all should strive to wear in this debate: open-hearted, level-headed, and what about conciliatory? Let's be more generous to each other and search for ways to cooperate. There's too much at stake.

Observe how the speaker doesn't defend the accusation of racism. This is because the taint of racism would remain if the speaker were to say 'I am *not* a racist'. Professional communicators realise that denying an accusation leaves the accusation floating around in the minds of those who have heard it. It is better to leave people thinking about the positive elements you have introduced into a debate. Say what you *are* and what you are *doing* and not what you're *not* and what you're *not doing*. Instead of:

No, we do not have a glass ceiling in this corporation.

rephrase it to something like:

We are an equal opportunity employer. We promote on merit.

Instead of:

Liberal Party economics are not an act of revenge by the greedy against the needy.

rephrase it to something like:

We are doing everything possible to give all Australians equal opportunity to become prosperous and financially secure.

When criticised, turn the criticism into a positive statement and tell people about the advantages and benefits that your position will deliver. This applies as much to issue-based debate as it does to workplace politics.

USE FIRST PERSON, ACTIVE VOICE

It can be important to convey the impression of action, involvement and decisiveness. Statements such as the one below reek of dispassion and distance:

The program will be initiated on a trial basis in Sale. The results will be analysed for their impact and will determine whether the system is implemented across the state.

Indicate involvement and action by adding verbs and associating yourself with the plans and tasks at hand:

I will trial this new program in Sale first. In three months I'll take a careful look at whether it delivers better services to those without a job. If it does, then every unemployed person in Victoria will gain from our experiences in Sale.

Project empathy towards the human side of things. The following statement creates an impression in listeners of distance and lack of human warmth:

The economic downturn in the housing industry has forced the downsizing on us. We couldn't justify an under-utilised workforce to our shareholders.

Take responsibility for having made a difficult decision. Remember governments, organisations and companies don't make decisions or formulate policy, people do! The following indicates not only respect for the sensibilities of those souls who lost their livelihoods, but also sustains the impression of good corporate citizenship.

It was a tough decision: one of the hardest things we had to do because we value the people who've helped the company survive. We had to let people go because there was no work and not enough money coming in to pay such a large wages bill.

KEEP IT RELEVANT!

One of the most important variables in motivating an audience or individual to think about your message is personal relevance. Personal relevance can stem from a variety of factors: linkage to personal beliefs and values, desired outcomes, membership of groups, possessions, hopes for the future, significant others and shared experiences, to name a few. Relevance strikes a responsive chord in your listeners. Suddenly, you and they are in shared and familiar territory.

When the relevance quotient of a message is high, people will be more motivated to scrutinise and think about its content. If your arguments bear scrutiny, then you can expect to achieve higher degrees of persuasion. The formula is a simple one: the more relevant your material, the more persuasive it will be as long as your arguments are properly structured and sustainable. You can increase the persuasive power and relevance of your message by choosing word clusters that draw your listeners into a shared experience. For example, instead of:

The benefits to consumers will be substantial if the taxation system is reformed.

choose to communicate the benefits to listeners by making the proposed changes to the taxation system personally relevant:

For every $100 you spend in the supermarket you'll get 13 per cent more for your money than you do now.

Relevance is the compass that keeps you walking down the Path of Least Resistance. The reason why relevance is so important is that it can override other negatives in your form and content. Research shows that if your material is highly relevant the attention of your audience is less likely to be diverted towards issues of likeability, status, the large wart on your nose, the extra 6 kilos you're carrying around your stomach, the mild speech defect you have, and so on.

If your material is of low relevance, your listeners are more likely to abandon efforts to follow your argument and focus on issues such as status, likeability and physical attractiveness. If you're one of the beautiful people or a world authority on your subject matter, that could work for you. If you're like most of us, however, you don't want your listeners to focus on any of those little foibles that we try so desperately hard to conceal.

Your commitment to your listener should be greater than your commitment to what you think is important. People react positively when you say, 'I know who you are, and I know what you want'. You can achieve high relevance when you infuse what you say with something of emotional and personal value to your listener. When you're constructing your arguments or building an argument on the run, ask yourself some of the following questions and build the answers into your message:

- How is what I'm doing reaching out and touching my listeners?
- How will this idea, concept, action improve my listeners' life?
- How can this dovetail into my listeners' needs?
- How can I show my listeners what this proposal can do for them?
- What are the emotional experiences my listeners could experience?
- What hot buttons could be pressed?
- How can I direct my message to the 'you' of my audience?

The following hot buttons have been shown to enhance relationships with audiences and elevate the relevance of messages:

- Tell your audience how your idea will enable them to have more control over particular aspects of their life, where applicable.
- Show them how your content can help them re-evaluate their life for the better.
- Make sure you take your audience to highly familiar and comforting places on a regular basis. Always introduce the new by first touching on the familiar.
- Help your listeners make new and exciting discoveries. People generally love new ideas and services that link into their perceived needs.
- Use words such as now, new, better, at last, breakthrough, cure and solution: 'Now here's a way that you can *finally* make that career breakthrough'. Build in discovery points to your presentation.
- Do things that will enhance people's status. Put your listener on a pedestal for investing their time to come and listen to you: 'Want to put yourself head and shoulders above the rest when it comes to knowing how to beat the competition at its own game?'.
- Talk about family bonding. While the traditional family is largely a myth these days, people hanker for the warm fuzzy feelings of old family values. How can we capture them again in modern Australian society? Show your listener ways to bond with spouse, parents and children. Make sure you don't preach.
- Launch into nostalgia, particularly for the 1960s to the 1980s. Tap into your audience's collective sense of personal history.
- Add fun, novelty and stimulation to your content and presentation. With all the manufactured gloom in current affairs and news, people value speakers who

help them 'lighten up'. The reason for this is simple: studies show that if pleasure and stimulation are associated with you and your message, that message will stand out in the mind of your listener.

■ Show people how your idea may save time.

■ Utilise the 'est' factor, and make sure you associate your content on occasions with an 'est'. Brightest, easiest, fanciest, fastest, funniest, happiest, shortest, liveliest, damnedest, tastiest, finest, safest, classiest, fairest, best feed into your listener's desire to be associated with quality and excellence.

■ Help your audience become the best and be associated with the best. Show and tell your listeners how they can be the best they can be. Include in your content elements that you know will help people succeed in life's endeavours, but make it short, concise and unambiguous. Constantly give your audience and colleagues 'gold stars' for being the great people they really are.

■ Demonstrate your innate nurturing instinct: for your city, its people, its victims, its defeats. Focus on how things affect people at the personal level.

■ Help your listeners build new personas. Help them discover the new them or how to reinvent themselves, at work, home and socially. This might relate to the changing working environment, business opportunities, how to start a new life today or, importantly, how to realise their full potential, be it physical, vocational or spiritual.

MAKE CHOICE EASIER

Double binds create the illusion of alternatives while, in reality, forcing a choice for a single option. Would you like to know more about the types of double binds that allow you to enhance ethically your powers of persuasion, *or* would you prefer to stick with hit and miss techniques? The choice is yours! Try the following double bind ten minutes before mealtimes on children who have reached the age of saying no and demanding choice:

Would you like to put your toys away now *or* before you sit down to eat?

This is hardly a choice, when you examine its linguistic components, but it works almost every time! You may imagine that adults would be impervious to double binds but research conducted from the late 1950s to the 1970s indicates that adults do, indeed, fall into the double bind trap. The illusion created by a double bind impedes/obstructs the critical-analytic functions of the left hemisphere (the logical 'side' of the brain in normally organised people) and induces an unconscious acceptance of plausibility.

In choosing to use double binds as a rhetorical device, you would be well advised to consider issues of people ecology. The test that non-toxic charismatic communicators apply to double binds, as to any rhetoric, is that of mutual desirability: Is the technique being used to empower people to make better choices or is it designed to fulfil the speaker's ambitions? Notice the double bind and forced choice involved in that question. Examine the following double bind and arrive at a conclusion by applying the people ecology rule:

It's either 'business as usual' and wait for the future to overwhelm us, *or* to begin to create a better future for the company and its staff by improving the way we work, inventing better ways of servicing our market and adding value to our product. Is there really any choice at all?

You may conclude that the above statement fulfils the people ecology rule because, arguably, it attempts to shift people from a less mutually desirable state of affairs to a better state of affairs. There are, however, other forms of double bind that are dangerous in the extreme, and you may need to understand how to counteract them to avoid being caught in their web. When double binds are applied for dishonourable reasons by people who are aware of their potency, challenge their apparent deception by asking, 'How can you narrow your options down to two?'. Understanding double binds empowers you to narrow down choice as an ethical persuasion tool. It also gives you the opportunity to detoxify the double binds of opponents who use them for unethical purposes.

LEARN YOUR ABC

It's a general principle that attitudes drive behaviour. So, how do you sew the seeds of attitude in a rich enough medium so as to harvest appropriate responses within particular realms of behaviour? There are certain specific circumstances that will improve the chances of individuals and groups accessing particular attitudes and acting on those attitudes. Attitude-behaviour consistency (ABC) theory suggests that two conditions need to be met for an attitude to drive behaviour. They are:

1. attitude relevance
2. attitude availability

Attitude relevance deals with usefulness, applicability and pertinence. You dealt with this aspect above and so, to complete the two conditions, we will focus primarily on availability. It's no good prattling on about attitudes driving behaviour if your target group doesn't know it has an attitude towards a particular issue. If an attitude isn't available, then you may as well forget trying to exhort people to behave in particular ways. How can you make attitudes available so people will be driven to act in a potentially predictable way?

An attitude is available when it gains your attention. You become aware at some level that you actually have an attitude on an issue, and the attitude is 'activated'. An effective way to introduce and activate an attitude is a technique known as 'priming'. Say a health agency is concerned about the increasing level of obesity among teenagers. It wants young people to resist pop psychology talk about 'loving yourself for who you are— all 140 kilos of you' and have a negative attitude towards obesity. Priming may offer the solution.

A group of teenagers could be 'primed' first by having them look at moving pictures with supporting dialogue of young, physically fit, vibrant people doing 'cool' activities, having fun and admiring each other's bodies. The priming process will stimulate attitudes about the type of body profile that is attractive, healthy and sexy.

The second part of the formula would be to ask the teenagers to take a position about the state of being overweight. Having been primed as to what constitutes the ideal, the teenagers will be far more likely to access the 'available' attitude and apply the criteria you have introduced during the priming process. The priming formula makes the preferred attitude available and significantly increases the likelihood of achieving a desired ABC (attitude-behaviour consistency).

Ethically, you would need to take the group of teenagers through two more steps to avoid the fat ones becoming depressed over their size. You would encourage the group to create strong visual images of becoming fit and healthy within a time period and of imagining how it would feel, what people would say and how they would look in a fabulous new outfit. Second, you would help them develop a process to achieve the desired fitness and move away from their current undesirable shape and level of fitness.

Finally, attitude-behaviour consistency theory works when the attitude is available and relevant in specific contexts. For example, an obese teenager may not think about the attitude you have installed if he is smashed out of his mind at a party at three o'clock in the morning and has an attack of the munchies. So part of your persuasion process must be to cover as many contexts as possible and link the attitude to a broad range of situations. A good way of installing attitudes cross-contextually is to invite people to consider all the contexts in which the attitude would best prevail.

SPEAK PLAINLY

Short words, rather than long words, included in short sentences, rather than sentences that take longer than fifteen seconds to say, assist your listeners to work within the confines of their working memories, and long sentences crammed with multi-syllables and unfamiliar words, perhaps accompanied by qualifications and subordinate clauses which, if people haven't given you their fullest attention, and let's face it they often don't, will lead to confusion and indeed loss of meaning, probably about half way through, can turn an address into a kind of marathon requiring the cognitive endurance of a Mensa candidate and ultimately everyone including yourself will probably have forgotten the starting point of the idea you sought to express (if, incidentally, there was one in the first place) before the end of your verbal onslaught is ever reached. Of course you get the point, don't you?

The most glaringly obvious verbal onslaughts are usually contained in written speeches. A point well worth remembering when you initially write out a speech or address is to use the written word purely as a phonetic representation of spoken language. In other words, do write as you speak and avoid writing content that makes you speak as you write.

When writing any part of a verbal presentation, bear in mind that people do not generally speak in sentences: they speak in *sense bursts*. In oral communication, people process words in chunks or phrases. Pick up a book of well-written poetry and notice how it's set out. Good, conventional poetry is far closer in style to spoken language than most of the stodge that professional speechwriters churn out.

REPEAT, REPEAT, REPEAT

How do you learn a new behaviour? How do you burn something into your memory banks? You really get involved in it and you do it, or say it, over and over again, don't you? To install a new behaviour or learn something new, your experience can tell you that practice plus involvement does, indeed, make it perfect. Charismatic communicators direct much effort towards finding elegant, and sometimes inelegant, means of impelling listeners to practise an idea and burn it into their memory banks during speeches and presentations.

The advertising industry has long appreciated the value of repetition. Research shows that if you want to link a product name with a particular need, you have to make between three and seven 'hits' before a target consumer will establish a mental link between a need and the advertised product. A hit is a consumer's exposure to the particular message. As you sit down to your television and get hit with the same ad night after night, you are, in effect, engaging in a form of practice at the unconscious level. So when, suddenly, you notice the tell-tale flakes of dandruff on your shoulders, you think of Selsun in a flash, and all that practice pays off.

Repetition works, plain and simple. In the great contest of influence and ideas, hawkers of competing ideologies do exactly the same thing: repeating simple messages over time to whittle away at their opponents' credibility and burn their message into their listeners' memory banks. Below are examples of standard repetition techniques. They all require a range of three to seven repetitions: the more the better, but do allow commonsense to prevail.

- Constantly refer back to a mega-frame or theme. Keep referring your stories, loops and arguments to your major point.
- Say the same thing over and again, using different tonality.
- Repeat a single message throughout your address, using different words and different examples.
- In major campaigns, design a powerful and succinct message with three major points and repeat it in all forums. For example: 'This budget goes for growth: growth in business confidence, growth in jobs and growth in our quality of life.'
- Follow the age-old principle of telling people what you're going to tell them, tell them it and tell them what you told them.

Repetition par excellence

Now, here's an example of possibly the most potent application of repetition you will ever encounter. The model is based on a presentation given by UK-based international trainer and management consultant David Shephard in 1997. So effective was his use of repetition that years after the seminar people still remember it vividly and practise what they learned. In fact, participants of the seminar use it as an alumni code for their experience.

Shephard was invited to be part of a two-week training course in human change technologies in 1997. The composition of his audience was biased towards practitioners in the caring professions, such as psychotherapists, psychologists and hypnotherapists. An essential point that

Shephard wanted to get across in his presentation was the need to break free from the habit of trying to match people's presenting problems, behaviours and symptoms to neat and predetermined categories.

Shephard wanted to emphasise the point that, more often than not, people have within them the means of their own recovery. If therapists were observant enough they could uncover these internal resources and utilise them to help effect change in their clients. In order to discover the truly individual dynamics of a client's problems, Shephard believed that practitioners needed to become uncommonly observant. Shephard was speaking to people in his audience who followed a professional pattern of reaching for the DSM IV (fourth edition of *Diagnostic and Statistical Manual of Mental Disorders* produced by the American Psychiatric Association) to categorise patients as soon as they felt they had enough information to do so. They were comfortable with putting presenting problems and patients into pigeonholes and labelling them with the constructs of the DSM IV.

Shephard's task was to demonstrate the therapeutic benefits of choosing a new focus, realigning attention back on the patient and the presenting problem, and avoiding the trap of stock diagnoses. The other message that Shephard wanted to get across was that 'real curiosity' was an essential tool in unpacking and modelling successful behaviours as well. Here is the basic template of what he did.

Define the task

Define specifically what you want your audience to be able to do. A good way of arriving at a definition is to ask yourself: 'If I could just instruct my audience to do something and have them magically obey my command— what would it be?'.

The answer to that question, in David Shephard's case, was 'Get real, real curious'.

Create a metaphor

Find an appropriate metaphor around which you can wrap a story. Shephard chose a childhood experience of overwhelming curiosity about what made a radio crystal set he had been given actually work.

I looked at this enchanting object that had music and voices coming through an earpiece and *I got real, real curious* as to how it created its magic.

The essence of the metaphor was the impelling force of curiosity, which drew him to look inside the crystal set to understand more clearly how it worked. You may begin to notice the parallels here between looking inside a presenting patient and looking at the workings of a crystal set.

The metaphor continued as a short story on how that initial childhood experience of curiosity marked the beginning of incredibly fruitful and interesting experiences resulting from his having learned 'the awesome power of curiosity'.

Repeat the key phrase throughout

Shephard went on to tell a number of short stories about various experiences. He told of encountering various people, objects and events, and having got 'real, real curious' about them and learned incredible things.

After having recounted two or three stories, Shephard let the audience complete his 'real curious' sentences. His stories got closer and closer to the audience's real-life professional experiences. Bear in mind that this was an audience largely composed of professionals, yet he had them acting as though they were children listening to a bedtime story and playing the role of a chorus filling in a recurring theme.

S: I met this man who had been through something like five different psychotherapists to cure his germ phobia. Hey, this was one hell of a phobia. This guy did phobias better than anyone I had ever encountered and, of course, I ...'

Audience: got real, real curious!

S: That's right! How did he do it so well? What made him such an expert? I had to know. Wouldn't you?

Appeal to personal experience and assign internal causality

The final part of Shephard's masterful use of the technique was to draw all the stories together with an appeal to internal experience and a strong suggestion that curiosity equals being a better practitioner. This latter technique of linking success as a practitioner to an internal quality, as opposed to an external reaction, is a powerful persuasion tool.

S: Your own experiences can tell you that curiosity is the key to uncovering vital information that other people miss. We can miss so much when we're not curious. Curiosity is all about focusing 100 per cent of your attention on the object of your curiosity. *As you become uncommonly curious about your patients, you can privately know that you're becoming a better and better practitioner. You'll know inside that curiosity is the key that opens up your clients' potential for rapid recovery.*

Someone presents you with a person quandary ... and what do you do?
Audience: 'Get real, real curious!'

The total duration of this exercise was about eight minutes and yet the time passed rapidly because the audience was enthralled and thoroughly enjoying itself. Years after the event, participants in the seminar still recalled vividly the experience they had. It was a turning point for a number of participants in the seminar. In discussing cases with each other it's not uncommon for them to say, 'And then, of course, I got real, real curious'.

Since the 1970s the evidence has been accumulating that repetition alone is far from the most efficient way of installing ideas and behaviours into long-term memory. It has been found that, without strong motivation, repetition can produce less than dazzling results. Involving an audience in some way and adding unusual or novel components to the process, as David Shephard did, can enhance self-motivation and help fully utilise the latent power of repetition.

USE THE PRIMACY/RECENCY EFFECT

People tend to remember more from the beginning and end of a presentation or learning session. The probability of recall is significantly higher at the beginning and conclusion of lectures, presentations, training sessions and even personal study. Recall and retention are lowest in the middle of a presentation.

Primacy

In the initial stages of your presentation, introduce your principal theme. Be direct and to the point. For example:

The global economy is setting up every company, every town, every region, every country into open competition with other countries, towns, regions and companies around the world. In true Darwinian form, this frenzy of competition will leave only the fittest standing.

Your financial security is truly on the line. What happens if your division is downsized, re-engineered or sold off because it can't compete with some distant town you've never even heard of? What can you do to prevent the cold winds of globalisation from freezing you out of a decent lifestyle?

Tonight, I invite you to consider a number of solutions that will allow you to place your security where it belongs: on your skills, abilities and the qualities within yourself that no amount of globalisation can take away.

You'll discover some simple answers that can immunise you from the heartbreak of redundancy and the anxiety that comes with job insecurity.

In the above example, the speaker introduces a major universal theme (security), is direct with his outline of the issue and sets the tone of the presentation.

Recency

In the closing stages of your presentation or speech allocate time for a summary of your major theme and the key points outlined during the presentation.

The solutions we have reviewed together work, and they offer you much greater chance of having work in the future. These three tenets of career security can allow you to anticipate surprise and to develop a personal plan that will deliver a secure lifestyle.

I am wondering whether the last thoughts you leave here with tonight are those of:

1. Learn about and become a user of information technology.
2. Keep up with the latest developments in your industry.
3. Become a lifelong learner.

By taking responsibility and making the choice to place your sense of security in yourself, your abilities and your ever-developing skills, you can insure yourself against the harsh effects of the global economy. And that's a worthwhile goal we can all embrace, isn't it?

USE MEMORY ENHANCERS

Use mnemonics to encourage listeners to remember information sets. 'Mnemonics' comes from the Greek word *mneme*, meaning 'to remember'. A mnemonic is an aid to memory— anything that helps you install something in your own or your audience's memory.

Spatial mnemonics

Spatial mnemonics mark out spaces for each of your ideas. If, when you are doing a presentation, you stand in a particular space to deliver the information, return to the same space to either recap or invite recall.

If you want your audience to remember a series of points, numbers, words or ideas, invite your listeners to associate each idea with a particular visual experience. For example, you might choose the rooms of a house, where recall is stimulated by revisiting a visual image of each room.

Acronyms

This mnemonic technique is a powerful way to install a sequence or process. You may have encountered the following goal-setting process described as SMART:

S = specific
M = measurable
A = achievable
R = realistic
T = timed

The key to using acronyms is to make the acronym 'sexy'. If the acronym can describe the process, all the better.

Visual representation

A picture, map, design or chart is often worth a thousand words. In presentations and speeches, as well as one-on-one conversations, the introduction of visual material promotes retention.

Association

Link new information with bizarre or unusual imagery or words. For example:

I call this the watermelon theory. Picture a watermelon and, as you do, notice that when you cut a chunk of watermelon it leaves an impression behind. You know the size of the chunk by examining the contours of the hole that it's left.

Same thing when people tell lies. People may give you highly selective chunks of information. Look at the contours of the information and you have a better chance of working out which watermelon it belongs to.

USE EMOTIONAL DIVERSITY

How is it that we remember the triumphs and traumas in our lives so well? Please recall a moment of, say, intense happiness or contentment in your life and you may sense that you have the answer within your grasp.

As you review that event start to notice the sensory information that's embedded in the memory. What pictures do you have— how bright and clear are they? What sounds are associated with the memory— what intensity, timbre or quality have they got? Most importantly, what emotions and states of mind do you experience when you see the event through your own eyes— how intense are those emotions and where are they located in your body? Can you also recall smells and tastes?

An easy way to install a memory is to associate an event with a SEE. The acronym stands for significant emotional event. Consider the significance of the emotion associated with the cherished memory you recalled. The intensity of the emotion you experienced at the time helped transfer the event from your working memory to your long-term memory. One big emotional rush is often all it takes for an event to be indelibly inscribed in your memory for life.

Another dimension in the transfer process is that shortly after the event you return to it and relive the experience. It's nice looking back on precious moments, if not for any other reason than to re-experience the pleasant emotions that were present at the time. The same process usually applies to traumatic experiences, except in cases where the emotions are repressed. In the immediate aftermath of trauma, we may relive it many times and experience the shocking states of mind produced by the event over and again. Regrettably, with trauma, we often create limiting beliefs and attitudes around the trauma and carry them for life.

Staged SEEs are an impressive method in the transfer of information from your listeners' working memories to their long-term memories. Have you seen the anti-smoking television advertisement in which various professional players in a lung cancer drama introduce themselves cheerfully with statements like 'I'm your oncologist and I'll be supervising your chemotherapy' and 'I'm your spiritual adviser and I'll be helping you come to terms with your death'?

These advertisements, while arguably so immoral that they would be knocked back by any responsible university research ethics committee because of the emotional harm they may inflict on respondents, work particularly well with people who have cancer phobias or who are motivated by avoidance. The SEE induced by the advertisement is real and likely to be relived, complete with associated pictures and emotions, many times over.

Now, think back to the series of 'bugger!' advertisements run in support of a popular car manufacturer's tray-top utility. The commercials became a household topic, not only because of the controversial use of the word 'bugger', but also because they were intrinsically novel and funny.

We will focus on creating moments of levity, novelty, humour and other positive emotions, leaving the anchoring of negative emotions to those bold or unethical enough to risk causing emotional harm to their listeners.

USE HUMOUR

Someone once said that humour is the ability to see three sides of the same coin. Humour can help people expand their models of the world. It may often assist an audience to experience the idea, argument, object or event from the 'third' perspective. Fun, humour, drama, wanton curiosity and the like can accelerate learning and create a more conducive environment for the taking on of new ideas. It's been estimated that strategically placed humour alone can improve retention and recall by up to 20 per cent.

Humour is a wonderfully uplifting device to install messages in the long-term memories of subjects. As far as is known, the creation of significant emotional events around laughter occasions no emotional harm and would breeze through any ethics committee hearing. Ask university graduates to explain how they excelled in some subjects and not in others, and you'll discover that 'enjoyment' and 'fun' are common denominators in learning excellence. Appropriately directed humour can also increase the 'liking' quotient in your audience. Humour, anecdotes and stories, however, must fall within the boundaries of your audience's sense of good taste. Human plumbing jokes may go down well at a local boilermakers conference, but at a black-tie event attended by inhabitants of our leafier suburbs they'd be about as funny as an outer Sydney postcode.

If your audience is feeling good, it will be more responsive to your message and less disposed to develop counterarguments to your presentation, pitch or speech. But, there's more. By managing the levity level of your presentation effectively, you can specifically 'anchor', or associate, your audience's good feelings to yourself and your idea. In Chapter 15 you will learn techniques of anchoring and for 'dropping' anchors at appropriate moments during your presentation. Here, you will acquire the knowledge to create emotional environments that are most appropriate and favourable to the absorption and retention of specific messages.

Here are some pointers designed to help you build humour and levity into your presentation.

Metaphor

Use metaphors creatively and humorously. For example:

They say bureaucracies are the hardened arteries of government.

Self-deprecatory humour

Engage in self-deprecatory humour. For example:

So, OK. I *am* the Prince of Darkness. But let me tell you, my duties these days are mainly ceremonial!

I know how difficult parenting can be. I have a teenage son and grown-up daughter, both in their twenties!

Quotations

Drop in pithy or funny quotations that link to your material. Always acknowledge the author:

As Amanda Lear says, 'I hate to spread rumours—but what else can one do with them?'. There's a strong rumour of a change in the regulations, and you might consider building up your inventory a bit to take advantage of it.

Humorous inferences

Draw humorous inferences from arguments you want to debunk:

Hey, outsourcing is great. The idea to outsource R & D can be just the beginning. Next, consider outsourcing your MD, your board and the marketing function. After that you could outsource your customers, and then your profits! Seriously though, why would you outsource company secrets and let outsiders learn how you maintain your competitive edge in the marketplace?

Link opposites

Link opposites in humorous ways. For example:

Getting into bed with Microsoft would be like John Candy having conjugal rights with Michelle Pfeiffer. Satisfying for John Candy, but a potentially crushing experience for Michelle.

Wordplay and puns

Engage in wordplay and puns with listeners or participants:

The police amassed a stock of more than 150 kilograms of marijuana, leaving no stone unturned in their blitz on dope dealers and importers. They decided to burn it on a remote part of Rottnest Island, thus also leaving no tern unstoned on that popular holiday resort.

Ensure your wordplay is not at the expense of someone in your audience. Never put your audience down, and ensure that your wordplay reinforces your major points.

Three-step-and-drop

Apply the three-step-and-drop technique. This humour model is based on the principle that once we're led along a particular path, mental laziness steps in and we allow the rhythm of the familiar to complete the process. For example:

Q: What do you call a tree that grows from acorns?
A: Oak.
Q: What do you call a funny story?
A: Joke.
Q: What do you call the sound made by a frog?
A: Croak.
Q: What do you call the white of an egg?
A: Yolk!

In the above example, you notice how tantalising it becomes to complete the sequence with the word 'yolk' instead of the word 'white'. The three-step-and-drop technique works in the same way. Find three points or ideas that lead your listeners into a pattern and disrupt the pattern on the fourth point. The following example demonstrates the technique:

The beautiful princess encountered a frog on a rock and kissed it.
The frog turned into a prince and fell instantly in love with the princess.
They courted, and in time the prince plummeted to his knees and asked for her hand in marriage.
[Drop] She said no ... and they both lived happily ever after.

Here is a more sophisticated example of the technique:

Gore Vidal is known internationally as a homosexual, a writer and an American. Naturally, when interviewing him it was necessary to broach deeply personal and potentially touchy issues. So, I just blurted it out and asked him how old he was when he first suspected that he was an American.

Punch lines

Develop elegant and pithy punch lines. Humorous punch lines after anecdotes, examples and stories can add perceptual scope and range to your content. Spend time to create and hone high impact punch lines. Notice how the following punch lines add dimension to the messages:

All good communicators start somewhere. The point is they start! They learn, they test, they develop their own style and technique. Look, I'm one of those people who take everything literally, and when my mother told me never to talk to strangers, I didn't. The result was that I never met anyone until I was thirty-four! I started then!

We are all responsible for our own emotional well-being. No one else can make us 'feel' good. Identify the periods in your calendar that are likely to produce emotional lows and plan to do something emotionally uplifting. This is especially the case during big 'family' occasions such as Christmas. It's not your fault you don't have family. Christmas is an international conspiracy designed to make single people feel like crap: don't let them make you one of 'their' statistics!

The best way I can sum up this movie is to say that I felt it was an absolute insult to my backside to have to sit through it for two hours.

Use one-liners

Build a reservoir of one-liners. Collect good one-liners and short, punchy jokes and have them at the ready. Adapt them to fit the sensibilities of your audience. Walk into a conversation, speech or presentation with a few short 'funnies' and be ready to use them appropriately when you notice attention is waning.

Levity and laughter are the best medicine, but unless you are a stand-up comic or after dinner speaker, ration your moments of levity for maximum impact. Avoid telling jokes or cheapening your presentation with antics that are not in alignment with your image or the importance of the occasion. Balance and compatibility are the keys.

Humour can also be used to galvanise the attention of your audience, interrupt fatigue cycles in presentations, relieve tensions, create supportive environments and help you establish rapport. Design your presentation, speech or conversation first, make a list of key ideas and points, and *then* craft your humour.

CONTRAST EMOTIONS

It's essential to avoid cycles of ennui in presentations and speeches because it is difference and novelty that promote recall of specific points. If your audience's emotional state remains constant throughout your presentation, chances are the key points of your message will remain suspended in the stale emotional ambience you've created. Boredom stifles transferral of information from working to long-term memory.

People have varying levels of tolerance for constancy. A CD with a selection of similar songs will often turn out to be too much of a good thing, one song debasing the currency of the next, and so on. Your favourite food, no matter how tantalising, will soon become ho-hum if you have it every night. So it is with a speech or presentation.

Novelty and difference become significant when you want your audience to remain attentive, stimulated and sufficiently aroused to be able to recall the crucial parts of your message. Commercial television news bulletins provide good case studies of how to manage contrast so as to maintain interest and stimulation. News values aside, news producers and editors spend a lot of time creating formulas for light and shade in a thirty-minute television news bulletin.

The programming code of a commercial newscast is to command the attention of an audience for the duration of the bulletin. According to the logic of commercial newscasting, the secret to evoking the 'Shut up, I'm watching' response is to present a cluster of mini-dramas that activate a range of emotional states. Sure, the emphasis may be on shock value and triviality, but sit through a well-crafted commercial bulletin and monitor the states of mind you experience. It works.

You may be disgusted at your propensity to be sucked into carefully packaged gossip and forty-second stories that merely scrape the surface of issues, but you have to hand it to commercial television. Its operators know which emotional buttons to press to keep you watching. The forms used to maintain your attention, however, are not themselves lowbrow or despicable, and they can be applied to any level of information.

So, watch commercial newscasts and pay attention to the contrast patterns used to maintain your interest. Forget the content and observe carefully how the structure and form of the bulletins take you from one emotional state to another. Notice also the expert use of cliff-hangers. See if you can map out the various structures used to get you to come back after the commercial breaks. They are rich pickings for those who want to learn rapidly how to maintain stimulation and interest in an audience.

The following pointers can be used to promote diversity of emotional experience in those listening to your speech or presentation.

Introduce an activity

Get your audience to do something that will be fun as well as instructional or will help them see your point. Properly directed activities that invite participants to view your main point/s from a number of different perspectives can be a highly effective way of stimulating interest.

There are numerous games and activity books available for trainers and speakers. Choose activities that reinforce learning themes or major points of your message. Select brief, rather than longer, activities and aim for novelty.

Tell a short story

Tell a story containing an anecdote that connects with your major theme/s. Stories by their nature evoke emotions and, if structured to elicit curiosity, are highly memorable.

Stories necessarily have to go somewhere. When telling a story in a presentation, you need to:

1. be economical;
2. keep it on track;
3. keep in mind your purpose behind telling the story.

A principal purpose of storytelling in presentations is to build and/or reinforce the overall objectives or arguments you have presented.

Use props

Use props creatively to make your points. Former minister and Labor Party president Barry Jones is reported to be a masterful user of props to capture interest and curiosity.

On one occasion, Jones took a new ceramic car part into parliament to labour the point of our need to think beyond the steel industry and invest in the research and development of new materials. In a classic version of 'I wonder what the cat's brought in tonight', Jones had his parliamentary colleagues spellbound by the object. His presentation stimulated considerable media interest and opened up a new chapter in the continuing 'clever country' debate.

Evoke curiosity

Curiosity can be evoked by the tactical use of cliff-hangers. For example:

In a moment you'll encounter one of the most powerful techniques for galvanising the attention of audiences you will ever encounter.

Can you guess how they responded to such a novel attack, and can you imagine how it had the entire executive floor scurrying around for whatever alluvial facts they could lay their hands on? I'll tell you in a moment what they came up with ...

The first stage is intelligence gathering, the second stage is planning and the fourth stage is delivery. Ah, you're wondering about the third stage?

Create compatible emotional states

Another effective technique is to create compatible emotional states in which to deliver your message, guiding the emotional states of your listeners at crucial points of your presentation, conversation or speech.

We learn in childhood how to create emotional environments that are conducive to self-preservation and persuasion. We master the use of humour to avoid unpleasant consequences or to soften people up for a big ask. We learn how to create doubt in others for self-serving purposes. We understand how to trigger curiosity and practise the art of surprise, and we instinctively know how to evoke fear.

So, it's a natural part of human intercourse to unconsciously induce particular emotional environments to achieve predetermined ends. You are usually unaware you are doing this or that you have a store of unconscious patterns you call up during your daily interactions with people.

The difference between impulsive and intentional inductions of emotional states is that the first are in our repertoire and the second require a measure of premeditation and rationality. Most people have a small repertoire of emotional inductions at their disposal and repeat them indiscriminately. An obvious solution to the problem of limited choice is to expand one's repertoire, isn't it? And in addressing the question of whether you need to pay conscious attention to the creation of emotional environments, ask yourself this question. At crucial moments when you may have to draw on every means available to persuade your listeners to understand your view of the world, wouldn't it be preferable to choose a compatible emotional environment rather than inducing one randomly?

The emotional states advertising agencies create to engage their target audiences are anything but random. The deliberate creation of significant emotional experience is a prime persuasion platform in advertising. From tampon commercials to anti-smoking messages, emotion is a key variable in the persuasion formula. If emotion can be induced to promote conspicuous consumption, isn't it reasonable and intelligent to place your important messages in emotional envelopes that guarantee rapid delivery to your audiences?

Please take a look at the following emotions. From the list you'll be able to identify emotional environments that are useful in creating more memorable experiences for your listeners.

agreement	eagerness	sadness
scepticism	cooperation	commitment
desire	mirth	determination
being poised for action	excitement	concern
fascination	self-confidence	disgust
protectiveness	indignation	exuberance
fun	doubt	laughter
curiosity	wonder	amazement
solidarity	enthusiasm	oneness
delight	surprise	thoughtfulness
empathy	joy	

Let's think of something to communicate to somebody and gain agreement on. Earlier in this book you read how charismatic personalities have the capacity to encourage their followers to believe in and have confidence in themselves or their abilities to carry out specific tasks.

Let's imagine your message is that your listeners can have every confidence in their abilities to develop the flexibility required to induce emotional states in their listeners at will. What follows is an example of an emotional induction.

In this example, we want to create the conditions for self-confidence, don't we? So the first thing you do is take another look at the emotions list and, as you do, you'll begin to realise that at some time you've experienced each and every one of those emotions. Therefore, emotional flexibility isn't an issue because of your experience of the emotions in the list. You've done all those emotions before and can exercise good judgment on the most appropriate emotional environments for specific messages.

Can it be a simple task of finding the right process to help your listeners ease into the chosen emotional state? That's a fairly significant thing to know, isn't it? Now think back to those times when you created an emotional environment from the limited range in your repertoire. See yourself having created a climate of, say, fear. You can do that can't you? How did you create a climate of fear? You may have told a story, recounted an anecdote, made a dire prediction or looked concerned and fearful yourself.

When you look at what you did in creating fear, you might hear yourself saying 'Hey, I already know a process' and feel pretty confident about being able to replicate the process when seeking to induce other emotional states. It would be fair to say, wouldn't it, that you have some fairly useful resources to call upon already? Let's just recap on the personal abilities and skills you already have:

1. You have experienced most, if not all, the emotions in the list, so you know what they feel like.
2. You've induced emotional states before.
3. You've called up into consciousness a process that you can begin to experiment with.

So, imagine yourself addressing a group or having a conversation, easily and fluently carrying out an emotional induction, noticing the positive impact it's having on your audience, and feeling the confidence that comes with the success. Yes? Of course, you can do it!

The example above is limited to the use of words to create an appropriate emotional environment. In real life, you have tone, body movement, facial expression, space, visual effects and much more at your disposal. Below is a model of an emotional induction. Expand on it. Experiment with different models, map the processes you already use, and observe other people's emotional induction techniques so as to build up a repertoire of processes.

1. Go through your speech, presentation or intended conversation and identify your key points. Then ask yourself what would be the most conducive emotional environment for the delivery of each specific point. Review the list of emotions for guidance.

2. Having selected particular emotional environments, begin to map out your induction process. What parts will make up the whole of the process?
   - a story, metaphor, statistic or anecdote?
   - visual aids?
   - props?
   - a step-by-step argument with discovery points built in?
   - audio?
   - activities with a predetermined learning point?
   - tone, building to a crescendo or dying to a whisper?
   - vivid language embedded in a story?
   - a pre-organised testimonial?
3. Rehearse the process you've created. Access the emotion you want to induce. Go back to a time when you felt it and feel it as you are peaking in your induction process.

Having rehearsed your process and polished your performance, try it on some supportive friends or colleagues and make any final adjustments.

Encourage 'soft' attention

Understanding how we pay attention to things appears to be quite deficient in Western cultures. We imagine the act of paying attention is a type of vigilance where all our senses are unfalteringly directed on the object, person or idea in question. This feeds neatly into the 'I speak, you listen' mindset and fails to take into account the small matter of human neurology.

Curiously, the instructions we are given, or may give ourselves, to pay fixed attention to something do not appear to match the reality of the structure of attention. Pick an object, any object, and try to pay attention to it for twenty seconds. What happens?

What you may notice is that your mind will wander, competing thoughts will interrupt concentration, your ears will pick up extraneous sounds, your eyes will lock on to other visual information, you'll feel an itch and attend to it, and so on. This is called distraction, and it directly challenges our notions of what attention is declared to be.

Please remember an occasion when your attention was locked on a movie or television program. What enabled you to focus so completely on the program or movie? Things were happening, weren't they? Nothing was static. You were able to fix your attention on the content at the expense of everything else because there was variety and novelty present.

While, at the abstract level, your attention was directed to the television show or movie, it was distraction that enabled you to attend so fully to the task at hand, wasn't it?

The lesson that audience attention can only be fixed when there is variety and novelty is an extremely valuable one to apply to the form of your presentation, speech or conversation. If you want to stimulate retention and recall, consider inviting your listener/s to look from an adaptive perspective at the information you impart. Let's explore a couple of examples of the adaptive technique.

As you're reading this section on attention and absorbing the point of supplying variety and novelty to attract your listeners' attention, pause and begin to think of ways you could distract them with novelty and variety but keep them on topic.

The last paragraph is an example of how you can introduce distraction, in this case an instruction to think about *ways* you could introduce novelty and variety, while still maintaining overall attention on the topic at hand. In fact, this example presupposes that you will continue to think about the key elements of the message.

- Invite listeners not to concentrate on the material you have delivered but to let their minds wander and wonder at the possibilities the information could open up for them. Follow up immediately with a short open forum to hear ideas from the floor.
- Introduce a game. Keep the abstract of your message in mind by defining the parameters of the game. 'Who can be the first to come up with five applications of this idea?'
- Present your idea multicontextually. Demonstrate the different contexts in which the idea may have application. Get suggestions from the floor.
- Ask your listener/s to notice and report on the different elements of your message.
- Talk about the 'Teflon effect', where a material originally invented for space travel found so many different applications. Ask your listeners to nominate how they will use your information in their everyday lives.
- Tell a story, leave out the ending and invite listeners to nominate the most effective ending to illustrate your point.
- Robin Williams demonstrated in the movie *Dead Poets Society* that students standing on, instead of sitting at, their desks could achieve a different perspective on an issue. Move your listeners around and ask them what they see differently from their new perspective.

Distraction, through novelty, difference and variety is a powerful means of maintaining attention. Ambiguity solves the riddle of 'soft' attention and generates potent results.

Memory and recall are reliable tests of your skills as an effective communicator. No matter what your subject material, the level of absorption of your message will determine if, how, why and when it is acted upon or used. The models and techniques introduced in this chapter can help you tip the odds in your favour and make your communication truly easy listening.

9 CHOOSING WORDS WISELY

> To know how to dissemble is the knowledge of kings.
>
> *Cardinal Richelieu*

Words have caused wars, racial hatred, international incidents, civil conflict and the division of our communities. Words, and our structure and interpretation of them, have also awakened the entire index of honourable human emotions and actions. Powerful things, aren't they? Depending upon whose mind and mouth structures and delivers them and whose ears and brain hears and processes them, words can make us soar with the eagles or hunt with wild dogs.

An evolutionary prank seems to have been played on the human species during its development of language. As you are about to discover, you can't help but communicate deception even when intending to deceive, you can't usually resist communicating hypocrisy when it's present and you can't help communicating the importance or unimportance of relationships and objects. You're often grossly inadequate to the task of hiding your prejudices, foibles, misgivings and desires. *You* truly are your message.

The following discussion on words is predicated on the idea that you are an ethical and moral individual and would much prefer your followers to soar with the eagles than run with the dogs. In this chapter you'll become acquainted with some words and linguistic behaviours that activate negative impressions and resistance. The examples you encounter can encourage you to open up your ears to track the barely hidden meanings found in everyday speech patterns.

CLOSENESS/DISTANCE

Let's take the example of a 'slip of the tongue' and examine some possible unconscious reactions to it. In the following example the speaker is referring to her partner of three years. What does her statement reveal?

I have a boyfriend who works in the computer industry.

Did a thought or feeling pop into your head, as it often does to people who read that statement, that the relationship between the couple was, at least from the speaker's perspective, not a particularly serious one? Reflect on the sentence and ask yourself what it suggests at a deeper level.

Psycholinguists may go as far as to suggest that the comment reveals the relationship is unlikely to lead to a life-long partnership. How is that so? Think about the words you hear yourself using to describe people, ideas and objects you are close to or own. Consider the words that you use to indicate distance from a person, thing or idea. Here are some examples:

Closeness	Distance
my	a/it
mine	the (as in 'the boss')
us	them
our	that (as in 'that child')
we	they

If you feel closeness or have an emotional attachment to something, you unconsciously structure your language to reflect the attachment. In the case of 'I have a boyfriend', distance can be inferred. After a three-year relationship, the speaker could be expected to reveal closeness and a degree of ownership of the boyfriend, both of which are expressed by the pronoun 'my'.

Further, if the relationship was a healthy one with a future you could have expected the speaker to say something like 'My boyfriend, Bradley, works in the computer industry'. The psycholinguistic patterns of closeness would demand the speaker make a social introduction of her partner at first mention, together with the closeness pronoun 'my'. Her statement reveals a clear tension in the relationship and an unconscious act of removing Bradley from the centre of her emotional life.

The above example demonstrates a deeper pattern that reflects a silent 'rule' of human language structure, generally understood at the unconscious level by most of us. An important variable in persuasion is your compatibility with people, emotions, values, ideas and objects that are held dear by those you want to persuade. Your emotions, values and ideas need to mirror closely those of your audience. If you demonstrate opposing emotions or values by using inappropriate distance language this will also be a major influencing factor on your listeners. For example, read the following quote from a speaker addressing a meeting called to oppose a neighbourhood development. What follows is a 'conversation' he had with the developer. Closeness words are in italics and distance words are in bold type:

I rang him up and said *we* have to have a *conversation* about **people's** concerns over this development *initiative*. I said that if *we* worked at it *we* might be able to come up with something that addressed the concerns of **those** who say **they** want to stop it in its tracks. So you can't say that I am not representing your interests in this matter.

Who do you think the speaker is trying to kid? His use of the pronoun 'we' denotes closeness not to the views of those who oppose the development, but to the developer. The noun 'conversation' is almost universally used when engaging in cooperative dialogue. It's a closeness word that denotes an absence of conflict. Had the word 'discussion' been used the speaker would be signalling the potential for debate and disagreement, as it's a mid-distance word generally associated with dialogue dealing with opposing views. The word 'initiative' caps it off and reveals where the speaker's loyalties really lay.

Now explore the distance words the speaker uses. The use of the distance word 'people's' indicates clearly that the concerns are not those of the speaker. The words 'those' and 'they' are pronouns of distance. Pronouns, by the way, account for more than 80 per cent of the unconscious confessions in a statement. The confessions the speaker made in the above quote were those of incompatibility with a group of constituents he needed to pacify. Do you think they received his real message?

What many deceptive speakers fail to realise is that the people they're talking to have had a lifetime's experience of deception, both on the receiving end and as perpetrators. The deliberate distancing from the scene of the crime is a favoured childhood ruse that remains stored in the unconscious mind. Your listeners may not be able to specifically point to the linguistic signals of deception, but rest assured that deep in the unconscious minds of many of them alarm bells will ring.

WHAT I'M SAYING IS …

Several years ago a world-class Australian athlete was tested for drugs and registered a positive result. The scandal occurred overseas and he went to ground, leaving others to speak on his behalf. The Australian media pounced on the story and, as is its custom, formed a pack and hunted down the athlete's parents. Resistance was futile. His parents went into damage control and called a press conference. Below is a segment of what they said:

What we are saying is that **** is not into drugs. He is telling us that he is not a drugs cheat. We're saying he has absolutely no reason to take steroids. It doesn't make sense.

The parents were either lying or suspected their son had, in fact, swallowed performance pills. How can you be so sure? The answer is that when people tell the truth about serious matters they close off all other options. Normally, if an individual is innocent or known to be innocent, a strong, unequivocal denial will be made. If the athlete's parents had said 'he didn't do it' or 'he is totally innocent', then you could assume an absence of deception.

Instead, the parents told Australian audiences what they were 'saying' and what the athlete was 'telling'. This can be seen as an unconscious 'leakage' of the truth behind the matter. The parents chose not to commit to a complete lie, as in 'he didn't do it', but to say something that required substantially less commitment either way.

There is a two-part principle in deception detection. First, when people make a truthful denial about an event that occurred in the past, they make an unambiguous commitment to their innocence. Second, their language reflects the true tense of the situation. If they are talking about a past event they will deliver their statement in either first person singular past tense, 'I didn't do it', or third person singular past tense, 'he didn't do it'.

There is no commitment present in the answer the parents gave and their tense is inconsistent. '**** is not into drugs' is third person singular present tense. In other words, **** is not into drugs *now* but might well have been yesterday or at the time the test was taken. The supporting statements are simply an attempt to give plausibility to the lie and contain no commitment to the truth.

The 'what I'm saying' manoeuvre is a favourite of politicians and other players in social and political debate. You can speculate that they've used it so frequently in place of what they really ought to be saying that it's become a habitual part of their linguistic behaviour. Nevertheless, it remains a marker for deceit deep in the memories of those who hear it, and often it serves to reinforce the cynicism Australians justifiably harbour about their elected representatives.

OOPS, WRONG PRIORITIES

The executive in charge of your conscious mind has to go to lunch sometimes, or may otherwise be occupied. Review the following quote and you may begin to wonder if the CEO of this speaker's conscious mind hadn't taken a week's holiday:

> I put everything on the line for this chance to show what I was really made of: my reputation, my job, my house, my financial future, the kids' welfare, the man I've been married to for fifteen years ...

Here, the speaker's unconscious leakage turns into a torrent. Adopt the position of the man married to the speaker for the past fifteen years. How do you imagine you would respond to this wonderful tale of womanly courage? Would you be inspired to spend the next fifteen years with her, or would fifteen minutes be about as much as you could take?

We may not articulate our priorities exactly in the order embraced at the deeper unconscious level, but in this example the extremes are so clearly delineated that it's patently obvious the speaker would rarely, if ever, put her family first. Adding insult to injury, the speaker unconsciously 'leaked' her emotional distance from her husband. 'My', as you know, implies closeness. The combination of turning her children into 'the kids', her husband into 'the man' and the passive language that follows is a certain indication of negligent parenting and a dead marriage.

Be careful in listing priorities. There are times in public and vocational life when you will need to understand and embrace the priorities of your stakeholders and colleagues.

I'LL TRY, NOT!

There's an old saying that goes, 'If you only try, you'll only fail'. Because the phrase 'only try' is so embedded in our linguistic culture, the author probably added the second 'only' to the statement in order to drive home the point being made. 'Only' is a word that minimises or discounts the meaning of the words or ideas that follow it. In the case of 'only fail' the language instructs the listener to view failure as trivial or inconsequential.

In many contexts the words 'merely' and 'just' also devalue the words and ideas that follow them. 'I was merely saying what I thought' reveals an attempt to minimise either guilt or responsibility and, in some cases, to transfer blame.

The word 'try' is code for expectation of failure. This word enjoys such ubiquitous usage that few listeners would ever interpret it at the deeper unconscious level to mean anything other than a signal of impending disappointment or lack of success. Put 'try' and 'just', 'only' or 'merely' together and you send a potent signal to listeners of dubious motives and doubtful resolve.

Linguistically deconstructed, the statement 'I was only trying to help' reads as follows:

only = attempt to minimise, trivialise or discount involvement
trying = lack of commitment, little expectation of success or lack of real intention
  to assist in the resolution of the issue or problem

Review the following sentences and intuit their real meaning.

1. 'We're merely trying to create a level playing field.'
2. 'What we're trying to do is balance the interests of the timber industry with those of the environmental lobby.'
3. 'I can only put your proposal to cabinet and test its reaction.'
4. 'We are trying to resolve a difficult situation.'

You may have intuited deeper meanings similar to the following:

1. We are covering up our callous disregard for the human misery caused by our policies by presenting a level playing field as self-evident imperative.
2. We know we don't have a hope in hell of achieving an equitable balance of interests but we have to be seen to be making an attempt.
3. I am not committed to helping you but will go through the motions.
4. We have little confidence in our ability and are softening you all up for an inevitable disappointment.

Notice how frequently public figures use words like 'try' and 'only', and begin to appreciate how, at a deeper level, you get a sense or feeling of a lack of commitment to what they're saying. It's amazing, isn't it, that seemingly intelligent beings can't imagine that you sense when they're wriggling out of making clear promises and assurances or setting you up for a lack of success down the track?

Charismatic communicators understand that pretending to commit to something helps whittle away the credulity quotient of their listeners. The key to maintaining your audience's credulity quotient in contexts such as the above is to make clear statements about what you can and will do:

- In place of 'try', say what specifically you will do.
- List the things you will do in sequence.
- Consider telling people how you will do it.
- Alert people to possible difficulties.
- Assess the likelihood of success.
- Rather than 'make every effort', say what the effort will be.

Commitment is a key factor in the attribution of charismatic qualities, as you discovered in Part 1. In becoming a person who does much more than 'try' you will begin to earn a reputation as someone who is trustworthy and who can be relied upon to give clear, unequivocal assurances that people can act on.

KICKING 'BUT' FOR SIX

Where 'only', 'just' and 'merely' depreciate or cheapen the words and ideas that follow, 'but' discounts, negates or contradicts the words and ideas that precede it. The word 'but' is also code for 'I've lied up to the word " but", and now I'm going to tell you what I really think', as shown in the following example:

I think this is a fabulous plan, *but* our priorities won't allow it at the moment. (This plan stinks and I'm not in the least interested.)

'But' is also used as a device to avoid outright conflict by giving the appearance of conformity or agreement. It's also a favourite artifice of boot-lickers and flunkeys, as in:

I totally agree with what you've said, *but* the troops will not buy the idea. (I disagree with what you've said and I think I've found the perfect scapegoats.)

The word 'but' has several close cousins that do the job equally well:

I think Margaret is a first-class person. *However*, she needs to improve her social skills. (I think Margaret is a bush pig.)

The wedding was wonderfully romantic. *Notwithstanding* that, I feel the bride should have got married in a dress rather than a swimsuit. (The wedding was ruined by that hussy who defied convention just to annoy her mother-in-law.)

I think your speech was fine, *still* I would have liked you to have paid tribute to the sponsor. (You idiot! Who do you think is paying for all this? Your speech has put the sponsor's nose right out of joint.)

Can you think of one person you know who hasn't used the 'but' defence at some time or another? Everyone knows at some level of their consciousness what the word 'but' signals, but there is a way to turn it to your advantage. At the unconscious level 'but', as was pointed out earlier, contradicts or cheapens the words and ideas that have gone before it. Knowing that, can you think of a way of turning it to your advantage? Exactly! Reverse the order of words, as shown in the example below:

I'd really love to go to the ballet with you tonight, *but* I'm feeling exhausted.

The listener converts this to:

Ah, you're feeling exhausted, bu-u-ut you'd re-ea-ally like to go to the ballet with me tonight! I really appreciate that. Now, what can we do to help you feel awake and raring to go!

You need to be playful or moderately light-hearted when you reverse the sequence. It can be quite useful to offer cooperation in jointly overcoming the initial objection. Content and context will determine whether you use the second part of the technique. Notice that the objection 'feeling exhausted' is transformed to 'awake and raring to go'. Invite cooperation in overcoming the objection or, in the example above, finding the right mood to go to the ballet. Taking a previously mentioned example, the reversal would read:

Hmm, the troops *may* not buy the idea, *bu-u-ut* [slightly light-hearted] as we agree this is a good idea, how can we make it attractive enough for them to support it?

THE NEGATIVE 'NOT'

Imagine this. You're at a party with your significant other. You begin to enjoy yourself and engage in friendly conversation. You create a rapport with other party-goers and become delighted at being the centre of attention. Your partner gives you the cold shoulder and, during the post mortem on the way home, volunteers, 'I didn't feel jealous. I just felt you were making an idiot of yourself.' What are you to make of that?

Often, people give glaringly obvious clues about the patterns they use to protect themselves against personal inconsistencies, threatening emotions, unpalatable thoughts and guilt. In the example above, a clear hint of denial is present. Assuming that the speaker hadn't been asked about jealousy, the voluntary admission of 'non' jealousy reveals at least sensitivity to jealousy by the speaker. How so?

The answer lies in the fact that it's impossible to process a negative unconsciously. For the speaker to admit to 'non' jealousy she or he must first have experienced an awareness of at least the idea of jealousy. Under normal circumstances, it would be reasonable to expect the speaker to report something along the lines of, 'I was happy for you to enjoy yourself, and then I noticed you went over the top' if, in fact, jealousy wasn't a consideration.

So, in the case of the statement 'I didn't feel jealous' the feeling, or abstract, of jealousy would have had to enter the speaker's awareness before it was denied with a 'not'. For you to not think about something, you must first think of it at some level, must you not? Police investigators often listen for verbal cues of denial. The statement 'I did not shoot the deceased' becomes a hollow denial when the cause of death has been kept a secret. Children often demonstrate a penchant for this form of denial when they respond to statements like 'Boy, are you in trouble now!' with 'I didn't cut all the hair off Taylor's Barbie!'. The key to detecting denial at this level is the presence of a voluntary 'not' statement, in no way instigated by another party.

Given that most people are well practised at using the negative 'not' in attempts to throw listeners off the scent, have a look at the following statements and sense how you deal with them unconsciously. Intuit their real meaning:

1. 'Of course, I was not offended by your question. This is just part of public life.'
2. 'What I'm not about is taking a piecemeal approach to planning in this city.' (as an opening statement)
3. 'I don't want you to think that I'm soft on young offenders, but you have to balance justice and rehabilitation issues.'
4. 'When I saw him standing there naked in front of me, I didn't know what to think.'
5. 'It's not that I don't think you deserve a promotion.'

Your intuitive responses to the above statements may approximate the following:

1. 'You bastard. I'll get you for this.'
2. 'I don't like taking a piecemeal approach to planning but I can't think of an overall or unified theme.'
3. 'I am soft on young offenders and I have a big emotional stake in their rehabilitation.'
4. 'When I saw him standing there naked in front of me, I knew *precisely* what to think.'
5. 'You don't deserve a promotion. I'm just too passive-aggressive to tell you.'

The negative 'not' is textbook unconscious leakage. It sends a clear signal to your listeners that you have at least thought of the subject matter denied by the 'not'. As you intuited the real meaning behind the 'not' statements given as examples, so will your listeners intuit the real and hidden meanings behind your 'not' statements.

'Not's in some contexts are more memorable than positive words. Some research shows that when people hear defensive statements or denials couched in the negative they're more likely to hear and remember the antithesis of what you said. What impressions do you intuit from the utterances of the following household names, and how would you rephrase them into positive language?

Hugh Grant when asked if he and Elizabeth Hurley were going to tie the knot: 'Umm, no. But it's not that I'm scared of growing up.'
Jessica Hahn, a central figure in the Clinton scandal: 'I'm not a bimbo.'
Michael Jackson when questioned on television about child abuse: 'I would not ever harm a child. Never.'
Richard Nixon's famous Watergate statement: 'I am not a crook.'

Hugh, Jessica, Michael and 'tricky' Dickie would have better served their interests by transforming their negative denials into positive speech. Had they done so, they might have responded along the following lines:

Grant: 'No, we are not planning to marry. We are both focusing on our careers at the moment.'
Hahn: 'I am an educated American woman.'
Jackson: 'Those allegations are false. No one values the sanctity of children more than I do, given my family background.'
Nixon: 'I make mistakes but I strive to conform to the expectations of the American people.'

INCREDULITY CREEP

Recall those conversations or speeches you've heard where your initial feelings about the speakers were positive but the longer they went on, the less believable you found them. Give your unconscious mind a pat on the back, because it was well and truly on the case. It was most likely picking up a host of linguistic cues that denote lack of commitment, the possibility of deception and other credulity stretching devices. Below are some of the more common examples that induce what is called incredulity creep, the gradual wearing away of credibility through unintentional admissions of dishonesty or, in some cases, habitual use of verbal crutches.

Honestly, truly, really, certainly, I kid you not!

Think about it for a moment, why would anyone preface or end a statement of truth with one of the above words? People usually take a direct path in expressing the truth. Any deviation, surely, is significant.

The statement 'Honestly, I have explored every avenue, and on balance this is the best option' is not the shortest way of expressing what the speaker believes is the truth. If uttered without any prior questioning of the speaker's honesty, the statement can be seen as a significant cue of sensitivity. In truth, you could expect the speaker to say something like, 'Out of all the options I looked at, this is the best one'.

The truth, as you inherently know, requires no heralding of its arrival. In the first statement, the speaker may well know that what she is about to say is, in essence, dishonest and so prefaces her remark with a protestation of honesty in order to deceive those listening. This is a common pattern of language identified by specialists in the scientific analysis of content for deception.

You should avoid prefacing your comments with such words. Ensure you don't use them as verbal crutches, because you will inadvertently trigger sensitivity to deception in your listeners at the unconscious level.

Believe me, believe it or not

'Believe me, there's no person better equipped to do this job than me.' Now, what do you imagine is the motive of the speaker in prefacing his remark with an appeal for you to believe him? Chances are you have already intuited that the speaker wants you to make an immediate decision for fear of the discovery of people who are, indeed, much better equipped to do the job than him.

In most contexts 'Believe me' and 'believe it or not' (remembering that 'not' cannot be processed unconsciously) are clues of deceptive behaviour or, in some cases, insecurity or doubtfulness about the veracity of the statements. People who have confidence in the truth or validity of their sentences rarely introduce a statement with an appeal to believe.

'Believe it or not' in some instances can be interpreted as an expression of indifference by listeners. It can also be intuited by listeners as a means of feigning nonchalance or even-handedness in order to cover up a strong desire for a lie, or in some cases a truth, to be embraced. Avoid these expressions at all costs and develop a habit of saying what you mean and meaning what you say.

Naturally, obviously, of course, clearly, it goes without saying

Often, the best deep-level interpretations people make of these words are that the speaker is prone to condescension or showing off what they know. One of the easiest ways to lose an audience's sympathy is to demonstrate a superiority complex through linguistic cues such as the above.

In some contexts, speakers use these words in an attempt to convince listeners that the ideas that follow are legitimate or normal practice. Don't you? And, can't you sense at some level when a speaker is using these terms to deceive or win you over on the basis that they're simply repeating common knowledge?

In some fields of linguistics, words such as 'obviously' and 'clearly' are termed 'lost performatives'. If you find yourself on the receiving end of statements like the above, recover the lost performative by asking 'Obvious to whom?' or 'Clear to whom?' and notice the interesting replies you elicit.

POWERLESS LANGUAGE

Researchers in the, umm, err, field of Persuasion, ah, Psychology have identified a number of kinda linguistic, you know, variables that, umm, have, I reckon, had a noticeable effect—OK?—on impression formation, umm, of course in the contexts in which their studies were conducted. You know what I mean, right?

Pardon? Could we have that again? Well, scholars who are studying how words and phrases affect impressions have uncovered some interesting evidence. They have found that irrespective of listeners' ability to process messages deeply, certain language forms described as 'powerful' are more persuasive than language forms described as 'powerless'.

Generally, people on the receiving end of 'powerless' speeches, such as the one you've just read, will view the speaker in a much less favourable light than those who hear 'powerful' speeches. Listeners have been found to attribute higher levels of authority, competence, credibility and assertiveness to speakers who use 'powerful' language.

Let's define the key differences between powerful and powerless language.

Powerful language:

- is assertive and straightforward;
- has a smooth flow of words;
- uses pauses for reflection;
- lacks hedging;
- contains few, if any, hesitations;
- displays easy command of language;
- conveys a sense of control of subject matter.

With powerless language, on the other hand, the speaker:

- is tentative in delivery, tone and demeanour;
- is often circumlocutory (talks around points);
- uses frequent punctuation of 'umm's, 'err's and other linguistic idiosyncrasies;
- is tentative in message content;
- hedges;
- uses 'tag questions', such as 'right?', 'OK?', 'don't you think?';
- may seem not to have collected their thoughts properly (seems unprepared);
- does not lead listeners to some closure.

Powerful arguments can fall on deaf ears if delivered in a powerless style. In one study, researchers selected a strong 400-word argument and subjected half their respondents to the argument delivered in a powerless style and the other half to the same argument delivered in a powerful style. They manipulated variables such as male/female speakers, distractions and focus, and male/female listeners. The upshot of the research was:

- Respondents who were distracted when hearing the message became more distracted by the powerless style.
- Respondents who heard the powerful style were more favourably inclined towards the message.

- Respondents rated the intelligence, competence, likeability, trustworthiness and knowledge of speakers using the powerful style more favourably.
- Respondents rated the argument delivered in the powerful style as stronger, more logical, more reasonable and more sound, even though the same argument was delivered in the powerless style.
- Respondents reported having more positive thoughts and fewer negative thoughts after hearing the powerful version.

It may strike you as astonishing that a few 'umm's and 'err's, the odd prevarication and hedge, and a few 'don't you think's, could make such a substantial difference to the way you and your message are perceived. But, put yourself in the place of the people who have to endure 'powerless' delivery of speeches ruptured by 'umm's and 'err's, of speakers who give off vibes of uncertainty and who seemingly reward the audience's investment of time and attention with rambling and unprepared content. Hardly the way to pay homage and respect to those you want to persuade, is it?

Preparation and rehearsal are the secrets to powerful delivery. Rehearse, rehash and repeat your content until you can deliver it flawlessly. Don't, like a helpless child, look to your audience for approval—assume you have it!

THE DANGEROUS LABELLING GAME

Albert Einstein, in *The Evolution of Physics*, observes that, 'Whoever undertakes to set himself up as judge of truth and knowledge is shipwrecked by the laughter of the gods'. The gods may well have endured an eternal nightmare of mirth because here, down on earth, the myths of absolute 'definition' and 'rocks of truth' can be seen to inform much of the competitive debate in companies, organisations and the public arena.

Group perceptual bias, or seeing things through a set of ideologically 'pure' lenses and believing it to be true, is a staple of contemporary thought and debate in this country. It can make life difficult for those who dare to question mindless adherence to trendy social theories and corporate conformity. It can turn the heat on those who propose better ways of doing things or, in fact, pointing out things that appear to be misleading, inappropriate or incorrect.

When individuals and groups are faced with unpalatable 'truths', or bad words that represent unpalatable truths or ideologically threatening opinions, they may go straight for the jugular of those who utter them. In our modern Australian society we consider ourselves far too sophisticated to burn at the stake, consign to the gallows or stone those who make us angry by using 'bad' words or deviating from shared 'truths'. However, there's a rich diversity of punishments reserved for 'deviants' who challenge the things most people take for granted as sensible, wise, self-evident, natural and true.

The psychology of intolerance and fear, the comfort of the known, vested interests and mindless 'common' sense, have usually meant that new frames of awareness are born painfully when *framed in typical argument forms*. If you confront a group of people who are entrenched in a particular practice or belief and say 'I am right and you are wrong', do ensure you are wearing a heavy-duty flak jacket. The retribution may come swift and fast and you could find yourself the target of some very sticky labels.

Sticky labels

Bad names play a powerful role in how we perceive things. Each of the following has the power to invoke strong emotional responses (usually negative) when heard. Try them out to see what internal reactions or representations they produce:

feminazi	anti-family
un-Australian	poofter
radical	thief
stingy	control freak
troublemaker	venal
yuppie	white middle-class Anglo-Saxon male

The name-calling technique seeks to deliberately link a person, or an idea, to a *negative* symbol. In political debate, the technique is usually applied when the user wants to discredit an opponent or an idea. John Howard's spurious use of the word 'un-Australian' on occasions was part of his patterned attempts to demonise his opponents.

The idea behind labelling is that an audience will reject a person or argument on the basis of a negative symbol. The psychology behind this technique is potent. It often allows the user to gain uncritical acceptance of their idea, or support for themselves, by anchoring an opponent or opposing idea with a negative emotion. The champions of this deceitful practice often view the technique as a kind of rhetorical fly spray, a quick and seemingly cheap way of exterminating their opponents. Extermination, history shows, has been one of the terrible consequences of the deliberate and systematic application of this technique.

One of the most dangerous linguistic weapons of the foot soldiers of the One and Only Truth is a process whereby people are turned into objects. You've learned that name-calling makes it easier to discount what those so named or labelled say. Labels are often used in another way: to soften people's resistance to harsh actions against people who have been labelled.

Two classic examples of this type of depersonalisation are the words 'dole bludger', applied against those who are said to be freeloading off the social security system, and 'scab', applied to those who strike-break. Both words can stimulate powerful negative emotions in large sections of the Australian population. The dole bludger label turns the recipients of survival money (notice the different emotional response you have to that description) into people who are somehow a little less human. Once dehumanised, those on benefits become much easier targets for harsh actions by governments and their supporters.

Over the past few years, numerous actions have been taken against those on unemployment benefits, all under the guise of rooting out dole bludgers. Similarly, harsh actions were taken against so-called union scabs during the waterfront dispute in the late 1990s involving Patrick Stevedoring, the waterfront unions and the federal government.

Charismatic communicators almost to a single individual avoid the ugly practice of labelling in their rhetoric. Somewhere in their lifetime they usually uncover the near-undeniable certainty that no man or woman 'is' anything in the way that a rock is a rock. They have come to realise that people who label others— as in 'he is a troublemaker'— fail to comprehend the difference between verbs of action and verbs of being.

Criminal thinking

As soon as you hear yourself describing a person or attributing certain traits to individuals with the word 'is', know that you are entering what is often termed 'criminal thinking' territory. The word 'is', where it describes a state of being, is an accident of language and is illogical. Your own experience will tell you that people are always much more, and often much less, than the labels given them.

Instead of saying what a person 'is', describe their behaviour. It's not only more intelligent to do so, but infinitely more accurate. Please review the statements at the top of page 175.

A problem you may notice emerging from the projection of false evaluations like those in the left-hand column is that they focus attention on superficial descriptions rather than deeper differences. Take the false evaluation 'Carmel is a doctor' as an example. She may well practise

'Criminal' thinking	*Critical thinking*
Carmel is a doctor.	Carmel works in a surgery and practises family medicine.
She is a liar.	She said there would be no budget cut for the division. Two weeks later there was. In my opinion she told us a lie.
He is a dole bludger.	He hasn't worked in paid employment for eighteen months.
They are Asians.	They came from Cambodia as refugees.
He is a racist.	He said that he resented his taxes being spent on handouts with no strings attached, and both Aboriginals and non-Aboriginals should have to work for their benefits.
She is grossly incompetent.	She did not provide the plan to us by the Friday deadline.

medicine or have done a PhD in disco dancing for all you know. Is she the same as all doctors? What else is she, if you were to know? The 'is a doctor' definition in no way describes the totality of her identity, does it?

It may be better to say 'Carmel works in a surgery and practises family medicine' because it describes what she does rather than offers a rubbery definition of her as a person. As you intuitively know, no definition of any person can ever represent that person in totality, so why label individuals so discriminatingly?

Charismatic communicators are not shrinking violets and are deeply critical when the need arises. The difference is one of quality in their thinking processes. They opt for consensus building when the goal is to change attitudes or win the hearts and minds of people. They seem to recognise the cruel consequences of demonising their opponents, and they know that polemics have a habit of coming back to haunt the perpetrators, be it in the workplace or on the national stage.

When honourable persuaders seek to shift opinion or change attitudes, most of their negation and criticism is in the early and middle stages of the persuasion process. In comparing the present state of affairs with a more desirable state of affairs (see the charismatic model in Chapter 7, p. 119) they often offer broad criticisms and insights into problems, issues and behaviours.

If people are the main obstacle, honourable persuaders will offer well-prepared critiques of their behaviours, actions and policies, but rarely will they attach negative labels or projective stereotypes. As you will discover later in this section, the easiest way in which to entrench the attitudes of those who support an opponent is to make a direct attack on them.

Own your generalisations

Generalisations are often a shortcut to credibility suicide. It's easy to attack or refute generalisations because no generalisation can be true in all circumstances. Generalisations can also reveal the intellectual poverty of an individual's view of the world. They can impoverish listeners' options and experiences by presenting them with narrow, and often mean-spirited, slants on issues, people, ideas and events. Take a look at the following sentences, and notice how the statements reveal dogmatic and, in some instances, rather ignoble sentiment:

'All men are bastards.'
'The pop music of today is rubbish.'
'Dutch men are so arrogant.'
'France is too expensive.'
'The Chinese are such incorrigible gamblers.'
'The Liberals are the puppets of global capitalism.'
'Australians overseas are as arrogant as American and German tourists.'

The easiest way to demolish a generalisation is to ask for exceptions. If, for example, in answer to the question 'Can you think of a few men on this planet who aren't bastards?' you receive the reply 'No!', you can be reasonably assured that you're talking to someone who needs help.

If you are on the receiving end of spiteful or degrading generalisations, a good means of defence is to unpack the process the speaker used to arrive at the generalisation. As a Dutchman, rather than trading insults you may like to inquire how many Dutchmen the speaker has encountered and by what standards she judges Dutchmen to be arrogant. The culprit will soon retreat into a more reasonable stance because the specifics requested will reveal the extravagance of the statement.

If you need to make observations about classes of people or categories of experience, own the generalisation. Be honest with your generalisations, report the underlying experience that led to them or choose not to voice them publicly. If you were to become a reporter of the truer nature of the generalisations given above, they would more than likely read something like this:

'I seem to have this trick of having relationships with men who turn out to be very disappointing to me.'
'I am having difficulty in valuing and appreciating the pop music of today.'
'My personal experiences with four Dutchmen I have encountered at close quarters have left me with the impression that they can be arrogant.'

'The price of a Coke on the Champs Elysees is six dollars!'

'Everywhere I went to play mah-jong in Shanghai, the players wanted to gamble on the outcome.'

'I find myself refusing to entertain any other options than that the Liberals are nothing more than puppets of global capitalism.'

'In Bali I met a number of Australians I thought were as unpleasant as I've been told American and German tourists are.'

Generalisations are an indispensable mental device that all human beings use to make life easier, and on one level are a means of not making the same mistake twice. As a child you may have placed your hand on the bar of a heater, burnt it and generalised that all heater bars are dangerous. This form of generalisation allows us to take one example, or a few examples and experiences, and make the presumption that all examples in a particular class or category of experience will be the same. These types of generalisation may save us from being burned in many contexts. So far, so good.

It seems than human beings have little trouble in sharing experiences of objects and a lot of trouble in sharing experiences of the less tangible things in life. Remove generalisations from the realm of the physical, as in a bar heater that has certain properties that we can all agree on, and they take on properties that are open to critical analysis, debate and the high risk of listeners making negative generalisations about you, the speaker.

KNOW-ALLNESS

We can never know, say, understand, imagine or experience *everything* about any one thing. Embracing this simple principle may place in focus what you find intrinsically objectionable about those who hold extreme views, profess to know everything there is to know about a subject or claim to have found a 'rock of truth'.

What do you imagine it would take to know *everything* about just one thing? To know everything about one single thing, you would have to know everything about its past, its present and its future, and every relationship it had ever had, has and may have. You would have to know every future permutation and every effect it may produce. You'd have to be able to come up with every use to which it could be put and has been put. You would have to know all its properties and attributes, and not only the ones you see with the naked eye. You would have to enter the microscopic and submicroscopic domain, know every molecule, atom, proton, neutron, quark and neutrino, and even know the ones that haven't been discovered yet.

The same principle applies to an idea or a conclusion drawn from certain experiences or so-called facts. Before you could claim to know everything about any one thing, you'd have to possess the certainty and knowledge of a god. Curiously, many people in the public arena are highly amenable to the idea of impersonating a Supreme Being. You hear and see them every day. They speak and act as though they have a monopoly on wisdom: that all other opinions, considered judgments and interpretations of 'facts' are extraneous or wrong. They claim to know everything (all) that is pertinent to a particular issue, problem or concept. They dismiss the points of view, experiences, beliefs, positions, attitudes, knowledge and judgments of others with unqualified and unconditional conviction.

These so-called gods scatter linguistic cues of certitude like confetti, creating the ideal conditions for polemics and resistance. In the following diagram are a series of 'know-all' statements that can induce high resistance in audiences:

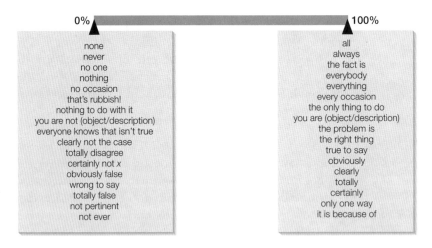

0%	100%
none	all
never	always
no one	the fact is
nothing	everybody
no occasion	everything
that's rubbish!	every occasion
nothing to do with it	the only thing to do
you are not (object/description)	you are (object/description)
everyone knows that isn't true	the problem is
clearly not the case	the right thing
totally disagree	true to say
certainly not x	obviously
obviously false	clearly
wrong to say	totally
totally false	certainly
not pertinent	only one way
not ever	it is because of

An easy way to detect 'know-all' statements is to convert them into percentages. Words that denote all, such as 'the fact of the matter is', relate to the arithmetical 100 per cent, while words like 'no one' or 'none' relate to 0 per cent. So, whenever you sense someone making 100 per cent or 0 per cent statements, you may be reasonably sure they're in know-all territory.

To practise know-allness with any degree of aplomb people have to become 'truth' believers; they have to take on prescientific notions of people and things 'out there' existing with such certainty in the shape and form described that they can be presumed to be 'true'. Quantum science tells us that we can never be totally certain about anything. Somewhere near certainty is about as far as we can safely go. But, practitioners of know-allness cannot function with uncertainty or conflicting truths. They would be shattered to discover a world where one and one may not always equal two, where fuzziness can reign supreme and where 'truth' can actually be in the mind's-eye of the beholder.

The quandary you may have with those who personify know-allness is that they frequently state their beliefs as 'truths', as 'God's-eye' perspectives, as completely verifiable declarations. This leaves very little room for those on the receiving end of their rhetoric to negotiate shared meaning. 'Know-all' statements increase the likelihood of evoking resistance in listeners who are paying close attention to your argument and, in some cases, in those who are seemingly not taking much notice.

Practitioners of know-allness usually exhibit the behaviours of those who think that people can be 'made' to change their minds. They act and speak as if others will be completely enamoured and overwhelmed by the sweetness of their truths and the majesty of their arguments.

BALANCING POSITIVE AND NEGATIVE WILL

Ethical charismatic communicators don't take on the mantle of the Almighty. They more often display what is called consciousness of projection: an awareness of how they filter information, events, ideas and propositions through their own unique maps of the world. They adopt a mental attitude consistent with an important trait identified in charismatic

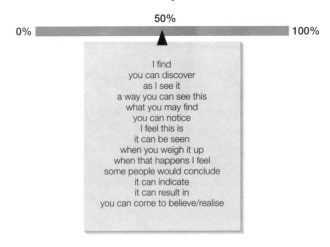

leadership: the assumption of personal responsibility for one's views and perceptions. Their language markers indicate a mature mindfulness of the diversity of thought, judgment and opinion. Their language tends to be accented by the linguistic markers in the diagram on page 179.

Whereas, 100 per cent and 0 per cent statements evoke tests of positive and negative will, 50 per cent statements don't invite people to think, feel, or say yes or no. They allow you to create an atmosphere where positive and negative will are at least balanced, or on average favour positive will.

As you sensitise yourself to know-allness, notice how people often make proclamations as though they have discovered the rock of truth. When you hear yourself and others making know-all statements, add an 'except', an 'unless' or a 'but'. You can come up with some rather novel and amusing statements, like:

'I'm absolutely certain of it, but I can't be 100 per cent sure.'
'I'm always putting my foot in it, except when I don't.'
'I never allow people to push me around, except when I do.'
'That is a totally crass way of looking at things, unless, of course, it isn't.'
'That's exactly what the problem is, in every instance that it is.'

It can be fun, can't it? And it may even add some levity to an otherwise straight performance.

WARS OF THE WORD

Powerful psychological forces and emotions are generated by the public debates of today, to the point where much of it appears to have taken on the characteristics of domestic disputation. What catalysts are producing this rise in the temperature of public debate? What is generating the heat, the put-ons and the put-downs? Sure, people can become passionate about their ideals, but many of the public debates of today go beyond the ardent exchange of beliefs and opinion. Why is the public exchange of ideas and opinions taking on many of the characteristics of domestic disputes in place of what you may imagine reasonable argument to be all about?

A perspective that may help you explain the perturbation and near-hysteria present in a lot of the political and social policy dialogue of today is the explosive cocktail of know-allness, the shared conceptual metaphor of debate as 'war' and a mass media which, ostensibly, imposes a form of rational and balanced discourse while cynically exploiting friction of domestic proportions for its 'entertainment' value.

A large body of research has been conducted into what is termed by cognitive scientists as conceptual metaphor. So as not to muddy the waters, think of conceptual metaphor as a template or lens through which you view the world. Cognitive scientists have been systematically unpacking the significance of conceptual metaphor in our daily lives since the 1960s. These scholars propose that metaphors are not simply playthings of the mind, but are a 'natural outgrowth of the manner in which our minds are constituted'. What that means is that conceptual metaphors are a product of your neurophysiology, that you have a genetic predisposition to attribute meaning to things by way of metaphor.

George Lakoff is Professor of Cognitive Sciences at the University of California at Berkeley, and he asserts that metaphor rules almost all our thinking. 'We may not always know it, but we think in metaphor. A large proportion of our most commonplace thoughts make use of an extensive, but unconscious, system of metaphorical concepts, that is, concepts from a typically concrete realm of thought that are used to comprehend another, completely different domain.'

Lakoff argues that these metaphorical concepts leak into our everyday language, but their most dramatic effect comes in ordinary reasoning. 'Because so much of our social and political reasoning makes use of this system of metaphorical concepts, any adequate appreciation of even the most mundane social and political thought requires an understanding of this system. But unless one knows that the system exists, one may miss it altogether and be mystified by its effects.'

Lakoff offers convincing demonstrations of conceptual metaphors governing what you perceive, how you negotiate the world and how you communicate with people. He says that conceptual metaphors prescribe the way you function right down to the minutiae of daily life. Conceptual systems are generally beyond consciousness and that's why you may not be aware of how you structure your meaning and how you apply conceptual metaphors.

But, of what relevance are conceptual metaphors to the pursuit of charismatic communication? Why is it important to know about conceptual metaphors, and what do you do with the knowledge once you've got it? Well, think about it. Conceptual metaphors are generally beyond consciousness and you're not aware of them governing your thinking or behaviour. What do you think would happen if someone applied a conceptual metaphor in a speech, conversation or debate, entrapped you within it, and slipped in a few self-serving suggestions? Because metaphor is part of the way you unconsciously make sense of the world, you'd be oblivious to what was happening and may be subject to covert influence *without ever knowing it.*

On the following pages you will encounter one such metaphor. This metaphor, when used as a deliberate technique by your opponents, has the power to embroil you in a cycle of self-destructive behaviour that can damage your reputation and credibility. Some unethical communication specialists teach this technique to public figures as a means of manipulating their opponents into showing their so-called 'true colours'. Experts call this technique 'conceptual entrapment' and it can be a frighteningly devious way of triggering the more primitive elements of your personality.

Conceptual metaphors can be deliciously seductive, so much so that they can obscure all other kinds of possible conceptions, options, ideas and viewpoints that exist outside them. People can become so entrapped within a conceptual metaphor that no amount of pleading to view things from another perspective will register. In politics, office environments, social policy debate and even in the home this may have extremely dangerous implications.

Declarations of war

Conceptual metaphors that are deeply embedded in our culture are relatively easy to identify because of the number of linguistic markers associated with them. Try the following statement for size:

He is mounting an *attack* [attack] on the fundamental rights we *fought* [engagement] for decades to *win* [triumph]. And let me tell you those *tactics* [war plans] will not get us to *give up* [retreat] one inch of *ground* [territory]. I mean, what a *pathetic* [insult] proposition. Let me *throw down* this *challenge* [duel]. Let him go and muster his *forces* [army] and prove what he says about a *legion* [troops] of Australians demanding a *showdown* [battle] on this issue. I can tell you this, we will not *yield* [cede territory] to anyone who wants to *destroy* [kill] the rights of Australian workers to withdraw their labour. We will *take to the streets* [counterattack] and there will be a *river of blood* [massive casualties] if he tries.

You can conclude that the metaphor used in the above statement is that of war. You may also have noticed that the speaker isn't simply playing with words as in a surface metaphor. His argument is structured, performed, voiced and understood in *terms* of war. Can you imagine him seeking to accommodate a range of views outside the ones expressed? Can you see him responding in any way that doesn't entail a fight, and a winner and loser?

War is the *partial* framework or template he uses to argue his point and agitate against deregulation of the labour market. It's a partial framework, or template, because he is using the metaphoric concept 'argument is war' to structure how he argues and how he makes sense of what he's doing as he's doing it. If it were a complete framework he would be out in the streets with an AK47. It would be real war and the body count would be astronomical! Tragically, the argument-is-war metaphor often leads to the real thing.

Sample any of the major social and political debates of today, identify the linguistic markers and you'll more than likely uncover clear demonstrations of the argument-is-war metaphor. This metaphor may well be the predominant structure we use for the debate of ideas and any exchange that goes beyond the boundaries of polite conversation in our culture. It surfaces as a deeply embedded cultural metaphor beyond the consciousness of most people who participate in the dialogues of daily life. You may notice its presence wherever there is divergence of opinion: from domestic arguments to the highest matters of state.

Recall your own arguments and use the following list to see if you complied with the key characteristics:

- You became *adversaries*.
- It became important to you, and/or your adversary, that they *surrender* their opinion and give *victory* to yours.
- The diversity of opinions produced *conflict*.
- You began to *plan a strategy* on the run and *marshal* your intellectual *forces* by coming up with ideas or points you could introduce.
- You noticed the *weaknesses* and lack of logic of the other person's *position* and you mounted an *attack* based on those weaknesses.
- You played with words, introduced red herrings and tried to *manoeuvre* the argument to put you in a *stronger position*.
- You attempted to *defend* your *position* by responding to the arguments and questions raised by the other person.
- If your *opponent* came up with a 'gob-stopper' you *retreated to safer ground* and *regrouped* for a *counterattack*.
- You both may have got bored, or tired, of the argument and agreed on a *stalemate*, or called a *truce* so you could bring in *reinforcements* at some other time.
- You could, with a combination of the above, have achieved *victory* and *won* the day or you, or your opponent, may have realised that, by continuing, a greater *loss* could ensue, and *surrendered*.

■ Your argument, or theirs, could have been so supremely logical or forceful that only a fool wouldn't have *sued for peace.*

Now, here's a question for you to ponder. What was it that seemed to draw you into behaving as you did during the argument? Think about other arguments you've had, and notice how an invisible and primeval force appeared to hijack the process. But, what about instances in which people deliberately apply the argument-is-war metaphor to trigger behaviour you wouldn't ordinarily exhibit in public? Could you withstand it?

Let's take a famous example of the deliberate use of the metaphor and examine the results. Cast your memory back to the occasion immediately after Bob Hawke's Labor Party leadership coup in the early 1980s. Do you remember the question Richard Carleton asked Hawke in his first nationally televised interview after deposing Bill Hayden? 'How does it feel to have blood on your hands?' was the question Carleton put to Hawke. Carleton's question provoked a response from Hawke that has gone down in history, clearly demonstrating that even one of Australia's most seasoned political scrappers couldn't withstand the power of the metaphor.

Hawke displayed behaviour that was patently inconsistent with the image of consensus politician and man of the people that he had cultivated since entering politics. Hawke's face twisted in rage and it was with almost superhuman effort that he resisted reaching out for Carleton's jugular. Voice and tone dripping with vitriol, he went on to attack Carleton in a textbook example of a person who had been hijacked by the argument-is-war metaphor. Fortunately for Hawke, the drover's dog was at hand and he went on to become one of Australia's most popular post-war leaders.

There were two elements to Carleton's question that embroiled Hawke in the metaphor. The first was the symbolic meaning of blood and the second was the direct attack technique Carleton applied to stir Hawke up. Carleton was dazzlingly successful in his use of the argument-is-war metaphor and in manipulating Hawke into revealing a side of his personality he most certainly would have preferred to conceal. Richard Carleton managed to complete the interview with his throat intact, but this could not be said for another reporter who tried argument-is-war provocation in the Northern Territory several years ago.

In a blatantly unconvincing display of journalistic interrogatory technique, the reporter elicited a 'fight' rather than a verbal response from a local politician during a recorded interview. The politician's reaction to the journalist's accusatory tone (attack) was to rise from his desk, lunge for the microphone and attached chord, and crudely attempt to garrotte the offending reporter, much to the glee and amusement of a worldwide audience who ultimately saw it on television. It was later reported that the politician explained to party colleagues that he didn't know 'what came over him'. His political career was ruined after the relentless and somewhat piously indignant reportage that ensued.

You can readily identify the point at which a discussion takes on the characteristics of war. You can listen to content and detect it through linguistic markers and the choice of language people use. You can also listen for context and notice changes in structure. And, when you find yourself or others entrapped in the argument-is-war metaphor, you will have a choice point, a point where you may decide to opt for a less lethal form of dialogue, won't you? Try consciously experiencing an argument as a dance, and notice how your perceptions and behaviour changes.

There are times when you can apply the argument-is-war metaphor legitimately, knowing that engrossing your audience in the metaphor can achieve mutually satisfying ends. In commercial and business playgrounds, the war metaphor can often motivate the 'troops' to pull together in a concerted effort to 'fight off' the competition. If you have cause to apply the metaphor to commercial competitors, use the list of key characteristics on pages 183–4 to create a motivational framework. The war metaphor can also be used to good effect to encourage unity of purpose in a variety of contexts, such as waging a war against poverty, fighting against dry land salinity and mounting a campaign to save an architectural treasure. But, please, don't declare a 'war on drugs', as it is tantamount to one generation declaring war on another. The war-on-drugs rhetoric pitches young people against authority and is more likely to encourage the behaviour than prevent it, as you will discover.

The war metaphor is deadly if applied within organisations to fuel interdepartmental rivalry or competition. You may notice that when people are hijacked by the metaphor quite severe behavioural changes occur. To put it bluntly, in many contexts the metaphor brings out the worst, most shoddy and most offensive elements of human behaviour. While foul and unprincipled behaviour may be acceptable when aimed against commercial competitors, it's hardly the kind of conduct you want to encourage within your own organisation. When this occurs, expect dysfunction of the highest order and a diminution of focus on the market and external competition.

War weariness

Historian Arthur Schlesinger once said, 'All wars are popular for the first thirty days'. It may well have taken Australians thirty years to tire of the endless war of words that has overshadowed public debate in this country, but tire they have. Perhaps one of the reasons for the strong aversion to public affairs so clearly demonstrated by television and radio ratings is antipathy and frustration at the phoney war of words. The 'phoney war', as a form:

■ operates on endless point scoring and disharmony;
■ centres on the interests of the power elite;
■ focuses on recrimination and blame;
■ tends to 'regress' people into past woes;
■ is 'problem' obsessed;
■ often leaves people with feelings that the 'world is falling apart';
■ acts to 'top up' people's negative emotion quotients: at some stage most people will opt out of an experience that makes them feel bad.

Australians are disengaging from the so-called big issues as presented by the mass media. 'Disengaging' basically describes the process of tuning out and of removing oneself from a source of irritation or negative feeling. A prime reason for doing this may be to remove at least some of the external reminders of the ugliness of life. How many New Yorks will it take before life seems unbearably dangerous?

Nationwide research shows that increasing numbers of Australians are becoming less involved in the bigger so-called issues on the national agenda. They have, in many ways, dissociated themselves from the 'hard' issues presented by out-of-touch news organisations. They appear to have become disinterested spectators in the phoney wars of words of the political elite, and their eyes glaze over when political and many social topics are broached.

If the evidence of disengagement is correct, then it can be assumed that a growing percentage of people will avoid leaders and speakers who place a negative, fatalistic or combative spin on content in public life and in the workplace. The public distrust of, and disgust expressed towards, many of the verbal thugs in the centre ring of public debate lends further support to the proposition that audiences attribute charisma and follow those who engage in the types of persuasion mentioned in the early part of this book, namely those who:

■ build trust through being consistent and conforming words to deeds;
■ find common ground through understanding the expectations, concerns and feelings of audiences and electorates;

- design arguments and positions that produce vivid and succinct word pictures of outcomes rather than recriminatory wars of the word;
- engage audiences in the shared construction of meaning;
- search for emotional unity by expressing appropriate emotional commitment and by sharing passion and enthusiasm for the ideas floated;
- address the hopes, fears, needs and aspirations of audiences and point the way forward.

The above is a universe away from the know-allness and war approach which demands that audiences and electorates become mere spectators to the gladiatorial battles fought by the social and political elite. Australians are saying that they won't stand for such an emotionally draining and alienating approach any more. They want mature leaders who connect with them and act not from self-interest but from a genuine concern for the welfare of others.

Win the war and lose the argument

If you are hijacked by the know-allness and war metaphor, your language structure will reflect it and that, in turn, will trigger know-allness and war behaviour in your opponents. When people are hijacked by the metaphor they will unconsciously view acceptance of your argument as defeat. Head-on challenges have the effect of *strengthening* the resolve of opponents to hold on to their publicly expressed views, opinions and arguments. After all, who wants to publicly admit to being a loser?

When a message openly, expressly and directly creates confrontation, the message receiver will be tempted instantly to resist the message because of the internal feelings of dissonance it creates. Direct confrontations, particularly those framed in the know-allness and war metaphors, have a dismal history of success. They create dissonance in the minds of those they're meant to capture, and perhaps this adds to explanations of why much of the millions of dollars spent in political campaigns may as well be given away.

A fascinating and highly instructional piece of research on dissonance involved a group of militant feminists. Researchers invited one group of self-reported feminists to attempt to resolve an issue of sexism. Another group of feminists worked on a different task and generally succeeded in providing an ideologically consistent solution to the problem.

The first group failed to resolve a very tricky sexism problem and demonstrated in their attempts to solve it the sexual stereotyping behaviours of the very people they branded as sexist. You can imagine that when confronted with this apparent inconsistency the first group would have experienced a fair measure of dissonance, part of which clearly was embarrassment. What occurred next, however, is most educational.

The researchers then invited both groups to read a court transcript of a discrimination case. They were instructed to judge who was at fault in the case and make an appropriate award. The group of feminists who were caught out using stereotypical and sexist thinking to solve the tricky problem was found to be much more likely to judge that sexual discrimination had occurred. They awarded much larger amounts of compensation than the group of feminists who had solved the initial problem in an ideologically 'correct' way.

In other words, those who were publicly shown to be politically and ideologically unsound became more feminist and extreme in their behaviour. An explanation for this phenomenon is that when individuals are confronted with examples of their own inconsistency, the emotional turmoil they experience is overwhelming. It's contrary to what they truly believe of themselves at a deeper level and directly challenges their social identity. In an attempt to recover from the deep assault on their egos, the ideologically incorrect feminists overcompensated. And so, it could be argued, do most people who are subjected to direct and open confrontation of their beliefs, values or behaviours.

The remaining chapters of Part 2 will show you how to develop low-resistance messages that do not directly and openly confront listeners. You will learn how to structure your content in a way that assists audiences to understand your message and makes it easier for listeners to embrace your ideas.

10 WORDS THAT WIN HEARTS

When high words confuse the talk, low words will untangle it.
Jabo proverb

Novelty of expression is a key marker of the charismatic speaker, but charismatic speakers tend to be highly aware of the dangers of polemics and of being labelled as heretics, iconoclasts or spin-doctors. Rarely do charismatic communicators reveal the arrogant signatures of modern-day prophets, or the stroppy rhetoric and behaviours of those who claim to have discovered the rock of truth. Rather, they act more as guides to higher and better ground, paying homage and attention to prevailing values and beliefs. They use the soft music of persuasion in place of the head-banging lyrics of self-righteousness, coercion and intimidation.

The truth dealers and warriors of words you encounter in public and private life seem to have at least one belief in common, that of having the power to change minds. They appear to operate on the belief that the supremacy of their truths, the elegance of their language or the forcefulness of their arguments will somehow trigger an electro-chemical reaction in the minds of listeners and miraculously transform doubters into true believers.

If that doesn't work, well, they can always use force, as they also tend to believe that for every argument victorious there is an argument, or person, vanquished. This win–lose mentality commonly works on the basis that persuasion is the art of using whatever means available to gain agreement or submission *regardless* of the best interests or needs of those who are on the receiving end of the message. It's deeply flawed reasoning at best and may ultimately undermine the position and ideas of those who use or embody it.

Practitioners of win–lose persuasion techniques tend to overlook a fundamental reality many of us share, which is that no one else can change our minds for us. Thankfully, we have to do the job ourselves. We may do it mindlessly or, indeed, mindfully but for better or worse we're the ones who ultimately make the choice of changing or not changing our minds.

Sometimes we foolishly submit to the forceful and seductive messages of others, only later to recant and feel embarrassed about our naïveté. People are 'stitched up' or shafted by all sorts of snake-oil salespeople, but does it change the reality that they made a choice at some level to do as they were bid?

How often has your anger or chagrin been directed towards those who tricked or persuaded you to go down a path that led to a dead-end or disaster? We habitually turn towards those who've misled us and project our embarrassment onto them. We choose to take the easy way out by vilifying the so-called cause of our discomfort rather than examining how we came to choose to be persuaded in the first place. Isn't it quite natural to vent our spleen at the trickster who deceived us in preference to examining our own role in the transaction? And, when you come to think about it, 'victimstance' can often represent a shortcut to regaining our dignity and avoiding the perils of self-examination. This is a common and occasionally hazardous trait of human nature.

Are you beginning to wonder about the importance of delivering 'enabling' rather than 'disabling' messages? Persuasion and influence involve the building of longer term relationships, and if you're winning at the expense of others with cheap ploys and sleights of mouth there will come a reckoning. People will do as you do and project their discomfort to you when they discover you've beguiled, bullied or duped them. You may be able to fool, or browbeat, all of the people some of the time, but ...

So, can you arrive at a definition of what the honourable communicator's role is in the influencing process? Let's also define what the listener's role is in order to understand the nature of developing healthy relationships between the persuader and the potentially persuaded.

As a *persuader* your tasks are:

- seeking to understand the higher principles, beliefs and values that inform your listener's view of the world;
- encouraging listener/s to *understand* your view of the world, your ideas, your take on things;
- finding the means of bridging the gap between your world view and that of others;
- choosing a form of delivery that produces the least resistance.

The *listeners'* tasks are:

- listening mindfully or mindlessly, depending on their mood or preference;
- filtering information through their personal world views and associating new information with what they already know;
- interpreting information on the basis of what benefits it will deliver;
- choosing what to do with the information: accepting, ignoring, rejecting or reserving opinion.

COINING THE RIGHT WORDS

A major step in learning how to intone the soft music of charismatic communication is to recognise that some words have greater value than others. In Chapter 9 you came to know that 'bad' words have about as much purchasing power as Russian roubles at Harrods. You may have also realised that words backed by honest intentions are more valuable than those that are not.

Better words have the potential to dramatically increase the value of your linguistic cash at hand. They can purchase more attention, more meaning, more understanding and more agreement. It can also pay you to remember that if you invest your words wisely and seek to expand people's choices with persuasive words, people will begin to view you as a true leader. After all, if people associate you with benefit and choice, they will be drawn to you for further guidance. The rest of this chapter is devoted to helping you develop a bankable vocabulary. And you would like that, wouldn't you? The following sets of 'persuasive' words have been found to reduce critical and analytic thinking. It goes without saying that you can choose to use these words with care and respect.

The world in full of 'I-me's

One of the most powerful words in the universe is the name by which you identify yourself. It will most likely be your first name, unless it's a nickname that you embraced fully as a child and carried into adulthood. The mention of your favoured name can stop you in your tracks. Notice how you're so highly attuned to hear that name that it can rise out of the din of a crowded room and fight its way to your ears. Equally so, you associate your favoured name with gaining the full attention of others. From birth, you heard the sound of your name repeatedly and connected it to your being the centre of its speaker's attention. Generally, you associated the speaking of your name with a positive emotion, like pleasure in being the focus of others.

If you use a person's favoured name, either at the beginning or end of a sentence containing a suggestion, you will significantly increase the likelihood of the message being received favourably. The knack is to insert the favoured name tactically into the sentence, as opposed to using random first name references. For example:

Alicia, when you add up all the benefits of studying part-time you may agree that it will give you the career boost you are looking for.

If this new system can deliver a 10 per cent savings in overheads, would you be interested, Bill?

Charmaine, can you work up a spreadsheet showing the space requirements for Option One, please?

Using an individual's name anchors a positive emotional stimulus (as in the comfortable feeling you generally experience when people mention you by name) with the suggestion or statement contained in the sentence. Politicians use this technique when attempting to get interviewers to soften their questioning approach, as in:

Kerry, you know that when you look at the numbers they show that Australians have never been better off.

Hmm, but, really, the core issue is about people's right to privacy, isn't it, Laurie?

When communicating with groups and larger audiences it becomes impossible to refer to individuals by name, but you may like to consider selecting key, or influential, members of your audience and applying the above technique. If you have framed your sentence appropriately, their nods of agreement will have a powerful impact on the rest of your listeners.

Given that you cannot mention each and every member of a larger audience by name, what can you do to create similar outcomes to the examples given above? Think about it. What pronouns do you use when you think about yourself or engage in silent self-talk? You generally use the first person singular 'I' or 'me', don't you? So, apart from having a particular affection for your favoured name, 'I' and 'me' are substitutes for the name that embodies your broader sense of self.

Can you play with this a little more? If someone is to trigger the 'I-me' in you, which pronoun would be best suited for the job? The second person singular pronoun 'you' would have to be first choice, wouldn't it? If someone addresses you using 'you', they're directly triggering your 'I-me' sense of your self, aren't they?

You may be thinking that 'you' is also a second person plural pronoun and, when it's used to refer to a group as opposed to each separate individual within a group, it can isolate the speaker from the group, rather than join the speaker and group in shared space, and right you are. So, the secret is to refer to the singular 'you', and not the plural 'you', when you're addressing groups, because you now know that you can speak with each individual as an *individual* if you use the 'you' pronoun properly.

The singular 'you' is one of the most important words in the English language because it triggers the 'I-me' in your listeners and sends a strong signal that your content is all about them, and not yourself. In using the singular 'you', can you sense how you're symbolically directing your attention towards each individual in the group? Have you ever, for example, attended a speech and felt that the speaker was communicating directly with you, or heard someone say, 'I felt I was the only person in the room and that she was talking directly to me'? Chances are the speaker framed most of their core message in the singular 'you'.

This simple technique replaces the traditional relationship with audiences where listeners' attention is directed towards the speaker. The reasons for doing this are becoming increasingly important. The singular 'you' is becoming more necessary as people's preoccupation with themselves and their problems increase. It seems people have less time and attention to give to others in today's high-pressure environment. Conversational narcissism, where people constantly refer conversations back to themselves in a relentless pursuit of attention, appears to be a by-product of contemporary life.

An argument you might find quite compelling and rewarding is that if you design a form of communication that mirrors your listeners' inclinations towards self-attention, your message will have a substantially better chance of being heard and acted upon. The second person singular pronoun 'you' is pure linguistic gold because it taps into this trend and purchases the attention of your listener/s. Moreover, it earns the higher interest of your audience because it triggers emotions similar to those evoked when people hear their own name. It places you, the listener, at the centre of the communication.

This book, but more especially this chapter so far, is written largely in the singular 'you'. And, as you're now becoming aware of how the singular 'you' pays homage to you, the reader, you may begin to marvel at how this simple word can place you at the centre of your audience's attention by placing them at the centre of yours.

Seductive words

Certain words and word structures have the power to engage mental processes that trigger memories, feelings and vivid imagery that override analytic thought. Have some fun with the following words. Put one or two into a sentence, and begin to sense how they can invoke *powerful* internal representations. Adding these words to your vocabulary can *guarantee* you *improved* access to people's attention. A small *investment* in your vocabulary can bring fantastic *profits* as you *discover* that some words have been *proven* to make your sentences more *powerful*.

In *truth*, the simple choice of a few words can *easily* and *effortlessly* enhance the *value* of your sentences and give you a *vital advantage* when seeking to persuade others. After all, you're looking for *results* when you seek to influence people, aren't you? The following words give you the *security* of knowing that big persuasion *benefits* can be *gained* from knowing a few *trusty* words.

Let's not labour the point, but you get the idea of how the inclusion of a few seductive words in the two preceding paragraphs can produce unrestrained curiosity and engagement in what is being said, do you not?

SEDUCTIVE WORDS

you (and variants)	sex	free
new	advantage	improved
proud	save	deserve
discovery	easy	benefit
fun	investment	proven
security	guarantee	happy
health	comfort	joy
profit	trust	love
money	results	right
safety	democratic	truth
value	powerful	vital
safe	gain	effortless
enhance	power	satisfy

These so-called seductive words tap into what are, more often than not, universal values. People, when hearing them, will be more amenable to your message. When used thoughtfully and ethically these words can help expand people's choices and options by triggering associations between the content of your message and universally embraced values, feelings and aspirations.

Don't!

The word 'don't' can be a means of accessing sentiments and actions that are the opposite of those suggested at the superficial level of your language. Please, don't feel as though you have to skim forward four paragraphs before returning to this explanation of 'don't'. Pause for a moment and review the internal sensation you may have felt when reading the previous sentence.

Some people may have felt a strong compulsion to review the material four paragraphs ahead, while others may have experienced a mild sensation to act. Which best describes you? If you remove the 'don't' from the above sentence you gain a very clear picture of the message your unconscious mind received. It makes sense when you realise that the unconscious mind has a hell of a time dealing with negation, doesn't it?

Pause for another moment and see if you can construct a picture of a red football in your mind's eye. Easy, isn't it? Now, see if you can construct a picture of the word 'don't' in your mind's eye? Impossible? As 'don't' is not a noun, you can't make a picture of it, and this is one of the reasons why it can be a powerful tool in persuasion. Look at the following sentences and don't think of some novel and fun ways that you can practise them in your everyday communication!

Don't feel as though a laugh is coming on when you look at me.

Don't feel as though you have to accept this phenomenon before you actually try it out and notice the effect it has on people.

You don't have to feel compelled to come to the video store with me ... really.

Don't choose to agree to this right away. Give yourself the time you need to do it.

Don't see yourself having the time of your life on holiday in New Zealand until you're totally amazed at how little it costs.

A disturbing thought may be occurring to you now, and that is if 'don't' works so powerfully when linked to positive suggestions such as the above, it must have the same impact when linked with negative suggestions. How do you imagine the unconscious mind processes statements such as:

1. 'Now, don't *worry* about that.'
2. 'Don't *do drugs.*'
3. 'Don't *touch* that!'
4. 'Don't use *long sentences.*'
5. 'Don't *forget* to go to the bank on your way home.'

Of course, your unconscious mind interprets negative statements like the above as clear instructions to do the opposite of what is suggested. You do indeed worry, you may not have even thought of doing drugs, you touch whatever it is, you use long sentences, and how often have you forgotten to do something after you've instructed yourself 'not' to forget? The lesson that can be learned with the word 'don't' is that its use dramatically increases the chances of listeners doing exactly the opposite of what you have asked them. Choose to give people things to do and think about. Leave them with a clear message about the action you wish them to take, such as:

1. 'You can feel confident about that.'
2. 'Get high on endorphins—go for a run.'
3. 'Here, touch this!'
4. 'Use short sentences.'
5. 'Remember to go to the bank on your way home.'

The following true story brings home in tragic detail the folly of using the negative version of 'don't'. A six-year-old was minding his four-year-old sister while their mother was doing housework. The children left the property and began playing by the roadside. The four-year-old wandered to the opposite side of the road. Her brother noticed her readying to return to his side of the road as an oncoming car drew nearer. He screamed, 'Don't cross the road!'. The four-year-old hesitated for a millisecond and proceeded to run across the road. The squeal of brakes, a sickening thud and shattering of glass illustrated the gruesome consequences of children learning the patterns and behaviours of adults and instructing others on what not to do.

'Can' really can and 'may' often does

In Chapter 9 you canvassed the issue of how 0 per cent and 100 per cent statements can stir up a contest of wills between you and your audience.

You were asked to consider enclosing the critical elements of your message within a pattern of rhetoric that invites at least a balance of negative and positive will rather than engaging in contests of wills with your listeners.

Please read the following two statements, imagining the comments are directed to you. As you're now quite used to the idea of 'going inside' to discover how certain words and sentences 'feel', recognise the difference in your experiences of the two statements:

You must improve your communication skills because you ought to know by now that you've rubbed so many people up the wrong way that the blame is yours to take. You have to become a much better listener. You should ask more questions instead of listening to people only as long as it takes to construct a reply and butt in as you usually do. You have to realise that this company places a high priority on communication skills. You'd better take that on board because your career will come to a grinding halt if you can't display these basic leadership qualities.

Can you imagine how reassured you'd be to discover you already have all the basic talents required to become a top line communicator? I wouldn't tell you that listening is the key because you can realise that for yourself, can't you? And when you consider it, asking questions can be one of the most powerful ways to gain the interest of people, because they sense you're interested in them. I reckon you might appreciate how these simple skills can accelerate your career prospects immeasurably. And I'm wondering what we can do next to help you achieve that.

Now, here's a question: Which of the two statements sets up a contest of wills between you and the speaker? And which of the above would leave you thinking more about the speaker than the content of the message? You've probably come to the conclusion that the first statement would. This is because the speaker attempts to impose values and judgments on your behaviour, rather than opening up options for you to consider.

If you encounter a statement similar to the first one in real life, chances are that you may feel quite wounded by it. You may begin to think unpleasant thoughts about the speaker and, as your resentment grows, completely forget about the contents of the message. You may answer back and leave the speaker's presence with wounded pride, vowing to continue the fight on another occasion.

The above is an extreme example, but the underlying structure of the first sentence is a splendid way of triggering resistance. When people tell you what you must, or ought to, do there's a high probability that it will clash with your map of the world and be in conflict with the way you see things.

It may not surprise you to learn that people of the shoulda-havta-musta-oughta mould tend to operate from a scarcity mindset. The rhetoric exudes references to compulsion, whereas those who use words such as 'can', 'may' and 'might' are more likely to operate from an abundance mindset. They can be seen as 50 per cent words that, on the balance of probabilities, do not engage speakers and listeners in contests of wills.

Please take another look at the second statement and ask yourself if the message is clear. Review both statements and consider which of them opens up a world of options to you. Which statement allows you essentially to choose to exercise your will in the way suggested by the speaker? Choice and the illusion of choice are important, are they not?

There are many examples of the use of 'can', 'may' and 'might' in this book. Take notice of the examples that could suit your conversational style and consider dropping a few 'can's into important communications and noticing the difference you can make. These words are called 'possibility' words. You can surely see how they align with opening up worlds of choice and possibility.

WORDS OF POSSIBILITY

can

may

could

might

possible

able to

Please consider

Mitsubishi Motors conducted an immensely successful advertising campaign based on two elementary but mighty words: 'please' and 'consider'. So successful was the campaign that the two words became popular buzzwords in this country. What made them so memorable when put together in the format of an advertising campaign?

The Japanese are past masters in the structure, practice and artistry of politeness. Mutsubishi's advertising agency was more than likely aware that the word 'please', congruently intoned, is second in emotional impact only to that of a person's favoured name. 'Please' and 'thank you' are words that have been drilled into us since early childhood and imply the bestowal of rewards and favours.

'Please' and 'thank you' convey appreciation and gratitude and are an invaluable duo in the verbal toolkit of the charismatic communicator. It's important that you use them congruously and naturally. A sharp or ambiguous 'please' and 'thank you' are likely to be interpreted as sarcasm. Ration your 'please' and 'thank you's and tuck them into sentences that ask something important of your listeners:

Please give these ideas your serious consideration.

Thank you for giving me the opportunity to explain how this proposal can win you customers.

Please allow me to help you identify your main issues so we can jointly work out a plan of attack.

Thank you for investing your time tonight. I believe you may look back in your future and see it as one of the better investments you've made.

The word 'consider' can be like music to the ears of anyone born after 1950. The baby boomer and ensuing generations embrace the principle of making up their own minds with more vigour and passion than probably any other recent generation. The dominant generations of today do not respect authority as previous generations did. Authority has to be earned and attributed, and many stern authoritarians have discovered to their cost that telling people what to do is the least persuasive of ways to change behaviours.

Inviting people to consider, once again, opens up the possibility of choice. People like, and often insist on, the idea of exercising choice and free will. 'Consider' also belongs to the family of 50 per cent statements. Please consider the following statements and begin to notice the ones that trigger the least internal resistance in you:

Here's a pricing option to consider that can push you head and shoulders above your competition.

You should discount those items because everybody's price conscious these days.

One way of looking at this that can give you real peace of mind is to consider having alarm sensors in every main thoroughfare.

You have to have sensors in all walkways, if you want my opinion.

It's OK to spend some time considering this before you decide that it really suits your requirements.

Look, there's not really an option here. You have to go with it.

CAUSE AND EFFECT

The need to have an explanation for everything seems to be a hereditary perceptual pattern of human beings. Linking a so-called cause with an effect is tidy, it offers a way out of contradiction, attempts to explain coincidence and allows us to wrap things up in 'common' sense. You'd be surprised, however, at how often it's out of whack with the ways things can really present themselves.

Cause and effect operates on both conscious and unconscious levels and can be represented by the simple equation 'when– then'. When 'x' is present, then 'y' follows automatically. Scholars too many to mention have ridiculed this simplistic yet ubiquitous 'truth' as illogical, absurd, foolish and potentially dangerous when in the hands of people who understand only too well its destructive and manipulative effects.

When you follow the useful premise that we can never know everything about any one thing, then the notion of cause and effect can appear as a rather intellectually cheap and silly but sometimes utilitarian way of explaining some, but not all, things. Notice how the when– then equation has been used in the above sentence. It tends to induce a sense of completeness and balance. It 'feels' right, doesn't it? Hopefully the fatuousness of cause and effect has been tempered by the employment of neutral language in the sentence. Let's explore some further examples of the when– then phenomenon and the outcomes it can produce.

In the aftermath of World War II, a group of New Guinea mountain tribes created a religion around fighter and other aircraft of war. The aircraft had become inextricably coupled with prosperity, and when the war ended the tribal equivalent of a depression occurred. The tribes subsequently created altars and shrines from pieces of aircraft and military hardware, constructing them to resemble aircraft.

Over time, an occasional aircraft strayed into the tribes' view. Sometimes the rate of occurrence increased. With each 'visitation' the altars and places of worship became more ostentatious and detailed. New sightings were held up as confirmation of the power of the ritualised religious behaviours occurring on the ground. The 'second coming', in this instance of more trinkets, more bully beef and more shiny things falling from the sky, was associated with ever-increasing levels of religious fervour.

You may laugh at the sheer idiocy of the cause– effect rituals acted out by a group of remote New Guinea tribespeople, but is it really any different in our so-called sophisticated and enlightened society? While the tribespeople may have associated their prayers with increased aircraft activity and the likelihood of prosperity, don't we associate a range of ritualised behaviours with promises of sexual potency, health and happiness, economic stability, wealth and social acceptance, and life eternal?

What is the difference between a New Guinea tribe believing aircraft are the cause of tribal well-being and prayer the cause of the return of the 'silver birds of prosperity', and the symbolic associations we make between flash cars and status, level playing fields and economic prosperity, soap and beautiful skin, and the endless list of spurious associations we accept without protest?

The reported apparition of the Virgin Mary on the glass facade of a California office building some years ago can be seen as an example of how a series of random events can be fashioned into a cause– effect pattern by some people. Belief, in some quantity, was invested in that pattern by many of those who had a propensity to look for cause– effect solutions. Once the pattern formed, the true believers would have it no other way than that it was a modern-day visitation, a miracle. As one believer attested, 'I saw it with my own eyes, and it's real. It's a sign'. Those who chose to believe the cause– effect pattern became quite agitated at the unpalatable suggestion that the apparition was a random scattering of bore-water mineral deposits reacting in some unknowable pattern on the glass of the building.

Cause and effect can be a useful device when applied to mutually desirable outcomes and when couched in language that moderates its potentially toxic effects. Adopting the position that cause and effect is a useful, rather than realistic, way of explaining some things can keep you out of harm's way when lethal when– then statements are hurled in your direction. It can stimulate both intellectual and rhetorical flexibility. It may also sensitise you to the potential traps of making cause– effect claims that can be disputed and debunked by your critics and listeners.

Be the cause of

You might choose to consider carefully how you use cause– effect as a rhetorical device *because* it has the power to trigger high levels of message acceptance and behavioural change in your listeners. Harvard psychology professor Ellen Langer conducted an experiment in which the simple word 'because' produced significant levels of capitulation in those studied. Langer's team tested three sentences on people who were queuing to use a photocopying machine. The researcher sought to jump the queue using one of the following excuses:

1. 'Excuse me, may I use the Xerox machine?'
2. 'Excuse me, may I use the Xerox machine because I want to make copies?'
3. 'Excuse me, may I use the Xerox machine because I'm in a rush?'

Which of the above sentences do you imagine brought about the least compliance? Yes, sentence 1 only achieved 68 per cent compliance. It may surprise you to learn that sentences 2 and 3 brought about equal and much greater compliance than sentence 1, 93 per cent and 94 per cent respectively. Adding a 'because' created more compliance irrespective of the plausibility of the reason.

Langer's study reinforced what good panhandlers and beggars have learned through their own research. Street kids, for example, soon learn that a sentence like 'Can you give me a dollar because I'm hungry and homeless' gives them a higher hit rate than sentences like 'Have you got any spare change?'. Where street charity is concerned the 'because' works in interesting ways. First, it induces mindless acceptance of the form of the message over the content of the message and increases the level of generosity and, second, it suggests at a deeper level that the donor can be the 'cause' of the relief of suffering: a fairly powerfully double-whammy in anyone's language.

In deciding to apply cause– effect techniques honourably, consider the following types of sentence construction:

Because you want your children to have the best chances in life, you can consider personal coaching as a means of giving them an edge.

You may feel much happier in a serviced building *because* of the greater sense of security you'll feel.

When you see your wonderful new figure in three months from now, *then* you can look back to now and think to yourself, 'Wow! This is the best decision I ever made'.

Can you give me some of your time *because* you'll be amazed at how this idea will solve some pressing problems for you.

LIVE EVIDENCE

The *Concise Oxford Dictionary* defines the verb 'vivify' as 'give of life to, enliven, animate'. In spoken communication, 'vivify' has come to mean the breathing of life into an idea, concept, story, point or argument through the use of sensory language. The purpose of vivification is to utilise your audience's capacity to create living representations of your content as you go along. Live evidence allows you to create a moving picture of supporting information, complete with surround sound, aromas, feelings and tastes.

Live evidence enhances message processing in your listeners and significantly increases the levels of acceptance and recall. Vivified messages are more effective in evoking audience interest than what are termed 'pallid' messages.

Before you go any further, you may like to pay careful attention to a very important feature in the use of vivid language. Vivified messages can either *undermine* or *enhance* your listeners' retention and processing. A major factor appears to be what is termed 'congruency'. Congruency, in this context, means creating live evidence where the images, sounds, smells, feelings and tastes are consistent with the message you wish to convey.

Here are examples of a 'pallid' message, an incongruously vivified message and a congruently vivified message. The subject is weight-control. Please review each of the examples and notice the internal images, thoughts and feelings each respective image evokes.

[Pallid] A growing body of research indicates that inappropriate diet and a sedentary existence can lead to various cardiovascular conditions. In addition, obesity is responsible for social, psychological and physiological disadvantage. Overweight individuals experience discrimination at many levels as victims of fatism. Overweight people also have a significantly higher risk profile for a range of life threatening medical conditions. Research has also shown that the morbidly obese experience a diminished quality of life through lower self-esteem, social derision, paucity of physical activity and compromised career prospects through negative stereotypical responses in the workplace. Sensible diet and exercise make life longer and better.

[Incongruously vivified] The fat man or fat woman, in their constant quest for the last delectable dark chocolate in the box, don't seem to even care about the effects their habits are having on their bodies. The only exercise they usually get is through wearing a track in the carpet from the couch to the refrigerator. As they munch through those delicious chocolate mud cakes dripping with luscious dark icing, and bite on to-die-for banana muffins, while swilling down a litre of icy cold coke, do they think about late-onset diabetes? Of course not, because the exotic and spicy smells, wonderfully contrasting textures and mouth watering tastes of food, glorious food hijack their attention. What's a bit of huffing and puffing, when you can repress your worries with a scrumptious pork fillet, floating on a lake of cream sauterne sauce. Who cares if one is the object of fun or loses out on a promotion when one has a walloping southern fried drumstick in one's hand, and one's mouth is ready to experience the crunchy sensation of the first bite. You only live to eat once, after all. But, sensible diet and exercise makes life longer and better.

[Congruently vivified] The evidence shows that too much food and too little exercise is bad for your personal and psychological health. In a movie theatre, the obese person goes to sit down and their thighs are far too wide for the seat. How embarrassing! They never go to the swimming pool for dread of people making fun of their bulky, cellulite rippling bodies. They're passed over for promotion and told at work that 'you don't have what we're looking for'. They labour under shortage of breath, huffing and puffing over a few stairs. Constant streams of sweat drip from their brows, giving rise to a peculiar and unhealthy odour. Contrast this with healthy individuals, brimming with energy, who can leap up a flight of stairs and climb the ladder of success with energy to spare: whose flesh is as truly willing as their minds. They know that sensible diet and exercise makes life longer and better.

Were you able to get much of a picture in your mind's eye when reading the first example? Pallid messages are discernible by the absence of internal experiences of pictures, feelings, sounds, smells and tastes. This is because the language is abstract and removed from sensory experience, as you discovered in Chapter 2. In reviewing the 'pallid' message you will be able to identify the paucity of concrete words and language of the senses.

What internal sensations did you experience when reviewing the second example? In the second example you can notice the use of tongue-in-cheek concrete/sensory language, but the images, sounds, smells and, particularly, tastes do not reinforce the underlying message of healthy eating and exercise. After reading the incongruously vivified version, did you feel even the slightest twinge of hunger? If so, the vivid imagery provided a strong contraindication and would fail as a tool of influence.

The third, congruently vivified, example creates pictures of lumbering, perspiring creatures huffing and puffing up stairs. Did you get a picture of that in your mind's eye? Didn't you hear some sounds and get a whiff of stale perspiration? The imagery is consistent and doesn't offer distraction from the intent of the message. It leads the reader, through the use of mild aversion, to the favourable conclusion that healthy eating and exercise is a valid message.

People subjected to arguments containing vivid imagery compatible with the overall thrust of the message show higher levels of message processing and retention. This is particularly relevant to people who have a tendency to process information automatically, as opposed to those who habitually give careful and conscious attention to information. Many of the language structures that induce automatic and unconscious processing of information appear in this section. In combining language structures that encourage automatic processing with vivid languaging techniques, you can significantly increase your powers of persuasion.

Vivification process

Vivification describes techniques of rhetoric that are, to use a metaphor, designed to place attention under arrest and, secondly, to maintain custody of such attention until your message has been completed and closure has been achieved.

There are two basic components to the vivification process, shown in the following diagram.

Sensory language describes words and phrases that mirror what your senses do: see, hear, feel/touch, smell and taste. Sensory language triggers imagination. Imagination in this context relates to your ability to create inside your head a five-dimensional theatre of pictures, sounds, sensations, smells and tastes, often with the presence of a narrator.

Imagination is a form of hallucination and, as with most hallucinations, an imagined event can create powerful sensations. Think of a bug that you're scared of, or dislike: a cockroach, for example. Picture it in your mind's eye and notice the feelings of revulsion or fear you experience as the cockroach scurries towards you. Sensory language can excite the imagination and arrest attention in the following ways:

■ Kinaesthetic. Evokes feelings and emotional interest, creates spatial experiences and imagined activity that involves touching, doing and feeling.

■ Visual. Evokes compelling images in the mind's eye of your listener.
■ Auditory. Evokes sounds and internal dialogue.
■ Gustatory. Evokes imaginary tastes.
■ Olfactory. Evokes smells.

Let's take sensory language on approval for a few moments. As you read the following sentences, choose to become aware of the sensations the words evoke.

You're walking down a dark, tree-lined street just after midnight. You're beginning to feel edgy, your body and mind are on high alert. You see bizarre shadows cast by the moonlight and you begin to wonder who and what is lurking behind the dark shapes that seem to dance in and out of your field of vision.

You're reminded of recent stories of muggings and attacks in the area; the cold, metallic tang of fear overwhelms your senses; and you smell danger in the chilled air you breathe.

The slightest sounds are magnified in your ears, and you begin to quicken your step as the need to take flight controls your body. Will you get home unharmed? Will tonight be the night that you meet your worst fears?

Your anger begins to rise in synch with your increasing pace: anger directed at those who put your safety at risk by turning the street lights out at midnight, for God's sake! The price you pay for this council-imposed curfew is fear! Is that what you want?

Contrary to what the councillors may believe, people are not all in bed by midnight. This is an inner-city suburb, not a dormitory! We want the lights on until five in the morning.

Were you able to picture the dark, tree-lined street? Did you observe the dancing shadows? Did you notice your ears sensitised to sound, did you taste fear and smell danger? What did you feel as you were reading? Chances are there were enough sensory words in the paragraphs for you to create a theatre of the mind and experience the predicament of walking alone through a dark street. If you've a mind to learn rapidly the sensory words that helped create that experience, please review the above and place the key sensory words into the five categories mentioned on page 205 and above.

It's believed that people have a dominant sensory system. While most people will make intellectual distinctions in all five sensory categories, some people make more distinctions kinaesthetically and pay more attention to doing and feeling, others are highly visual and place great importance on visual stimulus, while dialogue and sound are more important to others. It's been found, for example, that if you have a tendency to make more visual distinctions, visual words will be more effective in gaining and maintaining your attention.

People whose dominant sensory system is visual will visualise a word before they spell it, will more than often get distracted by messiness, and may forget names but remember faces. Visual people tend to speak more rapidly and don't like to listen long, like to see demonstrations, charts and visual aids when learning, probably think words are a bit cheap and opt for people showing rather than telling them, and so on. Is that you? If your dominant sensory system is visual, the following examples of visual words will give you greater clarity than other sensory words.

EXAMPLES OF VISUAL PREDICATE WORDS AND PHRASES

see	look	view
appear	show	dawn
reveal	picture	bright
eye to eye	bird's eye view	mind's eye
photographic memory	add colour	clear
foggy	dim	focused
envisage	envision	illuminate
clear cut	make a scene	flicker
perspective	in light of	looks like
spotlight	visualise	hazy
sparkling	crystal clear	flash
seems	appears	plainly see
under your nose	up front	well defined
naked eye	eyeful	frame
not a shadow of a doubt	glimpse	watch
image	sight	foresight
espy	short sighted	myopic
take a peek	make a scene	looks like
sight for sore eyes	luminescence	

If you're a person who makes more auditory intellectual distinctions you will be more attracted to words that have a 'sound' about them. Auditory people often think in sound, express their anger in verbal outbursts, forget faces but are good at remembering names, talk to themselves more and prefer dialogue in learning environments.

People with a strong auditory preference tend to like the telephone as a means of communication, may get distracted by extraneous noise, often cock an ear towards people who are speaking and use a lot of hand and body gestures when talking. If your dominant sensory system is auditory the following words will ring a bell.

EXAMPLES OF AUDITORY PREDICATE WORDS AND PHRASES

tone	loud	sounds
volume	heard	afterthought
hear	listen	make music
harmonise	tune in/out	rings a bell
dropped a clanger	silence	din
talk	resonate	deafen
dissonance	mellifluous	attuned
overtones	question	tell (myself/yourself)
blabber	clear as a bell	clearly expressed
call on	yell	melodious
describe	earful	mind's ear
express	give account of	hold your tongue
hidden message	heard voices	whispering
loud and clear	dressed loudly	keynote speaker
manner of speaking	power of speech	chattering
purrs	outspoken	rap session
word for word	within hearing	informed
voiced	vocal	utterly
telltale	tattler	tongue-tied
unheard of	noisy	shrieked

If your preferred sensory mode is kinaesthetic, you will show a definite leaning towards touching, doing and feeling. Actions speak louder than words to you.

You often do things because they 'feel' right, and you may not be able to visualise as well as a visual person.

The images you do see may involve action or movement. You tend to have a good memory for activities that you engaged in, may well like dancing, tend to buy clothing and shoes on the basis of comfort, don't read much, prefer examples with plenty of action in them and like to learn by doing. If your dominant sensory system is kinaesthetic, the following words will press your buttons.

EXAMPLES OF KINAESTHETIC PREDICATE WORDS AND PHRASES

feel	touch	grasp
get hold of	slip through	catch on

WORDS THAT WIN HEARTS **209**

make contact	throw out	turn around
hard	unfeeling	concrete
scrape	unbudging	pressing
take in	unyielding	solid
suffer	firm	warm
cool	all washed up	boils down to
chip off the old block	come to grips with	control
firm foundations	floating on air	forceful
heated	get a handle on	get a load of this
get in touch with	follow your drift	on your goat
hand in hand	hang in there	heated argument
hold it	hold on	hot head
keep your shirt on	know-how	lay cards on the table
fits	put across	light headed
moment of panic	I don't follow	pain in the neck
pull strings	sharp	dangling
slipped my mind	smooth operator	underhanded
scratch	firm	stand your ground
do	hands-on	on side

If you were a dog, or perhaps from a lost tribe in the middle of the Andes where life depends on acute smell and taste, chances are your dominant sensory system would be that of smell, with taste running a quick second. Most humans, however, process information predominately in the visual, auditory and kinaesthetic sensory systems. People do make numerous gustatory and olfactory distinctions, particularly if they're French or budding gourmets. If you were a talking dog and heard the following words, the speaker would come up smelling of roses and the experience would leave a very sweet taste in your mouth.

EXAMPLES OF GUSTATORY WORDS AND PHRASES

taste	aftertaste	relish
flavour	tang	savoury
lace with	savour	mouth watering
drooling	piquant	unsavoury
zest	tincture	season
spice	spice up	zing
drink in	sour	sweet
bland		

EXAMPLES OF OLFACTORY WORDS AND PHRASES

redolence	fetor	fetid
reek	bad odour	good odour
aroma	bouquet	smell
smell a rat	bad smell	odour
pong	perfume	get a whiff of
foul	fishy	whiff
stench	stink	scent
fragrant	acrid	pungent

There is another category of language that is described as digital. This is the language of dissociation, of concepts and of the abstract. While it is useful to use digital predicate words and phrases when you wish to dissociate yourself or others from specific content, it is not useful when creating theatre of the mind through vivification.

Word structures

While people generally have a preferred sensory mode it does not exclude them from gathering and processing information in other modes. Preference implies that more distinctions will be made in one mode than another. Distinctions in other modes will be made, but to a lesser degree. As with other typologies, there is a strong chance you will revert to your dominant sensory type when put under pressure or stress. The adverbs, verbs and adjectives you choose will reflect your sensory language preferences. A person with a visual preference will tend to use more visual words, and so on. In doing so, they may increase levels of stress and misunderstanding, particularly if other parties to the communication have opposing sensory preferences, as the example below demonstrates:

Look, from my *perspective* nothing could be *clearer*. The room has to have a *beige look*. Just *visualise* the furniture in here and you will *see* that beige is much more suitable for the fabric *colours*. You can *see* that, can't you?

Well, I *feel* you're *pushing* me into this. When I *walk* into this room I want to *feel* a *coolness* and I don't want it to have a *warm ambience* because that will be *stifling* in summer. I'm not *giving ground* on this!

Would the two parties having this discussion ever come to an agreement with a language gap so wide? Which dominant sensory modes are clashing in the above example? Someone would have to yield and choose a language perspective more suitable to the other person if they wanted to come to an agreement on decor, wouldn't they?

Often, behind major disagreements there is a clash of language or other typologies. Sometimes the more astute party, having recognised a clash of language modes, can solve the dispute by simply switching to the other party's dominant language pattern. For example, if you were to speak to a group of visual artists, you would be well advised to apply a preponderance of visual language to your arguments and talk the talk of your audience. Dancers and sculptors would demand greater levels of kinaesthetic language, and singers and musicians would tune into your auditory words and phrases.

It is one thing to mirror the preferred patterns of specific groups, but you might now be wondering how to mix your sensory language when addressing a diverse group or when you wish to expand the perspectives of a specialist group. Remembering that the role of a charismatic communicator is to help people expand their models of the world, consider the benefits of balancing visual, kinaesthetic and auditory language.

Each mode naturally offers a different perspective on the same topic. When deciding on which points to vivify in a speech, presentation or conversation, aim to give your listeners multiple perspectives with a flow of visual, kinaesthetic and auditory words. This not only offers three perspectives on the one issue, it also widens your catchment area by appealing to the three principal sensory modes. Bells will be ringing, people will clearly see your point and your message will get a warm response.

Putting it together

Let's assume that you haven't as yet incorporated any ad-libbing or information frameworks into your unconscious behaviour. Let's also assume that, until you do, you can choose to script and rehearse your vivified messages prior to unleashing them onto, let's face it, a wildly appreciative audience.

The following process can assist you in creating congruent vivified content. The model below is designed to appeal to both types of message processors: those who automatically process information without much conscious attention, and those who have a strong tendency to pay careful attention to the structure and content of your message.

PHASE 1

■ Think about what, specifically, it is you want your audience to understand, and write your points out as a series of short statements.

- Design an effective communication model using one of the templates in Chapter 8. Test the argument by asking a few subjects to carefully consider it. Make any necessary adjustments.

PHASE 2

- Vivify by applying a balance of visual, auditory and kinaesthetic (VAK) language to your message, using examples given in this chapter as a guide.
- A useful way to create sensory language is to take an idea or proposition, think of a supporting example and become either a participant in, or spectator of, the example. Feel what you feel and report it, see what you see and describe it, and hear what you hear and say it. The language you hear yourself use will almost certainly contain sensory language.
- Check your script for balance of VAK, make any adjustment and move on to Phase 3.

PHASE 3

- Test the vivified message with a few people to ensure that it creates internal images that are consistent with your message.
- Make any adjustment to your imagery to ensure all aspects of consistency are accounted for.

The process of vivification is part of natural language. What you have discovered in this section is that natural language patterns can be applied to create theatre of the mind that smoothly and elegantly transports your listeners into the picturesque world of the five sensory dimensions.

Much has been written on the ability of charismatic communicators to transform ordinary dialogue into extraordinarily moving and uplifting experiences. Far from being a mystery as it's often portrayed, live evidence simply reflects a sequence of successful and do-able behaviours, at the heart of which is what you have come to know as vivification.

11 TRIGGERING THE 'YES' RESPONSE

> If thou thinkest twice, before thou speakest once, thou will speak twice the better for it.
> *William Penn*

Imagine the immense delight you would feel to have an audience break into spontaneous applause after you'd made a significant point. You can appreciate that kind of response represents an audience 'going for' you and your ideas in a very big and tangible way. Consider, too, speaking in front of a group of people and triggering silent 'ah-uh' or 'yes' responses all the way through your presentation. The air would be electric with positive energy, wouldn't it? Now, what if you could create tactical sentences that excite those responses at will? You may say to yourself, 'Now that can be something really worth learning, can it not?'.

Review your experience of reading the paragraph above. Can you remember the number of times that you felt physically in alignment with its propositions? Maybe you felt a few 'ah-uh's as you quickly absorbed the points, or maybe the sensations of agreement and approval were a little stronger than that, providing more than enough reason for you to remain interested and continue reading.

The internal sensations you experience from a mild 'ah-uh' to a wanton 'go-for-it' impulse feel good. Consider the value of these positive feelings being associated with you and your content as you deliver your message. If people associate pleasure and stimulation with you and your message, three things happen.

1. People remember better.
2. People are much more likely to embrace your message.
3. People will come back for more.

The sensations associated with 'Yes!' and 'go-for-it' responses are an important consideration in the relationships charismatic communicators establish with audiences. They are particularly gifted in the assessment and management of emotion in those they seek to persuade. They take constant readings and actively engage in regulating the emotional mercury as circumstance demands. This gift can be seen as a combination of self-appraisal, the capacity to read and manage an audience's emotional state, and the ability to fashion words in such a way as to make them irresistible.

Having felt the power of 'Yes!' and understanding the value of incorporating 'yes' triggers into your speaking style, your next step is to learn some of the patterns and sequences charismatic communicators use to evoke those responses.

THE YES NOT

The word 'not' and its derivatives exist only in language. This is to say that 'not's are a construct and generally do not mirror the way your brain works. They are tough on your unconscious mind. That is why, for example, you can't not think of evoking 'yes' responses when instructed not to think about them, without thinking about them first and then attempting to stamp a 'not' on them. As you can see, it's not all that hard to tie your mind up in 'not's, is it not?

Some 'not's, however, are better than others. You may not have begun to wonder where this is all taking you, until now. And as you begin to consider the immense possibilities of this simple word, you can appreciate, can you not, how a few cleverly placed 'not's can bring about a strong sense of the opposite? OK, enough is enough!

The 'not's you are going to find relatively easy to integrate into your language style are connected to tag questions. Some tag questions, such as 'right?', 'OK?', 'You know?' and others that are part of powerless language, can reduce your effectiveness as a speaker. However, appropriately inserted tag questions containing a 'not' can have the effect of producing silent affirmations in your listeners, thus significantly increasing your effectiveness. It would be useful to be able to use a linguistic device such as 'not' and have your audience nodding in agreement as you go along, would it not?

During the important phases of building an argument it can be extremely useful to evoke your listeners' silent agreement on the points you introduce, to encourage them to feel a 'yes' coming on at various stages during the delivery of your argument.

A series of tag questions have been inserted at crucial points in this chapter to illustrate the usefulness of tag questions containing a 'not'. Perhaps you'd like to scan what's been written so far in this chapter to discover for yourself how a negative such as 'not' can induce internal sensations of agreement. Having completed your scan, begin to think about how you can absorb the following tag questions into your speaking style. Try a few out on occasions and notice the physical symptoms of agreement they evoke.

isn't it?/is it not?
doesn't it?/does it not?
don't you?/do you not?
haven't you?/have you not?
can't you?/can you not?
couldn't you?/could you not?
shouldn't you?/should you not?
won't you?/will you not?
hasn't it?/has it not?
aren't we?/are we not?
wouldn't it?/would it not?
you can add more to this list, can't you?

YES SETS

A yes set describes a method by which a series of universally 'true' questions or statements are delivered to elicit an agreement pattern. For example:

Politicians are less trustworthy.
Increasingly they're not of touch with average Australians.
More and more people seem to be showing discontent with politics.
Money is wasted on grand schemes.
But crime continues unabated.

Therefore:

Vote Labor and we will work together to bring you and your concerns back on the agenda.

In this example a series of five universally true statements were made that would invoke either internal expressions of agreement or, in some cases, a very loud 'Yes!'. The yes set is followed by a request, suggestion or proposition.

The minimum number of 'yes's you should aim for is four. On occasion you may wish to increase the number to enhance the rhythm of your statement. The theory behind yes sets is that by eliciting internal or verbal agreement, you build a sympathetic and receptive state of mind in your target audience. It's postulated that listeners, after having gone into an agreement frame of mind, will experience dissonance if they break the yes pattern.

It's also believed that in some contexts lazy thinking plays a significant role in yes sets. Try the following example, once again containing universally true statements, and notice how difficult it is to resist the pattern when you are locked into an agreement state of mind.

You've worked hard and paid your taxes.
You've made a contribution to the economy of this country.
You deserve a reasonable standard of living when you retire.
You want to have enough money to enjoy your life.
You want safety and security.

That's why National First Trust can be your first choice.

There's also a variation of the yes set called the yes-plus set. This set anticipates more mindful listeners noticing at some level that they're locked into an agreement frame and perhaps internally rebelling against it. The technique introduces agreement by negation: a no/yes response, as the following example demonstrates.

We haven't introduced ourselves yet.
There are people here who don't know each other.
And we wouldn't want to work with strangers, would we? (no/yes response)
You can see the value of getting acquainted.
Makes things better if we're on first name terms, doesn't it?

Therefore let's do the introductions.

Yes sets are particularly useful as icebreakers. They also come in very handy if you have occasion to address hostile audiences. By initially gaining the silent agreement of a hostile audience with a well-crafted yes set, you install in the minds of your listeners the notion that, while they may not agree with you, they agree with you. This is a crucially important element in the process of attitude modification, as you can appreciate.

YESSIR!

A conversational postulate is another form of communication that can produce a desired yes, or yes to a predetermined 'no' answer to a particular question. Could this useful technique be something you can come to *understand and gain some benefit from?*

You probably already know at a deeper level that questions like the above can produce agreement or disagreement, depending on the way the question is phrased. Do you sense that, from the examples already given, you can *get a hint of what a conversational postulate is?*

You might begin to *notice that sentences like the above contain some kind of command in them.* Can you please review these three paragraphs and *notice how they contain a command to which a positive response is generally presumed?*

In reviewing these sentences, you probably sensed that at some level you were being invited to feel a 'yes' coming on.

For example, the first paragraph contains the command *understand and gain benefit from this technique.* The second paragraph commands you to *get the hint of what a conversational postulate is,* and the third directs you to *notice that sentences like the above sentences contain some kind of command in them* and to *notice how they contain a command to which a positive response is generally presumed.*

In the remaining parts of this chapter you will randomly encounter conversational postulates. Now, can you begin to recognise how they offer a detour around issues of control and resistance?

Conversational postulates often allow you to give individuals and groups instructions and commands without having to deal with contests of will. They can set you on the path of least resistance. They're highly suggestive and useful when you consider it advantageous for your listeners to expand their world views or to think about options they may not have entertained. So how do you do them? Can you follow and practise the formula outlined below?

Simple conversational postulate 1

1. Think of what you want your listeners to do. For example: I want my listeners to recognise the importance of working on a neighbourhood security plan.

2. Turn the suggestion into a command. For example: Agree to start working on the neighbourhood security plan tonight.

3. Embed a possibility word such as 'can', 'may' or 'might' within the sentence (as outlined in Chapter 10) to transform the sentence into a 50 per cent statement. For example: I'm sure you can agree on how *important* it is to start working on the neighbourhood security plan tonight.

Conversational postulate 2
1. Think of what it is that you want your audience to say yes or no to. For example: I want my audience to say 'No!' to police having wider search-without-warrant powers.
2. Construct the appropriate suggestion or command. Make a sentence out of it. For example: Limit police search-without-warrant powers.
3. Express the instruction in a question that uses a possibility word or presupposes your listeners will agree with your yes or no proposition. For example: Can you notice how your interests and, indeed, personal liberty will be better protected by demanding the minister limit police search-without-warrant powers?

PACING CURRENT EXPERIENCE

Here you are reading this book<P>, and you notice that the subject heading is 'Pacing current experience'<P>. You may or may not be aware of what the heading means<P>. You're probably sitting down if that's what you're doing<P>, and as you're reading these words on the page<P> you're now being reminded that sometimes you find yourself drifting into shorter or longer intervals of thought about what you've read<P>.

The paragraph above is an example of pacing current experience. This technique is designed to imbue in your listeners a sense of being on the same wavelength, of seeing eye to eye or being in synch with a speaker. It is designed to bring about the perception of you and your audience singing a harmonious tune together.

As you learned earlier in this book, if your listeners see you as a fellow traveller, they will be much more receptive to you and your message. Pacing in this context is designed to elicit softer agreement responses rather than full-blown 'yes' or 'go-for-it' reactions. Nevertheless, a continuous flow of soft accord can snowball into a hefty 'Yes!'.

Please review the first paragraph and notice that the symbol <P> indicates a pacing of your current experience. You are reading this book, so that's one 'mmm', 'ah-uh' or 'yep' registered. You have noticed the subject heading, so that's two. You may or may not have wondered what the heading means— three. You probably are sitting down, tallying four. You were reminded, that makes five, and you were reminded that you do sometimes drift into shorter or longer periods of thought when reading a book, weren't you? In one paragraph you encountered a total of six examples of pacing your current experience.

As you replay your internal video of reading the first paragraph you can probably recall experiencing a feeling of soft agreement, can't you? Now, imagine listening to a speaker and feeling a flow of soft agreement as the speech went along. You can grasp the significance of soft agreement when you consider that the more you match your message content to the real experiences of your listeners, the greater will be their willingness to accept your persuasive appeal.

The key to pacing current experience is to reflect accurately your observations of the *real* experiences of your listeners. This means avoiding assumptions, judgments and interpretations. If you were to have read in the opening paragraph a statement like 'You're enjoying the prospect of reading about pacing current experience', chances are you would not have felt a 'yep', 'mmm' or 'ah-uh' coming on. The assumption, or in this case wishful thought, interrupts the rapport building sequence, because enjoyment may not have entered your picture. The chain of soft agreement would have been broken and a potential mismatch introduced. Some or many readers would have cause to disagree because the statement didn't match their experience. And disagreement is the last thing you want at critical junctures in your speech, conversation or presentation.

A safer way to pace current experience is to make your observations sensory-based. You'll only have to struggle for a little while, if at all, with sensory-based observations versus assumptions, judgments and interpretations before you get the gist and integrate them into your speaking style.

Sensory-based observation describes phenomena like activities, sights, sounds, experiences and smells that everyone can identify with. They are pure observations, rather than personal interpretations, and in the main they can't be disagreed with. Please look at the following statements and ask yourself which ones are pure observations, containing no assumptions, judgments or interpretations.

1. 'Gee, it's freezing in here!'
2. 'You're mad at me, I can tell.'
3. 'The sun is shining, the sky is cloudless and the temperature is 29 degrees.'
4. 'That's a much better tie than the one you wore yesterday.'
5. 'You people at the back are not paying attention.'
6. 'The drive home took an hour and twenty minutes to cover the distance of about a hundred kilometres.'

7. 'A wretched pong is emanating from the man on the centre aisle in the third row.'
8. 'He staggered along the footpath, bumping into three people, before he let out a cry and fell to the ground.'
9. 'Almost everyone said that they agree with postponing the launch until Friday.'
10. You all saw how John found the going tough and lost it altogether last week.'

Let's review the statements. Where a statement contains an assumption, judgment or interpretation, a rewrite will demonstrate how to convert it to a purer observation.

1. 'My breath is steaming in this atmosphere, I can see the goose bumps on my arms, and I'm shivering.'
2. 'Your frown is deep, your eyes are squinting, your nostrils are flared and your face is going red.'
3. [OK]
4. 'Your mid-blue tie is of the same hue as your suit and I feel [opinion expressed as opinion] it contrasts well with your white shirt.'
5. 'There is a person talking on a mobile phone in the back row, two people are exchanging words to each other, and the woman on the end is slumped in her chair and has her eyes closed.'
6. [OK]
7. 'As I walked past the man sitting on the centre aisle in the third row, I smelled an odour that some people may think is unpleasant.'
8. [OK]
9. [OK]
10. 'Last week you saw John get up out of his seat, throw his papers on the floor and hurriedly leave the room.'

Sensory-based observation allows you to deliver accurate commentary on the outside world without provoking disagreement among those listening. As with its critical thinking cousin, it focuses attention on the observable rather than the observer. It helps avoid the contests of will that often arise when judgments, assumptions and interpretation are introduced into the equation.

There are times in a speech, conversation or presentation when harmony and agreement are of the utmost importance:

- at the beginning of a dialogue;
- just prior to your introduction of a request, point, idea or proposal;

- at the end of a dialogue;
- at any time when you notice the tide of listener sentiment is turning away from you.

Here are some examples of the effective use of pacing current experience in real-life situations.

Hmm, there are thirteen of us here including me: a full complement.<P> We've come together to have a conversation about budgets<P> and, as you know, I'm here to help facilitate.<P> I'm looking forward to it because none of you has had a chance yet to put in your bid.<P> The agenda in front of you, you can notice, has each of your names on it.<P> You can see that you are grouped with the other two managers from your region, making up four budget or bidding teams.<P> As you agreed on the conference call last week, you have a better chance of funding your priorities this year by placing regional bids.<P> And ... [here begins the persuasion appeal] with the formula you have in front of you<P> I'm sure that you can follow its example and discover for yourselves step by step how easy it becomes for you to work cooperatively together to map out each region's funding priorities for the year.

You want to buy another house.<P> And while the vendor isn't here<P> it gives us an opportunity to look again at your needs. <P> You say you're really keen to have a corner block,<P> and you most certainly don't want to be near heavy traffic as the noise will upset you, won't it?<P> We're standing in the kitchen<P> and this room is at the back of the house<P> and it's Sunday<P> ... [here begins the persuasion appeal] and you can notice the obvious rumble of traffic on the quietest day of the week. You're probably not aware that the rumble will increase at least threefold during the week, and the noise will be unbearable in the front rooms. So you can appreciate that this is not the house for you, can't you?

You've read that pacing current experience produces soft agreement,<P> and you may not have known until now that half a dozen 'yes's, 'ah-uh's or 'mmm's build rapport and common ground.<P> You've reviewed sensory-based observation<P> and seen how it produces dialogue that cannot be disagreed with.<P> The examples of pacing you've encountered have shown you different ways in which it can be applied<P> and you have touched upon the key areas where pacing can be useful.<P>

Can you begin to see yourself using sensory-based observation to pace current experience when communicating with individuals and groups? As you do, you may wonder at the ease with which you can instil in your audience a feeling of common ground, of seeing eye to eye, of talking their talk. Imagine how useful this could be when you need your listeners to understand your view of the world.

Imagine how it can break down natural resistance when you need to advocate change, or to invite people to consider other options. It could increase your power to persuade immeasurably, couldn't it?

FUTURE PACING

Harmonious dialogue and good communication creates the scenery of change. In small, staged increments during a speech, presentation or conversation, the charismatic communicator attempts to create among followers disenchantment with the status quo, strong identification with a better future and a compelling desire to be led towards that vision. In order to accomplish a smooth transition from the status quo to a new position, a compelling and realistic snapshot of the future needs to be introduced and embraced by those who are being invited to change. You can come to know this process as 'future pacing'.

Future pacing can help prepare your listeners for the 'action' phase of the change process by showing them what they can do with new personal resources, new plans, new equipment, new ideas, and so on. It can lubricate the machinery of change by demonstrating the benefits that lie ahead when the vision becomes a reality.

Whereas pacing current experience encourages listeners to say yes to the observable present, future pacing is designed to elicit a committed 'Yes!' to an imagined future state of affairs. Future pacing allows you to create a concrete 'as if' world in which a predicted outcome can appear as a 'present' and highly desirable experience. A properly constructed future pace creates the conditions that motivate 'go-for-it' responses.

Future pacing must translate an abstract vision into a clear, specific, feasible and 'alive' option. This is where your knowledge of vivification (see Chapter 10) will become extremely useful. The portrait you paint of a future where the change has already occurred must be vivid and plausible. It's vital that your future pace includes a balance of visual, auditory and kinaesthetic language to make the portrayal of the future a true multimedia experience.

Future pacing involves two simple components:

- thinking about, and encouraging your listeners to think about, the future;
- plausible suggestion.

In a speech delivered to the party faithful in 1997, British politician Paddy Ashdown demonstrated the power of future pacing:

So where shall we be, we Liberal Democrats, as this historic game is played out in the months and years ahead? Some say we should be satisfied with our local strength and concede that Westminster will always be a side-show for us. Some say we should be content to be a good conventional opposition, and that is enough.

Well, no doubt our opponents would like to see us satisfied with such limited ambitions. But I am not. And I hope you will not either. I have bigger ambitions for the Liberal Democrats. I accept no glass ceiling for this party. [Speech interrupted by spontaneous applause]

Where we should co-operate we will do so wholeheartedly. Where we must oppose we will do so unflinchingly. [Speech interrupted by spontaneous applause]

Ashdown's future pace for the Liberal Democrats was the subject of extensive media reportage. It was purpose-designed for the thirty-second news grab, as were the rhetorical devices that triggered the 'spontaneous' applause. Ashdown created a compelling future vision for the Liberal Democrats by embedding suggestions of what the future would hold for the party and its supporters.

Let's take a closer-to-home example to illustrate the power of future pacing dialogue. A couple is arguing the toss over an issue that is affecting their relationship. The cannier of the two has a flash of brilliance and recognises the presence of a choice point: continue to inflame the situation by engaging in confrontational argument or embed a future-pace and change the dynamics.

Hey, something's just occurred to me [argument pattern is interrupted by question cue, as in 'What has occurred to you?']. You know, after we find a solution to this problem by making sure that both of us have our needs met [embedded suggestion on how to solve the argument] life is going to be so much easier and happier for us [future pace 1]. We have so many things that we already agree on [pacing current experience] and just imagine how good our relationship is going to be [future pace 2]. When we look back to now [embedded suggestion], we're gonna laugh and say 'phew, I'm glad we solved that one. It brought us so much closer together' [future pace 3].

Anyone who's had a major argument with a partner knows that argument is often associated with negative future pacing. When an argument erupts, warring parties often report their imaginations being hijacked by dire predictions of the future, such as there being no future at all or a miserable future marked by argument and conflict.

Charismatic performers customarily use negation in the initial and middle stages of a persuasion plan. Negation is distinctively employed by charismatic communicators in these first two stages as a communication strategy to neutralise conventional audience attitudes, to loosen personal links to the original attitude and to create a less neutral position towards the need for change. Negative future pacing can have a place in the first two stages of a persuasion plan. It is typically included in the construction of an argument where you examine the current state of affairs and invite your audience to contemplate the negative consequences of the status quo, as in the following argument.

I wonder where all this is going to take us [rhetorical question]? We have formed a pattern of argument. We have made a habit of automatically contradicting each other when we need to make joint decisions on the future of this company [pacing current experience]. We need to find a way of accommodating each other's needs and priorities [suggestion of win– win]. If we fail to find that way, you can see our future working relationship deteriorating into constant bickering, side-taking and white-anting [future pace 1]. The staff will notice this weakness and before too long they will exploit it [future pace 2]. But, worse than that, our deteriorating relationship will ultimately be reflected in the company's bottom line [future pace 3] and you can visualise what the MD will do to us both then, can't you [future pace 4]?

A powerful form of future pacing involves the creation of a road map to the goal, change, objective or vision you have set out. The following model takes you through the process step by step, by developing the last example into a positive future-pacing exercise.

1. INTRODUCE A RHETORICAL QUESTION OR CONVERSATIONAL POSTULATE
Can you see how it's to our mutual advantage to build a better decision-making environment?

2. CREATE A WORD PICTURE OF THE FUTURE
As we take these initial few steps to map out how we are going to cooperate [embedded suggestion], we will enter a new phase of working together [future pace 1]. You can imagine that when issues arise between us, an agreed process for clarifying them will make it easy to scope win– win solutions [future pace 2]. We'll be taking the opportunity to work more closely together and have productive conversations because we know that better decisions will be the outcome [future pace 3]. And I reckon that staff will notice that we've formed an alliance and will not be tempted to divide and conquer [future pace 4].

3. DEAL WITH PROCESS
So can we agree that when decisions require comment from both of us, we will call the other into the discussion and ask ourselves how we can make it work for both departments [process suggestion]? We can deal with the details by using cost-benefit criteria and working on the basis of overall impact on our cost structures [process suggestion]. Our decision-making process will be simpler and we'll both have an eye on the best outcome for our respective divisions [future pace 5].

4. SUGGEST A START AND REVIEW DATE
There's no better time to start this than now, is there? Can I suggest that we meet again in a couple of weeks, say the 25th, and review how it's gone [future pace 6 and ongoing cooperative relationship]. That way we will be ironing out any glitches as they happen and we'll both be confident in the long run that we're looking out for each other [future pace 7].

5. REINFORCE THE VISION
You know, I'm really appreciative that we have the maturity to talk about this and agree to cooperate [presupposes a link between maturity and cooperation]. I'm confident that as we begin to notice the benefits of close cooperation, we'll find that we're making each other's jobs a lot easier and more enjoyable [future pace 8]. I can actually see our profitability increasing [future pace 9] and I don't think the MD will be minding that at all [future pace 10].

The final stage of a persuasion plan essentially involves the consolidation of new attitudes and frames of awareness. Charismatic communicators substitute the negation with highly compatible positive images and strong future pacing. An important element of future pacing is to create plausible and desirable outcomes that solidify the links between the new values introduced and the world in which they will operate. The more compelling and realistic the message, the more vivid and value-laden the language, the higher the probability of a 'go-for-it' response will be.

PACING THE LANGUAGE REGISTER
According to experts in psychometric testing, between 65 and 70 per cent of Australians would report a preference for information to be couched in concrete terms. If you are a person who relishes communicating in abstract terms, you're likely to produce the same look of confusion in those listening as you'd get from a cow if you led it out to graze on concrete. If

nearly three-quarters of the population prefers to be spoken to in a practical and down-to-earth way, you have little choice but to break concepts, complex issues, ideas and events into understandable and concrete chunks.

Abstract language, when used to describe processes, allows people to use a type of linguistic shorthand when speaking and it is often described as 'jargon' by those who do not understand the language register being used. This form of expression is quite acceptable if you are communicating with a group of people who understand and use the jargon of your particular profession or discipline. It can, however, have a severe and negative impression on audiences and groups that are unfamiliar with your verbal shorthand. Unfamiliar jargon will distance you from your audience as it helps your listeners form negative impressions about you. It will also distance your audience from your ideas.

The following excerpt demonstrates the use of abstract language at its worst. Abstract language is in italic type:

We may have to change our current *attitude* and address the *critical socioeconomic imbalances* that are becoming more prevalent with the *effluxion* of time. We have to go beyond *selective interventionism* and most certainly resile from the *narrow social responsibility models* being practised at the moment. They are recipes for serious *societal disunity* and *fragmentation*.

We need to embrace *holistic solutions* that will allow us to avoid the *historical correlation* between *widening inequities in wealth distribution* and *revolutionary ferment*.

Holism cannot emerge unless governments realise that the *social contract* they have with the *electorate* to govern includes *responsibilities* to create and maintain an *equitable society* through policies that address *social justice issues* through *economic and social policy making*.

This statement may well be appropriate in a gathering of social scientists, but for most people it's inexcusable twaddle. This is because the language register is dissociated and specialised and fails to communicate the information in a way that connects people to reality. The speaker may or may not have been aware of the abstract form of this communication, but one thing is certain and that is a lack of awareness of the real effects of the message.

Another important consequence of the use of abstract language is that it can remove 'emotional actuality' from the communication. In the last example, it allows the speaker to dissociate from the harsher reality of the concrete actions and issues being described. So, how could the example be transformed to capture both abstract and concrete thinkers? Notice how the following statement converts gibberish into intelligible English by bringing concepts much closer to earth and reflecting the language patterns of general audiences.

The figures tell us a frightening story: the rich are getting richer and the poor really are getting poorer. Isn't it time to put away the big welfare stick and quell our hostility towards those who've committed no greater crime than that of being poor? Doesn't it make sense to question the consequences of the increasing gap between the haves and the have-nots?

Let's pause a moment and ask ourselves what 'have-not' actually means. It means not having many of the simple things that you see as a right and privilege of living in a country like Australia. Think of the basic things that you absolutely must have and then think of not having those basic needs fulfilled. Wouldn't you feel alienated and resentful?

If we ask ourselves these questions now, we may be saved from the inevitable repercussions of societies that choose to ignore the plight of the poor and disadvantaged. History tells us that the more people slipping into poverty, the greater the price to be paid. We will pay it with increased crime, more lives destroyed by drugs, more home burglaries, more civil disobedience, more violent attacks, more destruction of property and more fear.

If we take one page out of the history books, let it be the one that says that economics is the means of building better and happier societies and not creating a new class of the super-rich. If we have the will we can give poverty the same priority as efficiency and competitiveness. Let's throw dogma away and do our duty. Let's keep our side of the bargain to work on behalf of all Australians.

Linking abstract language with concrete reality in a communication allows a greater degree of meaning to be exchanged between the speaker and listener, as the example demonstrates. You may have also become aware that the language in the last statement is about half way between abstract and concrete. Speaking the same language as an audience dramatically enhances the relevance of your content. Relevance is a critical element in the persuasive power of your message.

A common misconception is that 'big words' can be equated with intelligence and mental substance. This perhaps explains why many speakers fail to filter out unfamiliar or confusing abstract language before it gets to the ears of an audience. To the insecure or immature speaker it can become a means by which they inflate their intellectual vanity or fake authority. Using abstract language may also fit in with misguided attempts to come across as intelligent and credible.

A point you can choose to consider is whether abstract language patterns actually allow you to sustain an image of intelligence, authority and credibility. It can be argued that abstract language does exactly the opposite. Any language that causes a separation between speakers and listeners can hardly be seen as smart. Any language that operates on a level of abstraction beyond what its general audience can understand will seriously undermine the authority of the message, and language that is unintelligible to large sections of its audience fails both the credibility and relevance tests.

Charismatic communicators and persuasion experts recognise the importance of not allowing their preferred thinking and language styles to obscure the task of creating meaningful experiences with their audiences. They know that their words will go unheeded unless they are crafted to pace the preferences and language styles of their listeners.

WHO HEARS IT

THE CHARACTERISTICS OF THE AUDIENCE

12 SHARING YOUR AUDIENCE'S SPACE

> Do unto others as *they* would have you do unto *them*.
> *Rex Steven Sikes*

Charismatic communication demands a transaction between speaker and listeners and, as with most forms of fair trading, customer satisfaction is predicated on exchanging things of equal value. For example, in exchange for a piece of electronic equipment at your local electrical store, you hand over its alleged value in dollars. In effect, the store buys your money with the piece of equipment. Similar dynamics apply when you seek to buy people's commitment to your proposals or ideas. So, what currency do you need to use to purchase attention and a fair hearing from your audience? The currency comes in three denominations:

1. discovery
2. groundwork
3. dialogue

You can choose to spend a reasonable amount of time in discovery mode. It's part of a process of learning about the people you intend to influence. It enables you to gain an insight into their personal world views, and the information you gather qualifies you to respect their models of the world and talk their particular dialect.

Groundwork is also a key element, as it represents the preparation phase of involving others in discussion and debate on the desirability and value of your position and ideas. It enables you to respond with feedback and engage in a mutual search for alternatives. It also provides you with the opportunity informally to test ideas on potential adversaries and modify your approach as you go along. You can test, revise, hone and polish your message before you arrive at a final product that incorporates the key needs of your target group. There are many benefits in accommodating other people's concerns, ideas and solutions into your final strategy or proposal. Your groundwork phase can often save you from embarrassing, and sometimes perilous, consequences.

Dialogue is the art of talking *with* people rather than talking at them or pretending to consult. It can occur during every stage of the communication process. Formal dialogue, as in a presentation or proposal, best occurs at the stage when you are certain of winning assent and support. Open dialogue encourages commitment and motivation. It alerts you to the emotional temperature of your audience or group and avoids having an idea or strategy stall through covert opposition and resistance at every turn.

GROUNDWORK AND DISCOVERY

It may not always be possible to know the individual needs, values or beliefs of larger audiences. So, some communications, presentations and speeches are necessarily 'catch-all' affairs, where you may use other powers of persuasion to draw listeners into shared territory to discuss the merits of your ideas. The size of the crowd, media speeches and interviews, diversity of the congregation and other factors sometimes make it difficult to gain an accurate measure of your audience. Nevertheless, it would be foolhardy to deliver a presentation to a group of people about whom you knew nothing.

Consider extolling the virtues of Australian beef to a group of vegans, advocating Judaism to a gathering of Shiite fundamentalists or telling Irish jokes at the Celtic Club. The point is that, if you want your listeners to like and trust you, you must tailor your message to the people you're seeking to persuade. Even rudimentary knowledge about your audience is better than none, but the more information you have about your listeners, the better you will be able to communicate your message in their language. After all, if a small or large group comes together to listen to you, it must, by definition, have something in common.

When you align your content with the audience's belief and value structures, you send the signal 'We are of the same mind'. High-order sameness, as you have learned, is one of the most important factors determining whether your presentation will win the day or fall on deaf ears. The more your audience views you and itself as being of one mind, the more receptive it will be to your ideas and proposals.

People make rapid, unconscious calculations on the degree of one-mindedness they share with others, based on finding answers to the following questions:

■ Does the speaker/leader think like I do, or think like I want to think, and have a similar attitude and approach?
■ Does the speaker/leader share and reflect my core beliefs and values?
■ Does the speaker share my traditions: roots, culture, education, background?

Approach, attitude, beliefs and values are significant elements people apply in determining one-mindedness. In important situations when much is riding on the success of your presentation, it would be folly to misalign or mismatch the beliefs and values of your audience.

There are two principal ways to discover and mirror the beliefs and values of your audience or target group.

1. Research and/or elicit them.
2. Mirror universal values and virtues.

In researching the values and beliefs of your audience, you can do the following: ask. Speak to the client group before the presentation and ask questions like 'What are the things that are important to you in bringing this product to market?' and 'Why is it important to you to be seen as an independent operator?'. The key part of your questions should be what, why or how something is important. If you listen closely to the responses, you will hear words that represent values, beliefs and deeply held attitudes. Ask questions such as:

1. Where do people stand on particular issues: their values and beliefs?
2. What are the interesting aspects of particular corporate cultures?
3. Where is the group focus at the moment?
4. What are the primary needs of the group? What does the group absolutely have to have in order to feel satisfied and fulfilled?
5. What particular challenges or special circumstances confront the group at the moment?
6. What does the group need to have in order to achieve its goals?

If you have been invited to speak to larger groups, make a point of finding out as much as you can about the composition of your audience. Ask organisers the following questions:

1. What are the basic demographics of the group: age range, gender, positional rank, social background, educational level, and so on?
2. What are the expectations of the audience? What do they expect of you and how has your presentation or speech been promoted?
3. Ask about attitudes, schools of thought or general political persuasions. A group of Labor lawyers will require a different approach from a group of CBD accountants.
4. Discover as much as you can about the group or organisation that has invited you to speak. What is its history, what are its aims and objectives and what is its main thrust at the moment?
5. Find out if there are any specific issues the group is lobbying for or has taken a position on.
6. Who are the group's patrons and senior members?

Once you have created a picture of the nature of your audience, you have an excellent starting point around which to structure the content of your presentation.

Inclusion and consensus building are vital in gaining attributions of charisma and developing followers. Followers in the workplace are people who subscribe to your vision, who will invest energy, patience, trust, emotion and dedication in you and your goals. Emotional attachment to your vision and supporting values is essential if you want people to work as a team towards the missions you establish.

Charisma and influence are the result of quid pro quos. In discovering the values and needs of your stakeholders, your part of the bargain is to do unto them as they would be done unto. You do unto 'them' by establishing congruence between their needs and aspirations and your mission, by finding ways to share high-order values, by respecting individual differences you encounter and by linking beliefs and interests with your activities and goals. Your stakeholders' response will be greater emotional and motivational arousal, higher self-esteem, more cohesion and greater confidence in you.

DIALOGUE

Successful dialogue always meets four fundamental tenets of effective communication:

1. credibility
2. emotional affiliation
3. 'live' evidence
4. common ground and shared benefits

The first issue you can choose to reflect deeply on when seeking to get people on board is that of credibility. Your own standing with individuals, groups and audiences marks the initial barrier to be overcome. Credibility is paradoxically both durable and fragile. It requires constant nurturing during the dialogue phase, particularly in the workplace. Once earned and maintained it can usually withstand the occasional expression of human frailty.

Many leaders, managers and public figures imagine they enjoy greater credibility than they actually do. They often assume that position and authority are all that's required in shifting opinion, motivating people and getting others to do what they want. As any reputable leadership tome will tell you, the 'pharaoh' era of getting results or attitude change through naked power and proclamation is long dead. And yet, the corporate world and public life are teeming with latter day Tuts and Cleos who imagine they can shape people's opinions and behaviours with a wave of their royal sceptres and threats of public executions.

Today, authority and credibility do not come with the leadership territory. The trend in Australia and most of the Western world over the last three decades is for distrust towards, and challenge of, authority. If you want people to follow your wishes in the twenty-first century, you may like to choose the leadership tools and language of today in place of the quaint relics of the past.

Credibility maintenance at close quarters, such as in the workplace or within smaller groups where contact is ongoing, is in essence no different from that of public credibility. It is earned from two principal sources.

First, if you have established a reputation of competency or knowledge in a particular field, your colleagues or listeners will generally endow you with an appropriate degree of credibility within that specialist field. You discovered in Part 1 that looking the part and mirroring sameness are also important factors in establishing credibility, but an essential element in both workplace and public credibility is continuous maintenance. Personal credibility is a quality that must be ceaselessly affirmed.

Second, if you have demonstrated over time that you can be trusted to serve mutual interests over personal interests, your personal credibility will be higher. If you're generally considered to be a person who doesn't close the door on your morality and ethics when you leave home for work, you will have a significant persuasion advantage.

Professional ability and work-based relationships are key factors in credibility in the workplace, whereas appearance and demonstrations of expertise are important to public credibility. In mapping out a workplace or public persuasion plan, the issues of professional expertise and personal relationships form a critical part of any strategy. You would be well advised to evaluate your ratings in both categories before embarking on any major persuasion undertaking.

The questions you need to answer as objectively as you can about your professional expertise are as follows:

- What are my target audience's perceptions about my knowledge and track record in the area in which I will seek to influence them?
- Is my expertise acknowledged and accepted?
- What other sources of knowledge and expertise can I reference and apply to enhance the credibility of my proposal, strategy or idea?
- Who else can I recruit to enrich the credibility of my idea or project?

For personal relationships, the questions to ask yourself are:

- Does my target audience trust me? Have I shown trustworthiness over time?
- Do those I'm seeking to persuade view me as someone who shares kudos with them?
- Do they view me as one of them and one who listens to them?
- Am I in political accord with the group on this issue?
- Am I in tune with them intellectually and emotionally?

Workplace persuasion often goes awry when inexperienced managers seek to use the force of their position to effect change without attending to the above elements. Public and work-based credibility can be monitored and managed, and it is the end result of what you are, what you say and what you do. If you desire to be a person of high credibility in the eyes of others, you can choose to have your words and deeds conform to templates of trustworthiness embraced by your target audience.

Managing trust and credibility

Some people imagine they carry credibility somewhere on their person. If that were the case you'd have most of the politicians and half of the CEOs in Australia lining up for credibility implants. Credibility isn't something you have. It's more like an honorific title bestowed on you by others. It is the end result of people placing their trust in you, and this is an important point to acknowledge and embrace. Credibility is earned when you adequately satisfy criteria for expertise and engender trust through building meaningful relationships with those you seek to persuade.

Credibility management essentially describes the relationship you establish and maintain with your audience. It is the result of the minute-to-minute management of your audience's credulity meter or the day-to-day management of honourable workplace relationships. Charismatic communicators tend to engage in continuous monitoring to ensure that the credulity of their listeners is not tested by either what they say or how they say it.

When credibility is absent, when credulity has been stretched to breaking point, your message will have about as much impact as that of a self-confessed serial burglar trying to convince a group of right-wingers that the three strikes law is unconscionable. At best you may evoke mute indifference, at worst open scorn, astonishment and, you'd better believe it, organised hostility. The following actions and behaviours enhance credibility and receptivity, both in the workplace and in public forums.

1. Begin your persuasion strategy with a passionate search for answers

Identify an issue, problem or effect and invite your listeners to help you solve it. Instead of announcing your perfect solution and imposing your map on your listeners' territory, invite your audience to join you in creating a joint map of the available solutions.

> Competition in our industry is overwhelming. Everyone is competing on price. But is a price war the answer to maintaining our market share, or can we up the ante and compete on other terms? Can we explore those other terms? Can we discover opportunities that, if exploited, would give us an edge over our competition, above and beyond that of price?

2. Demonstrate that you are putting your audience's interests first

Robert Cialdini, in his ground-breaking book *Influence*, tells the tale of a technique used by waiters in restaurants to anticipate resistance in patrons and transform it into compliance. The waiters offer patrons advice that appears to be against the restaurant's interests. For example, they may pick the most expensive dish on the entree menu and advise patrons against choosing it because it represents poor value for money.

Generally, patrons will respond to such apparent munificence by investing their trust in the waiter and relying on their advice about menus and wine lists, regardless of expense. Cialdini found that bills and tips tend to be larger at the end of the night.

No plan, idea or proposal is perfect. Your outcomes can be better, in terms of trust and credibility, if you point out the negatives and deficiencies in your proposal, rather than have your audience discover them for itself.

This new system will deliver fantastic efficiencies in the medium to long term, but it would be remiss, indeed deceitful, of me not to alert you to the short-term risks.

During the reorganisation phase there is a chance that customer satisfaction will diminish if we are not vigilant. The question is, can we live with the possibility of congestion while staff are learning new practices? The second point is that the initial investment is high and once made it is going to be very costly if, for some reason, you cancel the project. If you stay on track the savings will begin to build after year two.

3. Make your audience your primary focus

A trap that many leaders and speakers fall into is that of their 'I's being too close together. Even if credibility is high, a sure way to lose it is to come across as self-obsessed and seemingly unmindful of the audience's presence. It may pay to remember that listeners commonly interpret information through their WIIFM (What's In It For Me) filters.

Often leaders are so driven by their own ideas that they fail to acknowledge or validate the concerns and questions of those they're seeking to persuade. They dismiss or ignore the 'what if's and supplementary questions with what is often interpreted as extraordinary rudeness. Little do they realise that rail-roading is one of the most prevalent triggers of resistance in audiences.

If you want people to embrace your ideas or proposals it is better that your attention is directed almost exclusively to your audience, constantly drawing your audience into a space where you can work on and negotiate shared perceptions and meaning. Effective persuasion involves a coalition of both the persuader's and listener's views formed into one outcome.

Questions and interruptions should be treated as opportunities for dialogue. Questioners can be framed as valuable contributors to the process and not fobbed off:

That's a really incisive point and I look forward to answering it during the time we've put aside for questions.

If your address is all about you and your territory and pays scant attention to your listeners' territory, you will lose many opportunities to deliver your message direct to your audiences' hearts. Your focus, your body and your content should all reach out to your listener. The following quote epitomises the listener-friendly persuader:

I really appreciate your sharing your observations and doubts. Sceptics are a valuable commodity and I would encourage you all to become sceptical about what I say because, as everyone knows, sceptics actually try things out to discover for themselves if an idea can work for them. In trying this idea on for size you can help make it better.

4. Talk on the level of your listeners

You may experience warm, ego-driven fuzzies when you adopt a superior position to that of your listeners, but the point is that they won't. You may know more than your listeners, but your job as a communicator isn't to intimidate them with your self-importance, isn't to tell them how much you know and how little they know. If you want to be a peacock, go live in a zoo. Your role as an agent of influence is primarily to encourage your listeners to think much the same as you do on a particular issue, subject or proposal.

Use the language of inclusion. Speak on the level of your listeners and build the framework for your ideas around the goals, expectations, rewards, values and feelings of those you want to persuade.

When I first came across gap analysis, I thought it was something a proctologist did. Then I discovered, as you can, that it's an important tool you can use to better plan the kind of work you want your people to do.

There's nothing more frustrating—is there?—than wanting to meet the competition head-on and not having the skilled people to take the fight right up to them. Understanding the gap between the skills your workforce has and the skills they need gives you a very clear idea where you can best invest your training dollar and get the results you're looking for.

5. Be candid

John. F. Kennedy learned something that very few politicians ever learn, and that was that candour could be a powerfully persuasive commodity. His famous *mea culpa* after the Bay of Pigs fiasco demonstrated that admitting mistakes could minimise political damage and, in fact, increase one's popularity. Kennedy dared to do what countless politicians before and after have shown a stubborn reluctance to do, much to their ultimate cost.

Kennedy stated boldly that he was wrong and made a mistake in supporting the ill-fated Cuban invasion. His intuition was right. Admission of mistakes or wrong doing is not half as harmful as having them revealed by the media or one's political enemies. Kennedy gained greater public support after his confession because owning up had the effect of increasing his credibility.

How often have you witnessed political figures die lingering public deaths because of the insane political convention that demands defence of the indefensible? How often over the last decade and a half have public figures been sent to Coventry, not for their original offence but for covering it up and lying about it? Wriggling out of situations with attempts at distortion and deception blows your credibility out of the water.

Public figures frequently cultivate images that incorporate god-like qualities of self-possession and uncompromising virtue. This is often the first major snare they set for themselves. If you promote yourself as a reincarnation of St Peter, do expect to have some difficulty in admitting your cock-ups. In engineering your public identity, it's worth your consideration to present as an individual with a strong commitment to making life better for your constituents or colleagues rather than as a candidate for canonisation, if for no other reason than you have a shorter distance to fall.

If you make a mistake, take a leaf out of the books of a handful of impressive persuaders who have demonstrated that candour can win hearts. Former New York mayor Ed Koch masterfully avoided a media trial and execution over his decision to invest more than $300 000 in the creation of cycle lanes on Manhattan streets.

The lanes were duly constructed and, in typical New York fashion, everybody started using them: pedestrians and motorists included. General confusion about the purpose of the lanes prevailed: cars were clipping cyclists and cyclists were running down pedestrians.

The result was mayhem. This, as you can appreciate, was hardly the example of orderly and safe people movement envisaged by the planners. It was a waste of money and had the potential to seriously damage Koch's credibility as a responsible planner and manager of the city's finances.

New Yorkers were being daily reminded of the city's financial woes with vivid reports of the crisis. Any politician bold enough to squander money on what turned out to be a highly visible blunder was going to get a roasting. In the lead up to the mayoral election Koch's opponents had primed a group of journalists to turn the blowtorch to his belly during a Sunday panel show.

With a self-righteousness rarely demonstrated by anyone other than journalists and fundamentalist Baptists, the reporters on the panel launched their attack on Koch. In response to the opening broadside demanding justification of the expenditure of $300\000 on ill-planned cycle lanes when the city was in perilous financial difficulties, Koch replied: 'You're right. It was a terrible idea.' He continued, 'I thought it would work. It didn't. It was one of the worst mistakes I ever made.'

The panel of journalists was all primed up with nowhere to go. The panel had anticipated that Koch would reel off a string of justifications and excuses as most politicians are wont to do. But, in response to the rapidly weakening attack, Koch merely repeated his initial admission using other words.

The principal lessons to learn from the Kennedy and Koch examples are that pre-emptive admissions take the steam out of attacks from opponents and, second, that candour, particularly when it relates to a personal confession, can increase credibility.

6. Be sincere and say only what you believe

Decades of lies in advertising, poetic political 'truths', corporate mendacity and high levels of distrust towards the mass media have made your average punter a fairly wary individual.

According to recent social research, Australians are a fairly cynical lot. They have suffered much as consumers, as members of the polity and at the hands of those who toil in the fields of deceit and human exploitation.

The excesses of the past have made the job of ethical persuaders and speakers a difficult one, and perhaps that is as it should be. As novel as it may sound, real sincerity can now be classed, to use the parlance of professional salespeople, as a unique selling position, or USP. One of the easiest ways to reinforce your credibility at work or in the public arena is to build a reputation of sincerity.

If, for example, someone challenges you on the basis of inconsistency with a previous statement, be sincere in your response. Admit the inconsistency and turn it to your advantage.

You're right, I did say that because it was what I believed was true. I now have a different view since having learned some things along the way. So [chuckle] thanks for reminding me that I'm wiser today than I was then.

Never underestimate your audience's capacity to detect insincerity. The average person has had a lifetime's experience of being deceived and knows quite a few tricks in the book themselves. People intuit insincerity and have a feeling about you, and an impression of insincerity, once formed, is hard to shift.

Saying only what you believe to be true is a reasonably safe way of maintaining a reputation of sincerity. Think of occasions when you have been compelled to spout a party line without the support of your convictions. What were the internal sensations you experienced as you were delivering those messages? You could feel your lack of conviction, couldn't you? Be assured you transmitted it to others by the tone of your voice, your physical gestures and probably the passive language you used. In cases where you need to toe the party line it is better to state it as a fact: 'The company's policy is clear on this', 'Cabinet has decided ...', 'The decision has been taken. Now let's make it work for everyone'.

7. Make the claim fit the idea or product

Your credibility is not only based on expertise and personal status but is also tied up with the quality of your ideas and believability of your statements. Claims need to be supported, inferences and conclusions should be crafted carefully and your evidence backed up by credible research and back-grounding.

People can, and do, confuse fact with opinion, opinion with well-reasoned argument and inference with truth. You may find it extremely useful to have a clear understanding of the distinctions between facts, opinions and reasoned argument, because it may temper any tendency you may have to present opinions as evidence or make unsupportable claims.

Knowing the type of evidence you are dealing with enables you to build better argument. Understanding the differences could also rescue you from potentially damaging cross-examination. It also places you at a very distinct advantage when dealing with the argument of your competitors and opponents, because it allows you to more easily discover and point out the flaws and thinking errors in their argument.

Facts, reasoned arguments and opinions can be distinguished according to the type of question that elicits them:

■ Facts and truths: questions with only one valid answer in a given context (statistics, data, research, verifiable reports, universal measurements, and so on)

■ Reasoned argument: questions with better or worse inferences, conclusions and answers, depending on the strength, logic and relevance of the response (argument based on drawing legitimate inferences from hard data; the use of logic, precedent, knowledge and conventions to build a specific and sustainable case)

■ Opinion: questions inviting expression of personal preferences, assumptions, beliefs and values (comments that involve subjective assessment and make a statement about the person uttering them)

Many speakers fail in the persuasion process because they confuse the above categories. Remember that just because you believe something is true doesn't necessarily make it so. To support a point, idea or hypothesis you have to do much more than articulate what you think is true. You have to build your argument on solid foundations of fact, reason and emotion.

The claims you make should never stretch the credulity of your audience. A useful rule of thumb is to *match your claims with what you know your listeners will believe.* You may well be of the opinion that your idea is the best thing since the silicon chip, but if you don't have the evidence to support the assertion you would be well advised to consider tempering your claims to what you know will be accepted by those listening.

There are two ways in which to present opinions that increase the probability of them being accepted by your listeners:

1. If you have occasion to state an opinion, use non-declarative language such as 'It's my belief', 'I have found', 'It seems to me', 'I feel', and so on. For example: 'I feel the movie had too much unnecessary violence in it.' This signals that you are offering an opinion as an opinion and not stating it as a fact. However, there is still a risk that people will oppose what you say and derail your argument or discount your credibility.

2. The following technique substantially increases the likelihood of your opinion being accepted by your audience. Break the active language rule and strategically use passive language that displaces you from the ownership of the opinion. For example: 'Some people would argue that the movie contained too much violence.' To add power to your opinion draw your listener into shared space. Continue the statement with something like the following; 'And when you think about it you may find yourself agreeing that they are right. Take the beach scene. Was all the graphic footage necessary to make the point? You may think it wasn't.'

8. Maintain your integrity at all costs

If someone says to you, 'I shouldn't be telling you this, but did you know that ...', what message are they sending you? Sure, they may be sending you a signal that they trust you, but are they not also sending you a signal that they can't be trusted, that they can't keep a secret?

The same logic applies when you tell other people that you bend the truth to suit some occasions. One of the easiest ways to create distrust and suspicion in an audience is to suggest that lying to a third party or parties is an acceptable practice. Of course you wouldn't lie to the audience! But, the punters out there, that's a different story!

The fact is that if you encourage people to act dishonestly or suggest there are times when embroidery of the truth is an acceptable practice, your audience will begin to seriously discount your credibility.

9. Keep your promises and commitments

A major credibility annihilator is that of welching on a promise or overlooking a commitment you have made to colleagues, clients or groups. Charismatic leaders recognise that people often build their hopes around promises, and if a promise is broken, hopes are dashed: the next promise that's made won't be believed.

Promises often raise high expectations, particularly when made about career, livelihood, performance of products, and results and outcomes. If you don't come through on a major promise or commitment, the damage to your credibility will remain as long as there are people around to remember it.

There are occasions when promises can't be kept for all sorts of legitimate reasons. One of the few credible ways to break a promise is to go to the individual or group you made the commitment to, preferably before you are expected to deliver, and ask to be released from it. You will need to give plausible reasons and evidence to support your inability to keep your promise, together with an appropriate apology.

Research shows that charismatic communicators rarely break the promises and commitments they make. They're reported to place high value on promises and do not make them lightly. One of the reasons for this may be that experience has taught them that keeping promises builds strong bonds of trust between them and their followers. When trust is plentiful, you can promise results and people will act on your advice.

10. Earn the right to be heard

You learned earlier that expertise is a significant variable in the credibility equation. If anyone questions your right to speak on a subject, take careful notice. Don't dismiss it with an indignant 'humph' or an acidic comeback line.

Open questioning of your credibility is a valuable form of feedback and gives you an opportunity to turn resistance into acceptance. Note how the following speakers seize the opportunity to build on their credibility when it's questioned:

I support you 100 per cent in questioning my right to stand here. You've reminded me that I've been remiss in not explaining adequately my background knowledge and experience. The points I've been making here are drawn from comprehensive research I conducted over two years as Head of Research at the Centre for Asian Studies.

You're absolutely right in suggesting that I have to earn the right to be taken notice of. I strongly believe that it's important to question the credentials of people as you do, because it enables us to give proper weight to what people say, doesn't it? The proposal before you today is based on a highly successful model designed by experts at Flinders University and tested by GMH for three years.

There are numerous ways to enhance your expertise in public life and in the workplace. Gaining qualifications, writing articles, papers and books, nominating for awards, garnering the support of luminaries in your chosen field and achieving media exposure for particular endeavours are but a few means of building on your expertise-based credibility.

Developing a history of sound judgment in your area of endeavour, proving yourself to be knowledgeable and well informed on your subject matter, demonstrating a thorough understanding of your material and building a solid track record of success can also enhance perceptions of expertise.

13 THE LOST ART OF LISTENING

From listening comes wisdom; from speaking should come repentance.
Italian proverb

Sylvia has earned a handsome reputation for entering rooms voice first. People report that she talks exclusively for the experience of being fascinated to hear what she's going to say next. She seems to listen to others only as long as it takes for her to seize on a verbal cue, and then she's off like a runaway road-train. If, for example, you voiced profound grief over the passing of a dearly loved pet, your sorrow would pass over Sylvia unheeded. She wouldn't, for a nanosecond, fuss with hollow sympathy or feign a gloomy countenance, as would some uninterested listeners. Rather, she'd pounce on your statement as a cue to assail you with an entire repertoire of stories on pet loss, probably rounding off the assault with sweeping views on cat curfews, endangered Chinese pandas or worse.

On one occasion, a long-standing colleague invited her to lunch. They duly arrived at the chosen restaurant, took a table and began to contemplate the menu. The ordering process took some time to complete, prolonged by a monologue Sylvia needed to finish before she could possibly turn her attention to the selection of food. Several speeches after the order was taken, sermons in which her powers of free association were unleashed with the intensity of a full-scale military adventure, the meal arrived. She continued to address her colleague before, during and after mouthfuls.

Sylvia's verbal offensive started to take its toll on her luncheon guest who was overtaken by sudden and extreme fatigue. He may well have been unconsciously toying with suicide as a form of self-defence because, at a moment when his mouth was filled with food, his body signalled and acted on an urgent need of oxygen. A deep intake of breath ensued, powerful enough to draw and lodge a piece of food in his throat. The food cut off his air supply and his colour changed quickly to several unattractive hues of purple.

During his entire near-death experience, which included the customary sound effects associated with asphyxiation, gesticulations of distress and facial contortions of theatrical immensity, Sylvia continued with the enthusiastic telling of her story, oblivious to the changes in her colleague's demeanour. Diners at a nearby table noticed and stared incredulously. At the point when her colleague's life appeared to be hanging by a thread, he staggered from his chair, clutching his throat. Sylvia stopped mid-sentence. Taken aback, she looked at the pathetic figure doing what appeared to be a bizarre and provocative ritual and demanded to know 'What's going on?'. Fortunately, a waiter also saw him stagger out of his chair, rushed to his assistance, administered a lateral chest-thrust to dislodge the food and saved him from a fate only slightly worse than lunch with Sylvia. In recounting this brush with death, the victim has so far resisted all whimsical suggestions to file a complaint of attempted murder at his local police station, although it's believed Sylvia has now been removed from his Christmas card list.

To many, this is a funny story, told at the expense of the two principal characters in the drama. They may choose to overlook the deeper import of the tale, sympathise with the victim and ridicule the perpetrator. One point that stands out, however, is that Sylvia saw but didn't see, and heard but didn't hear. The images of a colleague in distress appeared in her peripheral vision and struck her retinas. The pitiful, albeit muffled sounds of asphyxiation reached her cochleae, but somewhere along the line the right neural connections weren't made and the event never entered her conscious awareness.

While the story may illustrate an extreme pattern of narcissistic behaviour, you probably find yourself thinking, 'I know people like that'. And well you may, if you know yourself well. At times, we can all become absent listeners, and manifest egoistic or narcissistic behaviours, particularly in domains of personal or social significance. The absent listener is one of four fundamental categories along a continuum of attentiveness, as shown in the following diagram.

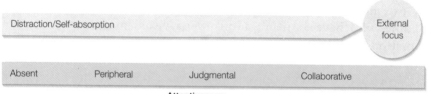

ABSENT LISTENING

Absent listeners are inside their own heads most of the time during their so-called listening experiences. This contrasts with collaborative listeners who place much of their focus externally on the speaker, using any remaining mental processing power to carefully construct a map of what the speaker is saying.

On her luncheon date Sylvia's behaviour was quite an extreme example of absent listening. Absent listeners commonly hear, but don't hear, and experience a kind of sensory numbness where other people are concerned. Common indicators of absent listening are the blank stare, little or no eye contact with jerky pretences of attention, signs of impatience, frequent interruption, the use of conversational cues to refocus attention on themselves and a propensity to free associate during what are often long speeches.

Absent listeners rarely have many long-term friends. They wear people down and are generally viewed as self-obsessed, unsympathetic and unwilling to enter other people's reality. They trigger absent listening in others, which in its deliciously ironical way is a just reward for their unwillingness to attend to the ideas and opinions of those around them. We can all lapse into absent listening on occasions, but with some it becomes habitual behaviour.

PERIPHERAL LISTENING

Peripheral listening is a dangerous habit because of the potential to mishear and misconstrue what people say. Peripheral listeners lend half an ear to a conversation while listening to their inner voice constructing and rehearsing responses and come-backs. Peripheral listeners often appear distracted and frequently misread the reactions of others. Spending too much time attending to what's in their own heads prevents them from hearing and accurately observing the words and actions of others.

Peripheral listeners regularly don't get the gist or underlying concept of what is being said. External distractions also draw them away from their primary listening task. While they lend half an ear to a conversation, the remainder of their listening capacity is easily diverted by extraneous noise and movement. This is particularly the case with people who have a strong auditory or visual preference. Internal sensations have the same effect on people who pay a great deal of attention to their feelings. They may find themselves submerged in a pool of their own emotions rather than seeking to understand the emotions of the speaker.

Peripheral listeners are the source of much frustration, because they pick up on surface content and react inappropriately, often taking offence, responding to points that weren't made and changing the topic at crucial points in conversations. They make very poor communicators and leaders because they rarely 'click' into subtlety and the thoughts and feelings of people around them.

JUDGMENTAL LISTENING

People on the other end of a conversation with judgmental listeners often describe the experience as incomplete, lacking in sentiment or unsympathetic. A common complaint is that the judgmental listener fails to understand the sum and substance of what is said. You can probably recall the extreme vexation of putting a case or important point to someone only to hear your words twisted and your points coming back to you tainted by poisoned or dispassionate reasoning.

Judgmental listeners tend to devote their heads to conversations, but rarely their hearts. They focus on literal interpretations of words rather than the underlying messages, or meta-language, contained in the words, and they seize on real or imagined holes in a speaker's logic. They lend their ears to the conversation, but rarely attend to physiognomy or body language. Concentrating only on the literal meaning of words leaves them plenty of brain capacity to pigeonhole those who are speaking, to think of contrary and challenging statements, to assess language and speech idiosyncrasies, and to wonder silently about what they're going to do on the weekend. At best, people leave the conversation heard but not truly understood.

Judgmental listeners may find themselves in conflict with other people because of their capacity to trigger increases or dramatic decreases in the emotional temperature of conversations. People often feel as though they are being badgered or harassed and may respond by getting upset or shutting down.

COLLABORATIVE LISTENING

Collaborative listening is elementary and not particularly easy. It's a simple manifestation of a deep commitment to understand as fully as possible another person's point of view. It involves putting aside one's own views for a time and jointly creating a map of the speaker's underlying message and feelings. Charismatic communicators to a person display the fundamental tenets of collaborative listening, creating deep rapport and lasting impressions of good listening.

Collaborative listening demands that you get out there, using your eyes and ears productively to gain understanding. By focusing externally, as opposed to focusing internally on their own feelings and thoughts, collaborative listeners are highly valued for their listening skills. They use elegant questions to free up the conversation, they get in synch with the speaker and provide appropriate verbal and non-verbal feedback. The speaker 'senses' the listener is fully attending to them, and this sends a powerful psychological signal to the speaker. People feel heard, know they're really being listened to, vest faith and trust in the listener and, significantly, are more likely to listen and act on what you say.

Collaborative listening is a frame of mind, an attitude that will inspire you to learn and evolve behaviours that elicit high-value information in secure, unthreatening milieus. It begins with you recognising that collaborative listening is a composite of high attention, or focus, on a speaker; thoughtful questioning; a rigorous approach to mental processing; and elegant feedback. In the rest of this chapter you will build the key elements of collaborative listening into a listening strategy.

Collaborative questioning

'Thou shall inquire, make search, and ask diligently' (Deuteronomy 13: 13–15) provides an ideal definition of how a collaborative listener goes about the process of gathering information from a speaker. Collaborative listeners avoid 'overloading' their questions with presuppositions, mind reads, inappropriate argument, challenges and premature judgments. Let's analyse the above quote to get to the core of what collaborative listening, and indeed questioning, means.

'THOU SHALL INQUIRE'

This can simply mean to examine or question. Sounds easy, doesn't it? But many people find it extremely difficult to examine without prejudice. They yield to powerful inner urges to filter information through their own personal maps of the world. Collaborative questioners, however, attempt to establish as neutral a questioning and mental processing environment as is possible in the context and circumstances. They choose not to contrast their world view with that of the speaker, suspending belief in what they think they know and their beliefs about the person they're listening to, so as to 'unpack', or reveal, the so-called reality of their subject's assumptions, judgments and conclusions.

'MAKE SEARCH'

This means look for clues. Think of a crime scene context. When competent investigators search a crime scene, they search for patterns, details and trails of evidence. They keep a keen eye out for anything, no matter how small, that may not belong to the natural environment of the crime scene. They make few judgments on what they uncover at the scene, but catalogue their discoveries for further analysis. Skilled investigators will resist the temptation to leap prematurely to conclusions. They will endeavour to treat information and clues impartially, as fragments of a bigger and yet unknown picture. This contrasts with those who fit the fragments into a picture they already have in mind.

'ASK DILIGENTLY'

This is asking and not 'telling'. Any question will guide a speaker towards a particular spectrum of answers. For example, asking a person a simple question such as 'What food do you eat?' directs the person towards a general domain of inquiry and legitimately presupposes the person makes distinctions and choices in food. However, the question 'What meat do you like best?' assumes the person likes meat. It presupposes the person eats meat, has likes over dislikes and makes distinctions and choices in a particular category of food. The second question narrows the answer spectrum and 'tells' the subject something. It makes assumptions that may not be valid and loads the question with the paraphernalia of the listener/questioner's prejudices. A collaborative listener asks 'purer' questions that help the speaker clarify their views, feelings, beliefs, values and positions.

Questions can take the chill off the frostiest of communication environments. If constructed appropriately, they can create an atmosphere of warmth and comfort, essential prerequisites for fostering trust and harmony. Questions can also ignite distrust and disfavour if they are posed in a threatening or accusative manner. Collaborative questions, on the other hand:

- drive and clarify thinking;
- empower both the questioner and the questioned;
- help open up options for the person being questioned;
- help diffuse conflict;
- help take the sting out of criticism;
- demonstrate a real and genuine interest in the individual being questioned.

Many individuals adopt absent or peripheral listening stances because of competitive, egotistical and control issues. They need to be in the limelight, they need to browbeat or dazzle their listeners with their eloquence, and they need to control conversations because of mistaken notions about power and status. They fail to understand that power resides in those who ask questions, not in those who answer them. The asking of a question directs a conversation along the path of the question, controls it so to speak, and it's indeed a mystery why more of those who terrorise others with their eloquence haven't concluded that real terror can only be struck with questions.

Conversely, real rapport, understanding and mutuality can also be unleashed by carefully chosen questions. Let's play twenty questions to illustrate the difference between conversational terrorism and collaborative questions that engage the listener and speaker in a mutual search for understanding. Review the following list and note the ones that you consider would open up a collaborative conversation.

1. How can you say that?
2. I'm really interested in hearing the reasons behind what you said. How did you come to those conclusions?
3. Why are you always trying to defend yourself?
4. What do I need to know to expand my understanding of your role in this situation?
5. Have you considered the consequences?
6. What are the likely reactions to your decision?
7. Don't you think you should approach it this way?
8. What approaches do you find available to you?
9. Are you going to follow process A or B?
10. Which process will deliver the results that you want to achieve?
11. Will that not increase the pressure you already have on your budget?
12. How are you tracking on your budget?
13. Why must you do it that way?
14. How did you make the choice of using this method?
15. Why are you leaving work early every day?
16. What are your feelings about working with the company at the moment?
17. Can't you organise your staff so there isn't a blow-out in overtime?
18. Can you tell me your ideas about staffing and overtime?
19. Doesn't that fall low on our list of priorities?
20. Why is it important for us to consider this option above others?

You've probably concluded that the questions come in pairs and that the odd numbers represent questions that evoke varying degrees of terror, whereas the even numbers represent collaborative questions. Notice the true diligence in the even-numbered questions. Notice how they open up a conversation and give speakers the opportunity to draw from their own experiences to answer them, as opposed to answering them within parameters you have set.

The odd-numbered questions are 'telling' in as much as they either instruct people how to answer the question, nominate the type of answer you're looking for or contain an accusation of some kind. Putting someone on the defensive is hardly the stuff of open communication, is it? Questions tell a listener a lot about you. Questions loaded with assumptions and judgments, such as the odd numbers, not only draw a flow of information from the person questioned, but *transmit* a flow of information to the person on the other end of the question. A questioner, in many instances, can be the most serious impediment to conversational harmony and the recovery of accurate, high value information.

What kind of message do you think a listener transmits, for example, when using stock questions such as:

'Don't you think you worry too much?'
'It'll be fine, can't you see that?'
'Aren't you getting a bit too upset over this?'
'You're overreacting, don't you think?'
'Can't you just ignore him?'

Judgmental questions such as these invalidate a speaker's thoughts and feelings about the topic under discussion. The point is they do worry, they can't ignore it, and the level of emotion expressed will be in proportion to the degree of concern they have about the issue. Questions such as these will raise the emotional level of the conversation as it dawns on the speaker that you are reading your map on their territory.

Another common form of conversational terrorism that essentially teaches people how to be weak and dependent is the practice of offering advice and solutions at inappropriate times. This style of neurotic intervention robs speakers of their potential power and sets up master– serf or guru–novice relationships. It is a favoured practice of 'rescuers', and while they may gain some psychic jollies from the encounter, it can help set up unhealthily dependent relationships. A collaborative listener uses questions to guide speakers so that they find their own solutions when the moment is right. They use questions such as:

'If you were to know, how would this best sort itself out?'
'What are some things you can do to make the situation different?'
'Ideally, what would you like to happen?'
'Let's imagine you've solved the problem and look back at what it might have taken to reach a solution. What things would stand out?'

'What may be some of the things you need so that you feel in control of the situation?'

'How would you like to see this change?'

Often people are not looking for solutions, they simply want to be listened to and, more importantly, listen to themselves talking out their quandaries. As a general rule, it is better not to give advice or provide solutions until a speaker specifically asks for them.

There is a very simple formula you can adopt to generate questions with a low terror quotient and high degrees of quality and depth. This formula will deliver more useful information and greater rapport, and also a few surprises: ideas, background, motives and maybe ways of looking at issues that you've never thought of before. A visual representation of the formula appears in the following diagram.

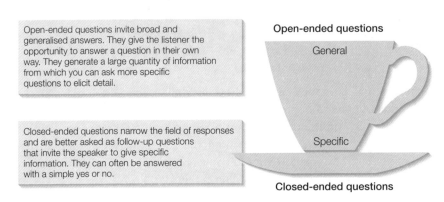

Open-ended questions invite broad and generalised answers. They give the listener the opportunity to answer a question in their own way. They generate a large quantity of information from which you can ask more specific questions to elicit detail.

Closed-ended questions narrow the field of responses and are better asked as follow-up questions that invite the speaker to give specific information. They can often be answered with a simple yes or no.

Open-ended questions

General

Specific

Closed-ended questions

The representation of a cup on the right metaphorically describes the volume of information that each class of question produces. With open-ended questions your cup may well floweth over with information, but with closed-ended questions you can reduce it down to a few drops of important information about a specific topic. When your cup is full of information, you have numerous choices available to you, from which you can choose the topic most appropriate to the circumstances of the conversation. You can then begin to reduce it down into relevant specifics until you have a clear understanding of the subject matter.

Open-ended questions are extremely useful in setting people at ease and creating conversational harmony. Collaborative listeners use them both as a means of getting in synch and getting to the bottom of what a speaker is saying. Please review the following example of a chance encounter and notice how the questions send a signal of genuine interest, keep the conversation going and don't scare the speaker off. Pay attention to the volume of information elicited, and try to work out whether an open-ended or closed-ended question is being asked.

F: Hi, I'm Felicity, and like you I'm one of the orphans in this bar. And how do you make ends meet?

G: Hi. Graham. I'm a barrister.

F: That sounds interesting. Tell me about the areas of law you practise in.

G: Well, mainly company law for the money, but sometimes I take on a criminal case that I'm really interested in.

F: Hmm, criminal case. And what does it take to arouse your interest?

G: You know, I often ask myself that. The case, I guess, has to have something really challenging about it, and then I have to feel that the defendant is the underdog, and is somehow a victim of circumstances. I also have to believe that mounting a good defence will somehow make a real difference.

F: Ah-uh. How do you know if the case will be challenging?

[and so on]

In this example Felicity transforms the general response 'I'm a barrister' into a conversation in which Graham feels comfortable enough to reveal his detailed reasons for taking on criminal cases. You will notice that none of Felicity's questions contain any information about Felicity or her views. The questions are focused solely on Graham, placing him at the very centre of Felicity's attention.

Felicity followed the three cardinal rules of collaborative questioning:

1. Start a conversation with an open-ended question and continue with open-ended questions until you can safety boil down to particular droplets of detail.
2. Keep the questions pure and free from contamination by your view of the world.
3. Formulate your questions from the responses you elicit.

In placing Graham at the centre of her attention, Felicity sends a strong signal to him that what he has to say is important and counts in her estimation. Felicity would have known that it was only a matter of time before Graham began to show interest in her and asked her questions. Collaborative questions have the power to particularly jolt peripheral and judgmental listeners out of unproductive listening modes.

The cardinal rules of collaborative questioning translate into the following model.

1. OPEN-ENDED QUESTIONS

These allow you to gain an extended take on an issue and are more likely to encourage the speaker to volunteer information. The open-ended questions you can use most frequently start with the words:

what	how	tell me about
can you explain	can you tell me	
why (as in why is that important to you)		

2. CLOSED-ENDED QUESTIONS (1)

These allow you to clear up any misunderstandings and are most effective when you need to elicit specific information. The questions you can use to drill down into specifics start with the words:

when	what	where	how	who
specifically (can be added at times to elicit detail)				

3. CLOSED-ENDED QUESTIONS (2)

These severely limit the available responses and may narrow the conversation down to yes/no answers or challenge the other person. The following words signify extremely tight questions and are best used when you want to clarify or feed back points to the other person:

do is	did	were	so		
have	was	would	are	but	could

4. 'TELLING QUESTIONS'

The following question types are 'telling' questions. You may choose to rarely, if ever, ask questions that start with words like:

doesn't	isn't	surely	don't	aren't
can't	why (accusative)	won't	wouldn't

5. OTHER QUESTIONS

Other question types you may choose to avoid are:

- double, or multi barrelled (the other person may only answer the easiest question)
- overloaded or long (the other person may get confused)
- leading questions (rapport may be broken and the other person may clam up)
- statements dressed up as questions (the other person may disagree and view your questions as a challenge)
- assumptions containing biased words (the other person may sense you are railroading or disagree with the premise of your question)
- free-ranging or all over the place (the other person may become confused or think you're not really listening)

- either/or questions (the other person may sense you are entrapping them in a double bind)

Gaining an accurate picture of a speaker's point or story is important if you want your resulting actions to reflect a real rather than imagined scenario. Peripheral and judgmental listeners often assume they know what a speaker means and expose themselves to serious consequences. Three major areas where assumptions can lead you on a wild goose chase are simple deletions, comparative deletions, and what can be termed 'nouning'. Here are the types of question you can use to help the speaker determine the essence of the issue. Please exercise care and ask these questions after you have heard the speaker out.

Simple deletions
Simple deletions are when a person leaves out specifics and you assume they mean the same thing as you.

A: He is out of control.

B: You were saying that he was out of control. Can you tell me how was he out of control?

A: I felt quite uncomfortable.

B: What specifically were you uncomfortable about?

Comparative deletions
Comparative deletions are when a comparison has been made but you accept it without understanding what is being compared.

A: New Omo washes brighter.

B: Brighter compared with what?

A: I want to create a better working environment for all our employees.

B: Better compared with what?

Nouning
Some speakers have developed unconscious ways of avoiding responsibility or conveying a belief that there is a lack of choice. For want of a more scientific description, let's use the term 'nouning' to describe what they do.

Think of it this way. A verb describes 'doing' something: an action or a process. A noun, on the other hand, describes 'things': objects. When people feel they have no choice or are at some level escaping responsibility for the things they're involved in, they often reflect that by *turning verbs into nouns.*

To neutralise the process and gather important information, turn the noun back into a verb in a non-threatening question, as shown in the following examples.

A: I need lot of *assistance* in getting my staff to adopt this initiative.
B: Who should *assist* in what way?

A: We've always had a tenuous *relationship.*
B: In what way do you go about *relating* to each other to produce that result?

A: *Life* wasn't meant to be easy.
B: *Living* how? *Living* where? *Living* with whom?

A: Their *perceptions* are so far off the mark as to be ridiculous.
B: How does their way of *perceiving* lead you to that conclusion?

A: The *decision* on whether we dissolve this company is up to Martin and Gloria.
B: How specifically are you going to leave the job of *deciding* up to them?

Collaborative listeners do make the mistake of assuming things but, over time, they begin to become sensitive to their own assumptions and those of others. They know that assumptions need to be gently unravelled to improve the quality of information they elicit.

Collaborative information processing

People speak at an average of around 140 words a minute, whereas the human brain has the capacity to think and listen from three to four times that rate. Judgmental listeners use the time differential unproductively as you've learned. Conversely, collaborative listeners use the time lag to gather information into patterns as they hear it, to review or paraphrase in their mind what the speaker has said, to arrange information into key categories or priorities, and to listen for underlying values.

Collaborative listeners know the differences between fact, opinion and reasoned judgment and they listen for uniformity in the speaker's ideas, noting when inconsistencies occur. Collaborative listeners never hoist speakers on their own petards, preferring to gently scrutinise any reasons for inconsistency or incongruity. In developing a collaborative listening mindset, collaborative listeners listen for specific things.

- Listen for values as represented by key words. Values words are emotional hot buttons and collaborative listeners keep a keen ear out for them. Revisit Chapters 2 and 3 for techniques to elicit values.
- Make an internal or written mind map of the ideas you hear. Sort for major points and issues, hierarchies and key explanations or reasons offered by speakers for their position or opinion. Feed it back to them on occasions to clarify.
- Listen for important metaphors and note them mentally or on paper. They may be crucial in understanding where the speaker is coming from.
- Ask yourself what the speaker really means. Try out your judgment by asking, 'Is this what you mean?'.
- Listen for two-value logic to give yourself a sense of the speaker's commitment to their message, such as right/wrong, for/against, benefits/disadvantages, true/false, good/bad and positive/negative.

Emotional meteorology

Collaborative listeners read people's emotional states and pay homage to them. They realise that it pays to make sure that people are in the right mood to receive a message by taking their emotional temperatures first. The following example shows the importance of forecasting emotional climatic conditions before communicating major messages.

The chief executive of a brokerage company routinely delivered a Christmas address in which he reviewed the successes of the year, handed out awards, announced a bonus and gave a pitch on the goals and challenges of the coming year. Traditionally, his speech was one of appreciation for the contribution staff had made to the continued growth and success of the company. The 1999–2000 year was a bumper year for his company, and both the executive management group and other staff members reasonably expected that the compliments and bonuses would be generous.

The chief executive rose to speak. The first words he uttered were 'I hate to tell you this but there's no bonus this year'. He went on to explain that 'Now is no time for us to engage in self-congratulations because this company is on the brink of disaster'. He outlined ominous changes in the marketplace where new competitive practices would threaten the company's future viability. He said the company's revenue streams, namely brokerage fees from share transactions, commissions from managed trusts and fees from other placements, were under attack. He pointed to online organisations that were offering to refund up to 100 per cent of the entry fees and a discount war that had erupted on share transactions. He concluded that the year 2000 would be a watershed year for the company and effort would have to be doubled to maintain market share.

The mood of the Christmas party changed from one of goodwill to all men and women (including the CEO) to that of silent outrage and disgust. This stunningly courageous albeit dim-witted chief executive destroyed in minutes what had taken years to build up. He broke implied promises, dismissed the rightful expectations of his staff and hit them between the eyes with the fact that his speech was very much all about how he was feeling and not about how they were feeling. He mismatched utterly the mood of his audience and paid a heavy price.

After a bumper year, you may expect that he would give due praise. On the contrary, he implicitly accused his staff of letting competition creep up on them, taking no personal responsibility for the state of affairs he outlined. He grossly overstated his case, and the speech can be seen as a statement all about him and what he thought.

After the Christmas break, staff and managers congregated in small groups and commiserated over the lousy Christmas they had had. In the ensuing six months the company lost a number of key personnel, staff morale was conspicuously lower and the CEO's prophesy of doom manifested itself in a drop in business and falling revenue. Failure to read and understand collective emotions can exact a high price indeed.

Had our valiant CEO taken the time to test the emotional waters with key staff, he would have discovered a prevailing pride and satisfaction in the results achieved over the calendar year. He would have recognised the need to acknowledge the significant efforts made to exceed revenue and sales targets. He may have chosen to celebrate the accomplishments of his teams and reward those responsible. Instead, he delivered a mighty slap in the face to loyal and hardworking staff.

Only after having completed his vote of thanks should he have raised the prospect of impending commercial threats. He would have been well advised to set a date early in January for strategic development meetings and permitted his staff to enjoy their Christmases, returning after the festive season with renewed energy for the challenges ahead.

The most effective communicators select influential and savvy colleagues and get an emotional reading from them prior to engaging in processes of persuasion. They forecast how various ideas and proposals might impact emotionally on staff. This practice enables them to acknowledge, and mirror in their proposals, the emotional state and expectations of those they are seeking to persuade.

Collaborative looking

Collaborative listeners look, not stare, at those they're listening to, averting their gaze at appropriate moments to prevent any suggestion of intimidation, to take the occasional note and to react to what the speaker has said. They look for congruity between the speaker's tones, facial expressions, body language and words, intuiting any lack of harmony between content and the way it is expressed.

Judgmental listeners usually listen only for content and the logic of what speakers say, whereas collaborative listeners open up their eyes and ears to take in the total multimedia experience of listening. A lack of harmony between the content of the message and the way it's expressed registers and is processed unconsciously. You will usually receive an internal signal if content and expression are not in harmony: a hunch, a feeling, a sense that something is amiss. Take note of these feelings when you have them and backtrack by asking the speaker to give it to you again, carefully noting and gently exploring any disharmony.

There are many publications that deal in detail with non-verbal communication, or body language. Borrow one from your local library, avoiding the more simplistic publications in favour of those that can offer you a reasonable depth of understanding. We'll take a short-cut by exploring one technique that is guaranteed to give you a sense of the importance of the non-verbal component of listening. It's called micro-muscle mirroring and it takes a little practice before you are able to gain an inner sense of what's happening in a speaker's body.

- Notice the angle of the speaker's spine, whether it is to the left, right or vertically positioned. Position your spine exactly in synch with the speaker. Notice how it feels.

- Slowly begin to arrange the rest of your body as a mirror image of the speaker's. Don't ape, do it subtly with an easy flow to your movements. Notice the feelings you have.

- Observe and hear the speaker. If they make a gesture, do a micro-imitation of it by imagining you're making the gesture and letting it proceed only to the point of feeling your muscles getting ready to imitate it. Do not do the gesture, just feel your body get in readiness for it. Sense the feeling associated with the gesture and notice what thoughts you have. Your speaker may notice your micro-movements at the unconscious level and may feel a sense of rapport with you.

- Tune into the speaker's voice and at times, particularly when the tone gets louder, raises in pitch or becomes passionate, do a silent micro-imitation of it without giving voice to it and sense the emotions you have. Listen to any attendant thoughts.

The micro-muscle mirroring technique should be practised in unimportant situations. After about fifteen separate practice sessions you will probably have integrated this skill into your everyday listening behaviour. You will notice how you gain a powerful sense of where a person is really coming from, because emotions are expressed through the voice and body and generally resist attempts by their host to mask them.

Collaborative direction

There are times in listening mode when you need to direct the conversation along a particular path, otherwise much time can be wasted in free-ranging conversations that don't lead to a conclusion. Use the following pointers to move the conversation on, only when you sense that the speaker has explained their underpinning meaning.

To cut through the detail

Some speakers insist on regaling you with minute detail. The worst thing you can do is stop them midway and ask a different question. They will most likely start at the beginning again and go over old ground until they reach the point where they were interrupted. A better way to interrupt is to propel them to the end of their story by asking questions like:

'And where did this all end up?'
'What happened at the end?'
'And what did you feel about all of this afterwards?'

To keep to the topic

If you're confronted with a free-range speaker who takes you for a guided tour of the entire barnyard, use the following types of question to keep them on topic:

'Hang on, you were making a really interesting point. I want to hear all of it.'
'Let's deal with that later, so can you tell me what happened next.'
'Hey, I'm a bit slow. I still haven't got the gist of your last point and I need to ask you about it.'

To get specific answers

If you're looking for specific answers about issues and events or need to close a conversational loop, try the following questions:

'In closing for now, can you tell me what we both can do right away to address your concerns?'

'If we can go back to the second point you made, what do you envisage is the answer to the problem?'

'Before we go on, can we come to an understanding on your roster?'

'Can we get some closure on your first point?'

Collaborative feedback

Whether it's a smile at an amusing anecdote, a simple nod of the head to signal that you're following what is said or a verbal response signifying agreement, you are communicating information to a speaker. Feedback can be divided into two broad categories— verbal and non-verbal— and it achieves several important objectives in listening and information gathering. First, it is a means of signalling to speakers that you are listening intently to what they say. Second, feedback helps you clarify any doubts you may have and to straighten out any words or phrases that have double meanings. Third, feedback is an important device to ensure you understand what a speaker feels about a particular topic.

Feedback questions are essentially designed to clarify, inform the speaker that you've been listening attentively or discover underlying feelings. Some distinct question types used to deliver particular outcomes follow.

Feedback test

These are the question types when you determine that you need to let the speaker know that you understand the detail or gist of the content.

I'm hearing that you would rather go for the second option but with these two modifications ... Is that an accurate reading?

As I interpret it, you're saying the issue revolves around the board looking for the right reasons to sign off on the project. Am I hearing you right?

Precision audit

When you need to clarify or check your understanding of what is said, need further information in order to understand, need to uncover underlying assumptions or to explore the content further, rephrase the content as spoken and pose a question to confirm your understanding.

What I believe you're saying is ... Am I on track?

Can you give me a couple of examples of what you mean to help me understand?

Can I assume that Jack said he wouldn't cooperate?

Use what, how, when, where, who questions, asked in a curious tone.

Feelings check

When you sense that an acknowledgment of feelings will cool the emotional temperature, when you want to signal that you understand how the speaker feels or to demonstrate that you have been paying close attention, use these types of questions.

You feel upset that they didn't listen to you?

The team feels it's unfair to be asked to meet that deadline?

I sense that you're really looking forward to the awards?

It feels as though you were happy enough to travel interstate until they decided that everyone had to travel on their own time. Is that right?

When you want to take the emotional temperature of the speaker, notice that they're telling you what they think but not what they feel or you need to get a handle on the speaker's motives, beliefs or attitudes, try open-ended questions such as the following:

What are your feelings on that?

What did that make you feel?

When that happened, what was your gut reaction?

How do you feel about transferring to Operations?

You ignore the emotional aspect of a conversation at your peril. You learned earlier that checking and forecasting the emotional temperature of an individual or group is essential in change communication. If you want to effect rapid change or action you need to know how strongly, or indeed weakly, people feel about the subject at hand.

The strongest resistance is always informed by a clash of values, beliefs or attitudes. Strong resistance is often revealed by the expression of emotion. People use feeling words to express the level of emotion they experience in situations. Words such as the ones in italics in these sentences:

Politicians don't *care* about the voters.
I'm *sick* of all the changes around here.
The communication plan for this project is *laughable*!
If I get one more complaint I'll *explode*.

If you ignore statements like these and move the conversation on, strike a mark against yourself as a collaborative listener because the statements cry out for feedback. An effective way to give feedback is as follows:

1. Pick up on the emotion and internally describe it.
2. Link the emotion to the content and put it into your own words.
3. Ask clarifying questions.

So, taking a couple of the preceding examples, your feedback sets would sound something like this:

A: Politicians don't care about the voters.
B: You're feeling ignored by our politicians?
A: You bet I am!
B: What would they have to do for you to feel included?

A: The communication plan for this project is laughable!
B: You're really concerned about the communication plan?
A: I'm staggered by its ineptitude.
B: How specifically would it need to change so you felt comfortable with it?

Non-verbal responses are the final element of collaborative feedback. If you have chosen to use the micro-muscle mirroring techniques mentioned above, you wouldn't be able to stop yourself from delivering congruent non-verbal feedback. Micro-muscle mirroring requires you to feel approximately what the speaker feels as they're communicating. Your facial and physical responses will be in complete accord with the speaker's emotions and content if you are employing the technique.

The most effective way to give verbal feedback that is harmonious with content and emotion is to merge all the components of collaborative listening with micro-muscle mirroring. Having done so, your nods, physical reactions, 'ah-uh's, 'mmm's and other elements of non-verbal and verbal feedback will be in total synchronicity with the speaker.

GO FIRST

An interesting aspect of human behaviour is our tendency to read our maps onto the territories of others. We appear to assume that others will react to us as we react to them. For example, if you are primarily a judgmental listener who criticises and challenges during the listening process, chances are your behaviour will be informed by a belief that other people will do the same to you. This quirk of human cognition sets up a loop of destructive behaviour before the conversation has had a chance to begin.

An important factor to consider is that you— all of your behaviour, verbal and non-verbal— are your message. If you take on the attributes of a collaborative listener, your behaviour will begin to be informed by a belief that others will afford you the same courtesies. And so, you have the power within you to create either an environment marked by conversational competition and conflict, or one enriched by curiosity and genuine warmth. Choose to put aside your preconceptions of others. Take the initiative, go first into collaborative listening mode, and notice how others will follow.

MOTIVATIONAL FILTERS: HOW PEOPLE ACT ON WHAT IS SAID

14

Man is a dog's ideal of what God should be.
Holbrook Jackson

An effective way to help people engage in self-motivation is to totally honour their models of the world. One means of honouring individual models of the world is to elicit and mirror them. In group self-motivation, however, it's generally impossible to know each individual's patterns and this is where a working knowledge of motivation filters becomes invaluable.

Motivation filters guide a great deal of human perception, motivation and behaviour. Filters is an apt description of the patterns you will encounter in this chapter, for they describe what information people will pay attention to and what information they will ignore or filter out. Like categories, prototypes and frames, motivation filters give quality to our internal and external experiences. Filters are buried deep in your unconscious mind and they help define the kind of person you are. They also help determine how you will act and react when confronted with a broad range of stimuli.

DIRECTIONAL FILTERS

You are going to explore four key filters, the first of which is called a 'directional filter'. A good way to develop a working knowledge of filters is to elicit your own, so please think back to the last time you were totally motivated about something. Did you just coolly think motivated, or were you consumed by a powerful impulse, a burst of energy that made your body-mind come alive in action *towards* the object of your desire?

Now, take what are called negative emotions, such as disgust, fear, distress or jealousy. Go to a time when you were seemingly ambushed by one of those emotions. What happened? How did your body-mind synchronise a response? And did that response involve an action that, if successful, would have transported you *away from* the source-location of those bad feelings? For many people it would have.

Verbally matching a person's directional filter in a given context will arrest your subject's attention completely. When you match a person's neurology with language, your communication becomes irresistible because it is in complete accord with the way they think. Linguistically mirroring the motivational filters of those around you generates a strong 'rapport': it instantly places you on their 'wavelength' and can help avoid misunderstanding. Toward and away-from filters can be explained by taking the extreme opposites and demonstrating how they work.

Toward filters

Toward people can be smitten by what is possible. They move towards things they value, and they embody what is described as an 'attraction-reward' personality. The easiest way to get them to do something is to offer a 'carrot' or a reward: something that is valuable for them to receive. They move onward to beliefs, values, aspirations, hopes for the future and new ideas, which may deliver sought-after objects, states of mind, experiences and the like. They are seekers of benefits, make assessments about potential enjoyment, they 'go for' things and, in the extreme, are often driven by greed, acquisitiveness or power.

These types of people tend to be effective at ordering and managing priorities. They tend to be energised by the possible and the goals they're involved in setting. In certain contexts, they can be blinded to the possible downside of an issue.

Away-from filters

Away-from people are actuated by what they don't like. They're motivated by avoidance strategies. At a restaurant, they're likely to run down a menu checking off each dish they don't like. They can often make a choice of something they don't like least or they don't know they don't like. They can be seen as having a 'repulsion-punishment' type of personality, in as much as they're primarily concerned with evading unpleasant feelings, people, places, things, ideas, events or information.

The choice of a career change, for instance, would be made on the basis of having to get out of an untenable work situation, rather than seeking to improve their career prospects. If you elicit and discuss their values, you're likely to discover that a strong attraction to honest people, for example, could well be motivated by a passionate aversion to liars.

The easiest way to motivate this type of personality is to paint a vivid portrait of dire consequences: plausible threats, appeals to their deepest fears, warnings of failure and horrific images really freak them out. These people are sitting ducks for fear motivation techniques. Some of the more fundamentalist religions, for example, play on the thoughts–emotions of extreme, and not so extreme, away-from personalities by graphically depicting the horrors of Hades.

Persuasive language

The brief portrait just given describes the behaviours of those who fit into extreme toward and away-from motivational categories. Most people don't. The majority of people will probably express a preference but have a motivational mix based largely on their neurology and unique life experiences. They will have a tendency to favour one more than the other, or in some cases may be equally toward and away-from in their orientation. Context is absolutely critical.

To appeal to someone who, in the context of your message, is driven by an attraction-reward, or toward, motivational filter, pick a 'virtue' theme such as freedom, security or happiness. Then link it with one of the following language sets. For example: 'This new system of work will *help you gain* much greater financial security.'

TOWARD LANGUAGE

get	achieve	obtain
attain	include	help you to
enable	benefits	reward
achievements	advantages	pros
incentive	fulfil	accomplish
gain	acquire	secure for yourself
procure	bigger rewards	

To motivate an away-from person in a given context, you would need to choose a 'base' theme and link it with one of the following language sets. For example: 'If you want to *avoid* the prospect of *losing* what financial security you have, you will need to consider adopting these new work practices.'

AWAY-FROM LANGUAGE

avoid	prevent
avert	solve
won't have to	fix
eradicate	not have to worry about
avoid dealing with	this isn't perfect
let's define the problem	let's find out what's wrong
there'll be no problems	let's avoid the pitfalls
thwart	quell
stop that from being a problem	work out what we don't want/like

Most audiences and groups will reflect a diversity of motivational filters from extreme toward to extreme away-from. It makes sense to include language for both ends of the index, such as 'We want this legislation to *achieve* justice for our constituents and to *prevent* some people from being treated as more equal than others'. This statement covers the index of directional filters. It can gain the agreement of both types by giving away-from people something to move away from and toward people something to move towards.

The key to the effective integration of directional language into your message is to demonstrate how your idea, proposal or action can produce results that achieve some benefit (toward) and can help people avoid disasters or undesirable outcomes (away-from).

How change agents create resistance

A fair proportion of public speaking and presentation delivery involves advocating some form of change. If ever there was a good case for knowing your stakeholders and understanding how toward/away-from directional filters work in various settings, it is in the area of industrial relations. Industrial relations provides a good case study that you can generalise to other situations.

On many occasions the dimensions of the dispute are broad. This is where an understanding of toward and away-from patterns can become an extremely valuable tool. As a general rule, unions:

- fight *against* the erosion of working conditions;
- act to *stop* workers being unfairly exploited;
- lobby and take action to *prevent* redundancies;
- work *towards* achieving pay increases;

- try to protect their workers *from* unsafe working environments;
- confront deviations *from* the status quo.

Whereas, executives:

- want to work *towards* new awards that reflect current economic conditions;
- talk about *reforming* the labour markets;
- are comfortable with talking about *change*;
- work in an environment where *goals, strategic plans, business cases and objectives* are a part of a common language.

Often, though not always, a major part of the conflict in industrial disputes centres on disharmony between the obvious toward patterns of employers and the equally apparent away-from patterns of union negotiators. If the parties cannot speak the same language, is it a wonder that communication frequently breaks down?

If in their communication patterns and speeches both parties were to recognise the palpable differences in directional filters and couch what they want or don't want in the language of their opponents, they might encounter far less resistance to their proposals and ideas. For the exercise, take some of the elements in the preceding lists and convert them into the opposite language. For example, in the following an employer's message has been transformed into union-speak:

What we are about is *trying to prevent* a significant *loss* of our skilled workforce because of uncompetitive practices. We need to *avoid losing out* to our overseas competitors. We want to *thwart* a situation where cheap imports *destroy* local jobs, and we want to join forces with the union to *stop* exporting our jobs to South-East Asia.

As you master the skill of integrating toward and away-from patterns into your messages you will begin to notice that resistance dissipates, enabling you to overcome the force fields that often block your message even before it's been heard.

INTERNAL/EXTERNAL FILTERS

How do you know if you have done a good job? Your answer, like many of the verbal responses people deliver, will give vital information on the way your brain works. In this case, it will tell you, or an astute listener, 'where' you go in a given context to make a judgment about something.

The internal/external filter relates specifically to the locus of judgment and the forces that motivate people. It focuses on *where* a person gathers the information to act or make a judgment about the responsibility for the actions they have taken. So, back to the question 'How do you know if you have done a good job?'. Do you just 'know'? Do you go inside and match your efforts with some criteria, or do you have to have input from others? Perhaps a bit of both?

In a specific context, your answer will fit into one of the following two categories.

Internal filters

People who reveal an internal pattern are motivated from within. They gather information, detail or stimulus of some kind from the outside and they *take it inside* to evaluate and measure it against standards they hold to be true.

A person with an internal frame of reference will 'know' if a good job has been done, and it will be based on an internal system of criteria developed over a lifetime. It changes in different contexts, and it's possible for someone to be internal in the extreme, say, in their job, but highly external in, say, their most intimate relationships.

Here are some further distinctions:

- If something does not 'align' with their internal system, they will generally reject it.
- They are essentially motivated by what 'they' think.
- They process what other people think by measuring it against their standards.
- They are likely to interpret orders or instructions as 'interesting suggestions'.
- A person with an exclusively internal frame of reference will have difficulty acknowledging the validity of other opinions and will baulk at instructions or directions.
- They make excellent self-starters in some contexts.
- A person with a strong internal frame of reference will generally go ahead with a plan, idea or action regardless of what other people say.

When these people receive external negative feedback they will most likely question the feedback giver/s, rather than question themselves. If half a dozen people say to an internal person, 'That hairstyle doesn't suit you', the internal person is likely to think 'Hmmph, I know six people who have no sense of style or taste'.

Internal people are at risk of too great a degree of belief in their own judgments. They can ignore the qualified advice of others and may react adversely to deeper questioning of their motives and decisions. Charismatic leaders tend to be strongly internal, motivated as they are by a powerful internal vision. They have, however, taught themselves to constantly visit external space to monitor how their ideas, actions and proposals are travelling.

External filters

People with external frames of reference are the opposite of internal people. They typically answer the question 'How do you know if you have done a good job?' with statements like 'When I get good feedback', 'When I meet my budgets', 'I got a bonus' and 'The boss said he was happy with my work'.

Do you notice the difference? People with an external frame of reference, in given contexts, rely on outside information. They are motivated by factors from the outside, such as what people say and think about them, data, figures and targets.

External people actually *need* the opinions, instructions, direction and evaluation of others. They are sometimes described as 'high maintenance' people by those of the opposite type. They require fairly constant feedback in order to remain motivated, and they may become disaffected, agitated or even depressed if deprived of regular input from others. It's been found that, in the absence of external data, they may experience states of mind not unlike sensory deprivation.

People with external frames of reference:

- can be highly suggestible because they rely on the opinions of others;
- can crumble under the power of a controlling partner, superior or colleague;
- often mistake information as an 'order' (for example, in response to an observation like 'It'd be nice if this room was brightened up' they may go and redecorate);
- sometimes have difficulty getting started on a project without specific instructions;
- generally take instructions well and will carry them out to the best of their ability in order to gain approval;
- when they receive negative external feedback, are most likely to question themselves ('What did I do wrong?' is a common response).

External people are more likely to take on the judgments of others, particularly those whom they respect. There is a real danger they will not verify information for themselves.

Persuasive language

Getting through to an internal person can be difficult because they will match the main thrust of your argument with internal standards they may well believe to be universally true, or at least true for them. On the other hand, you need to exercise care with an external person lest they take your comments to heart or interpret them as a command.

Here are the language patterns to use to influence internal and external types.

INTERNAL LANGUAGE
only you know this is right for you
only you can decide
you may consider this point
try it out and notice how it conforms to your principle of ...
this fits your basic point of ensuring ...
here's some information to help you decide
this could match your criteria if you think it does
can you have a think about
for all the information you need to decide, just ask me
when you think about it you may notice
here's something for you to consider

EXTERNAL LANGUAGE
people will like your approach
this should get you lots of kudos
a lot of people are thinking this way
the majority would approve
the jury is in on this one
research shows that
the general feeling is
this has X's seal of approval
everyone is excited about this
this is the trend
these testimonials show
you'll certainly win brownie points from the other managers
people will respect you for this decision

The profiles you've just read describe individuals who are at one extreme or the other. Many people are both, that is, they take notice of external information and then go inside to match it against their personal criteria. Context, once again, is an important factor.

A good way to honour the diversity of internal/external thinking patterns is to include both language patterns in your communication. Look at the following example and see if you can detect the patterns being used. One pattern is in bold and the other is in italics:

The *data shows* that there's been an enormous explosion of Elvis impersonators. When **you think about it** and match the trends with **what you know** about maths, you can **find yourself easily agreeing** *with the experts who say* that by the year 2020 one out of five Australians you meet will be a clone of Elvis Presley.

REASONING

At the extreme there are people who demonstrate by their actions a strong belief in choice and there are people who communicate by their inaction a belief of limited or no choice. The former are motivated by possibility, the latter by necessity. Possibility/necessity can mean the difference between an unlimited model of the world, or world view, and a limited model of the world.

People who feel they have a strong degree of control over their life will generally presume they have numerous options to choose from. Conversely, people who feel they have little control over their lives may believe there are few or no options available to them. By extension, those who say there are many choices are more likely to perceive the world as a place of abundance (unlimited choice), whereas those who say there are few, or none, may view the world as a place of scarcity (little choice). Generally, people who believe in a given context that the world is a place of scarcity will think, act and talk like it is. The opposite applies to those who believe in abundance.

People disclose their possibility/necessity preferences by their verbal and non-verbal communication, and in their behaviour. The extremes are relatively easy to gauge. They reveal themselves in archetypal conduct, particularly when a clash of patterns occurs. Consider the following statements and ask yourself which of the two statements you're more likely to utter:

People who have to stick rigidly to the rules and follow the same procedure all the time frustrate me.

I wish some people would just stick to the tried and true ways of doing things instead of causing confusion by coming up with endless so-called improvements.

A way to easily remember the patterns is to think of a person who has a possibility pattern as someone who likes plenty of options. A person with a necessity pattern can be remembered as someone who likes to stick to procedures or the rules. It becomes clear in the first example that a person with possibility (options) pattern has become frustrated with someone who insists 'we do it the way we always do it', whereas a strong necessity (procedures) person is railing against those who want to change things all the time.

Charismatic communicators are invariably 'possibility' types. They are necessarily high options people who believe that the world is filled with untapped opportunity. However, they understand that it takes different types to make up the world and, in many cases, they have forced themselves to both understand and practise necessity behaviours in order to achieve balance. The following profiles will assist you in identifying the types.

Possibility

Unlimited possibilities and ideas energise possibility people. This is often why charismatic leaders are seen to be powerhouses of enthusiasm. To them the world is filled with options and they spend much time in seeking them. They are more likely to have too many options than too few. While their underlying vision may remain constant, possibility people are constantly thinking of different ways of achieving it, which is why they need a necessity person close by. Possibility people:

- are more likely to do what they want to do;
- like doings things in different ways;
- generally feel there is always a better way of doing things;
- indicate through their behaviour an abundance mentality;
- have difficulty in following procedure and will probably attempt to modify it;
- are more than likely to indicate having control over their choice of environment or lives;
- indicate a strong interest in what might be;
- find challenging or circumventing convention and the status quo almost irresistible;
- are much better at developing new ideas and creating systems than they are at maintaining them;
- can be overwhelmed by options to the point of being indecisive;
- are interested in answers to the question 'Why?'.

Possibility people are excellent at designing and initiating procedures, plans, processes, strategies, research, development and installation or set-up, that is, the creation of new systems.

Necessity

While possibility people are looking for things that break the humdrum of daily processes, necessity people prefer routine because it gives them a sense of order and continuity. Necessity people get frustrated with possibility people, and vice versa, because of a lack of mutual understanding of each other's patterns and the value of the other's contribution. Those embodying the necessity pattern:

- often indicate a scarcity mentality, believing there is little choice (their models of the world can be narrow and self-limiting);
- are extremely good at following procedures, plans and accepted ways of doing things;
- will do something once they are shown how to do it;
- are seldom motivated to discover the reasons behind doing things;
- are motivated by obligation, known options and ways of doing things, responsibilities, rules and pressures;
- will feel stuck, frustrated or lost without having a procedure to follow;
- will start a procedure and finish it;
- will feel offended by suggestions of breaking established rules;
- are interested in answers to the question 'How?'.

Necessity people like following established procedures, keeping to the rules and engaging in processes that have a beginning and end, that is, the maintenance of existing systems. If, for example, you want to encourage necessity people to develop more options, you will succeed if you give them a step-by-step process to follow. You could teach them the process of stepping up, down and sideways, for example.

Persuasive language

POSSIBILITY LANGUAGE
opportunity
new idea
choice

let's challenge the status quo or rules
find a new and fresh way to do it
this will give you an opportunity to be part of something wonderfully new
let's look at alternatives
that's one way
here are the options
there must be a way
choices waiting to be discovered
give you the control you have earned
this will give you all the flexibility you need
design new systems
find new approaches
this will appeal to your creative urges

One way to encourage a possibility person to play by the rules is to establish some. The first rule you may like to introduce is that of closure. Many possibility people become nervous when a deadline looms because they know the time is approaching for a commitment to one option.

Along with a deadline you may choose to work with them on a list of criteria against which they can judge their options and choices. Criteria are important to possibility people. Make the criteria explicit and make sure you impress upon these people that they will be assessed on how well they go about meeting them. In the following example, the possibility language used to motivate an individual to adopt a procedure is in italics.

We need to *develop a strategic approach* to after sales service. There are *lots of things we can do*. Our job is to look at *all those options* and come up with a concrete plan by Friday next. Here are the benchmarks: (1) no labour increase, (2) more client contact, (3) it must demonstrate how to go about building a better 'relationship' with our customers to get repeat sales. How *you go about this is entirely up to you* but next Friday is the deadline.

Encouraging possibility people to meet the expectations of superiors and team members can be better achieved by involving them in the process of designing or developing the 'rules of engagement'. Give them the task of eliciting group values and criteria, making the point that servicing relationships and building new ones on shared criteria can give them more flexibility and open up more options. Link this with admonitions that once they've designed the rules they can lead by example.

NECESSITY LANGUAGE
the right way
tried and true way
proven approach
here's how to apply this
the procedure is
we don't have a choice, do we?
we have a responsibility to
our duty is clear, isn't it?
keep this on track
maintain the system efficiently
we need to follow these steps

So, how do you help a necessity person expand their model of the world and begin to search for choices that may be available to them? Telling them 'There are choices out there' won't usually work because they'll filter what you say through their 'no choice' pattern. What you can consider doing is giving them a *procedure* to generate choice.

Procedures tap directly into their natural way of viewing the world. By showing them how to go about 'doing' choice you utilise their existing model of the world to create an expanded model of the world. You can include a few irresistible language patterns to motivate them:

We have a *duty* to find different *procedures* to deal with today's commercial *demands*, but we have to go about it the *right way*, don't we? And the *right way* is to *first* work out precisely what the present state of affairs is. *Second*, find out where exactly we need to go with this—where we want to be at the end of it—and *third*, look at different ways to get there by applying these criteria [list]. So in the *end* you have a *step-by-step plan* to follow to generate more options.

Notice how the language used conforms to the necessity pattern. If you assist people to follow the plan and show them how to generate specific options, you can be assured they will add it to their repertoire. In following a plan to generate options they can begin to see the world as a place with more choice. This consideration becomes vital when you are seeking to motivate groups and audiences. Possibility people will click into options and rhetoric about creating better futures. With necessity people, you must follow up by demonstrating an achievable process they can undertake to reach the goals you have outlined.

See if you can meet the challenge of creating a statement that encompasses the preferences of both possibility and necessity people.

Think of an idea and write a statement that will irresistibly attract both types. An example of such a statement follows. Both patterns appear in italics type. Which is which?

There are some things in life that are *tried and true* and one of them is that you *don't fix something that ain't broke*, do you? What you do is *systematically* explore the *possibilities* it offers and match them with what the market wants. If the market doesn't want it any more, then *you design something* that the market does want and you develop *a plan* to bring it to market. *You work together to identify the most pressing need in the marketplace by (1) establishing a niche, (2) designing a product to fit that niche, and (3) developing a step-by-step process that creatively places* the product in the *forefront of the market*. This is what *innovation* and being *leading edge* is all about—*opening up new opportunities* by having *a process* you can follow to bring *new and exciting* products to market.

RELATIONSHIP FILTER

A question: What is the *relationship* between the boxes in the following diagram?

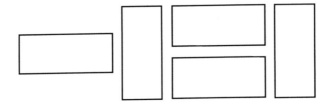

Some people will look for similarities in order to make sense of something. They will *match* pieces of information such as the boxes to each other. Did you? Other people, when trying to understand something will look for what is different first. They will *mismatch* the information. Did you look for differences first? Some people will do both, and will match (look for similarities) and mismatch (look for differences) and may constantly switch between the two, giving some weight to a preferred pattern. Are you like that?

The answer to the question depends on what relationship pattern you use. If you primarily look for sameness, your answer may be something along the lines of 'All the boxes are rectangles of the same dimensions'. If you sort by difference, you may say 'The first box is positioned horizontally and in the middle and, therefore, is different from the other two horizontal boxes, and the vertical boxes contrast with the horizontal boxes'. If you use a combination of the patterns you may conclude 'All the boxes are the same but the boxes are positioned differently'.

Relationship patterns are very important, particularly if your role is to sell change to an audience or group, and so you can invest some time in understanding this pattern. The way people sort for sameness, difference or a combination of the two has a significant bearing on the human process of understanding, learning and decision making. It can be seen as a major influencing factor on a person's personality, because this pattern reflects an individual's internal time clock and determines how receptive to change they will be.

The answer you gave to the question 'What is the relationship between the boxes?' communicates whether you are motivated by a need for stability, evolution, revolution or a combination of all three. In other words, the degree to which you either seek 'matches' or 'mismatches' in your life experiences is revealed in this pattern. As in all other motivational filters, your judgments on a person's pattern are context dependent and you cannot generalise your observations without losing precision.

The following lists give the minimum number of categories required to enable you to elicit and utilise the patterns effectively in work and speaking contexts. There are four patterns.

SAMENESS

- Sameness people look for, and often only see, similarities or sameness. They attempt to ascertain whether some event, action or idea is the same as their previous experience.
- Sameness people on many occasions deliberately or unintentionally (unconsciously) delete substantial amounts of information they encounter: most of the things that are different.
- They attempt to *match* almost every experience with what they know, and if it doesn't match they will resist it.
- They may want the world to remain the same and often tend to be conservative in their views and behaviour.
- They do not like change and may actively fight against it.
- They deeply desire stability and may stay in the same job for many years.
- They probably account for many of the work-related stress cases in the 1980s and 1990s.
- They may *accept* a major change about once every ten years.
- Their major change cycle is generally set from fifteen to twenty years. They will rarely *initiate* or provoke change outside their change cycle.

SAMENESS WITH EXCEPTION
- These people observe sameness first and then differences.
- They like things in a given context generally to stay the same.
- They can accept some incremental change about once a year as long as it's not too dramatic.
- They are evolutionary in the sense that they want their circumstances to develop over time.
- They need moderate amounts of change and innovation over time in their work to maintain their contentment and interest.
- They may change jobs or roles about every five to seven years, which represents their major change cycle.

DIFFERENCE
- Difference people love difference and are classical mismatchers.
- They are motivated by the prospect of change.
- They generally only see differences, more than often deleting all similarities.
- They can have difficulty seeing patterns, and this may put them at a disadvantage when evaluating behaviours, information, data and ideas.
- Difference people are the ones who want to reorganise, and when this pattern is combined with the options pattern they can be considered 'lethal' by some people because they often want to initiate change for change's sake.
- They are compelled and motivated to do things differently all the time because of their need for variety.
- If they have to learn this mismatching pattern to be successful in their work, expect a career change after a number of years.
- They really get on the goat of sameness people, and vice versa.
- They like their change to be revolutionary.
- Their major change cycle is around twelve to twenty-four months and if they cannot get a role change in their current job within their cycle they will change jobs.

SAMENESS WITH EXCEPTION AND DIFFERENCE (DUAL PATTERN)
- People with this pattern enjoy change and revolutionary shifts, but they are also at ease with evolutionary shifts.
- Their pattern is revealed in the flexibility they show towards various scenarios.
- They will match or mismatch depending on circumstances.
- Their major change cycle is around three to four years.
- Their language contains either difference plus sameness with exception terminology, or vice versa.

Persuasive language

The terms in each of the following lists will appeal to people with that pattern.

SAMENESS

it's the same as	the common thread is
it boils down to this	in common
maintain the essential principles	as we always do
many similarities	as before
consistent	regular way
unchanged	as you know
maintaining	continuing
identical	exactly as before
usual approach	familiar

SAMENESS WITH EXCEPTION

more	worse	deteriorated
better	less	improved
superior	greater	advanced
the same except	upgrade	rebuild
progress	gradual change	evolve
growth	augment	build on those foundations

DIFFERENCE

new	novel	changed
unlike	transformed	different
revolutionary	radical	unlike anything else
from left field	whacky	unique
one of a kind	total transformation	big shift
switch	brand new	completely fresh idea
unheard of	a complete about face	big turnaround
highly distinctive		

For sameness with exception and difference, use the language of sameness with exception combined with that for difference.

Implications

Let's imagine you are a sameness person working in the same job, doing essentially the same thing day in and day out. How do you think you'd react if some external consultant came in to 're-engineer' your work environment? Picture the consultant being quoted by your superior as saying, 'We're going to revolutionise the way work is done in this place, and we're going to turn everything upside down to make it more efficient'. You'd probably experience one of two major emotions, or maybe both: you'd want to fight it or you'd feel extreme fear for the future. If the focus on change continued, a betting person could make money on wagering that you'd be on stress leave in three months.

Now, what if someone came to you as a consultant and said 'I'm here to help make the company continuously improve its performance, but I'm very keen to make sure that everything that works well remains the same'. While you may feel a little uneasy about the prospect of change, those soothing words would probably allay your fears. When you got down to it, you'd probably find those words more accurately described the state of affairs anyway.

Use of language can have a major influence on the way people react to change. Chances are that, even with radical re-engineering projects in the workplace, many procedures, processes, models and approaches to the work at hand will remain the same. So why portray something as completely new, radical or revolutionary if that is not a *reasonable* reflection of reality in the given context?

Situations such as that just described happen all the time. People of different patterns induce fear and anger in each other by not appreciating the change cycles of others. Flip the coin for a moment and imagine yourself as a strong difference person. How would you react if a new manager came in and said to you, 'We're changing your job description. You're off the trouble-shooting staff, so now you won't have to be a generalist any more. You'll be doing the same thing every day because we want you to specialise.' Who would be looking for a new job tomorrow?

The following rules of thumb may assist you in your communication.

Sameness

People with this pattern are the most likely candidates for stress leave during periods of sustained change. The worst thing you can do is say things like 'We live in an environment where the only thing that doesn't change is change'.

If you want to minimise your workers compensation cases involving stress, you can profile the relationship patterns of those who will be affected by significant or revolutionary change. Having identified sameness and sameness with exception people, you can initiate a program that focuses on the parts of their jobs and lives that will remain the same.

In addition, you can link into their other motivational filters when explaining how things will 'develop' for them. Use *their* language patterns and not yours, and you may discover greater acceptance and less deliberate sabotage and resistance.

Sameness with exception

Use a similar approach to that for sameness people. You may want to show this group how things may improve for them, give them better opportunities or make their life or work more stimulating. Use other comparative devices and you will notice less stress and more cooperation.

For this pattern you may like to forget about using terms such as 'change' and 'change management'. Try descriptions like 'the continuous improvement' and 'job enhancement'.

Difference

These people love change as long as they're part of it. Involve them in the process, particularly if they are toward or possibility people. You will have a problem if the change results in fewer differences.

In the context of work, expect high difference people to leave your employ if the change doesn't offer them new experiences. If they are valuable employees, find them jobs that fit their pattern.

Expect difference people, especially those who have possibility patterns, to create a revolution around them. As a party trick, say the old Monty Python line 'And now for something completely different' and notice whose attention you've gained!

If, in a speech, you paint a scenario of revolution or dramatic change, rest assured you'll have difference people hanging on your every word.

The double pattern

When communicating change to people who have this pattern, mention the evolutionary and revolutionary aspects of the change. Don't overdo revolutionary 'sell'.

This pattern type seeks change and diversity but also values security or stability. Make sure you satisfy any need for stability.

Only a small percentage of the population is comfortable with change, and yet the role of leadership in today's environment is to respond to change and pilot teams, groups and entire populations through so-called commercial, political and social white waters to safer, more secure positions. The rhetoric of politicians, business gurus and social engineers is saturated with references to change, the need to change tack at a moment's notice and respond rapidly to economic, market, social and political forces.

It's estimated that around 5 per cent of the population exhibits sameness patterns, around 60 per cent of the population processes information using sameness with exception patterns, and 20 per cent has the difference pattern. Around 10 per cent of people use the double pattern, although whether they pay attention to evolution or revolution will depend on context.

You can probably guess that the most vociferous advocates of change are those who manifest the difference pattern. They are the people whose hearts quicken with excitement at the mention of change. Their language reflects how transformation and revolution energise them. The problem is that their words are like a spit in the face to most people. They are often unwitting provocateurs of resistance and may become very unpopular.

In practice

An easy way to identify the patterns is to ask the question posed at the beginning of the section on this filter. Ask what the relationship is between this plan and that plan, this and that idea, or the job you're doing now and the job you were doing last year.

Difference people will generally not understand the question and will go on to tell you what is different, sameness people will focus on similarities, sameness with exception people will pay attention to sameness and note some differences, and the people with the double pattern will mention both. Use the following general pointers when communicating with groups and individuals whose sameness/difference patterns you have identified:

Sameness

■ Point out how things are similar, the same or identical.
■ Mention what things have in common.
■ Talk about the things that haven't or won't change.

This digital editing system is just another way of doing the same thing. You still have to edit pieces together, you still have to cut out extraneous noise and you can still use multitracking. It just does it digitally.

Sameness with exception

■ Describe how things will evolve over time.
■ Qualify sameness with words like more, worse, deteriorated, better, less, improved, superior, greater and so on.

■ Give comparisons.

■ Focus on the means more than the end.

This editing system will let you do more things more quickly. It's essentially an analogue tape editing system but operates on a computer. You'll be able to do better edits, close gaps to a thousandth of a second and it will give you a superior product.

Difference

■ Focus on how things are different.

■ Use words like new, novel, changed, unlike, transformed, different, revolutionary or radical.

■ Concentrate on the end and not the means.

Digital editing will revolutionise the workplace. It will save money in tape and will dramatically speed up finished product getting to air. Everyone who has a computer with a sound card will be able to do it. It will transform the turnaround of interviews and allow you to do so many creative things on air.

Double pattern

Use both sameness with exception and difference language.

Digital editing is like tape editing, only you use a computer. It improves the quality of your edits and lets you do your editing faster. The differences are that you have to get the quality of your sound right before you input into the computer.

All four statements are true but they have been fashioned to match the sameness/difference preferences of specific individuals or audiences. The key to matching relationship filters is to notice the preferences of categories of people in particular contexts.

For example, people's patterns may change as they grow older. The sixty plus demographic is more likely to exhibit the sameness or sameness with exception patterns in a variety of contexts because older people become more patterned in their lifestyles, resisting the unfamiliar in favour of routine. If you decide to talk to older citizens about radical reform, do make sure you have an anti-lynching contingency plan in place.

People who work in the general labour force in jobs that involve processes are more likely to have both necessity and sameness or sameness with exception patterns than jobs that require innovation and responsiveness to change. Talking with workers on the shop floor requires different language than an address to the middle to senior executive ranks.

While a revolutionary sermon may be entirely appropriate to a gathering of business executives, the further you go down the line the less revolutionary your language should be. A radical revamping of an organisation's business concept may require enormous change and perception of change at the top. But, when you deconstruct the actual processes and activities required to initiate change at the shop floor, many activities can be perceived as remaining the same, as the digital editing examples show. If you look for no change, even during revolutionary times, you will find many examples of it.

Your sensitivity to the motivational filters of your audience can give you immeasurable opportunities for influence and persuasion. Charismatic communicators demonstrate through the structure of their communication a willingness to enter people's reality through their perceptual windows. Mirroring the motivational filters of individuals and groups allows your message to honour the diverse ways people absorb and process information. Get it right and your message will be truly irresistible.

15 THE PROCESS OF ANCHORING

> In order to realise the worth of the anchor, we need to feel the stress of the storm.
>
> *Anon.*

Many couples have a theme song, a song that captures the romance, excitement and carnal tempests of their early dating experiences. The song comes on the radio a decade or two later and, as the music plays, they find themselves transported back to a starry-eyed epoch of animal passion and fumbling, adolescent courtship. Somehow, the song reactivates the moods, behaviours and freshness of feelings associated with their falling in love.

Some couples conveniently stow 'our song' near the top of the pile of their music collections, ready to be played as part of the opening ritual of a night of romance. The couple may not understand how the act of playing their song rekindles their fires of passion, but they certainly know the effects it produces. Couples routinely fire romance 'anchors' to create moods highly accommodating to interludes of passion. They intuitively recognise that a variety of stimuli trigger a range of fairly predictable behaviours that lead to that incomparable, but tragically short, exchange of body fluids we call an orgasm.

Indeed, our daily lives are awash in anchors. Words, smells, sights, tastes and sounds continuously distract us from the now and transport us to various spaces and places of our personal history for short, sometimes unwelcome, but often instructional visits. Picture the objects of your most dearly held phobias, of flying, of mice, of creepy crawlies, of speaking in public, and notice the sensations come flooding back. Now think of the smells that trigger strong memories and feelings, like grandma's unmistakable odour of lavender, the smell of a steam train, the fragrance of a long departed lover, the musty redolence of an old book.

Sounds can also bring the rushing forth of long-forgotten emotional states. The sound of the old family home door chime, the theme song from *Titanic* or the ominous music of *Jaws*, the remembered tones of a parent's encouraging voice and the hysterical screech of a police siren, all transport us into other times and spaces saturated with associated emotions.

The touch of someone's hand, the remembered sensation of treading barefoot in dog poo, the warm radiation of the sun's rays on a late summer's afternoon, the sharp sting of a rose thorn can trigger, when recalled, a return to the states of mind and body experienced during and immediately after the events in question. Did you inwardly squirm at the mention of dog poo?

When we turn on our televisions, it's anchors aweigh! The theme songs of long-running series, the canned laughter of sitcoms, the catch-cries of game show hosts and a plethora of advertising stimulate responses we're not even aware of. For some instructional fun, complete the following phrases:

You deserve a break today. You deserve a ...
At moments like these you need ...
Oh, what a feeling! ...
It's amazing what a difference ... makes
Things go better with ...

In these examples you were given a stimulus and, if you're a commercial television consumer, your responses would have been right on cue. Take the first example: the advertiser anchored, or associated, the idea of taking time off and giving yourself a break with something as highly irrelevant as chocolate confectionery: an anchor in action, and damn the calories.

These behaviours reflect what is known as operant or classic conditioning. At its most basic, conditioning describes the use of an environmental cue (such as Pavlov's bell-ringing cue to his dogs) to stimulate a specific behavioural response (the automatic salivating of Pavlov's dogs). Anchoring is not dissimilar to classic conditioning. However, in classic conditioning the stimulus is invariably an external cue, such as a bell, a noise, a light or an object, whereas anchoring offers the use of internal cues: those stored inside your mind and body, such as pictures, sounds, feelings, tastes and smells. The second important difference is that in classic conditioning the subject has no control over the cue and subsequent response, but in anchoring the subject can choose a specific response linked to a predetermined stimulus.

In classic Pavlovian conditioning, repetition and intensity are claimed to be a primary means of installing the stimulus–response pattern, and so it can be with anchoring. Anchors set with one significant emotional experience, one novel stimulus, can install a powerful association between two things. If the stimulus is repeated a few times, the association can last a lifetime. Phobias are an example of lifetime associations between a stimulus (say, snakes) and a response (fear and extreme anxiety).

Covert anchors (unknown by the subject) and overt anchors (known to the subject) can be installed and applied to useful therapeutic effect. There are numerous cases of phobias melting away, unresourceful states of mind being replaced by resourceful states of mind, and patients generating more and better behavioural options.

The opportunities offered by ethical anchoring are many. In the fields of education, sales and marketing, and in the practice and theory of charismatic communication, anchoring is a highly useful device in creating states conducive to learning, buying and influencing. In this chapter, you will explore anchors as they apply to creating states of mind and body that are invaluable in learning and persuasion. It is also important to understand the process of anchoring, as you will learn in Chapter 16 how to install a confidence anchor to use as a personal resource in public speaking.

SETTING AN ANCHOR

The first thing to grasp in the anchoring process is how an association between two things can be established. Please review the following representation of an emotional episode.

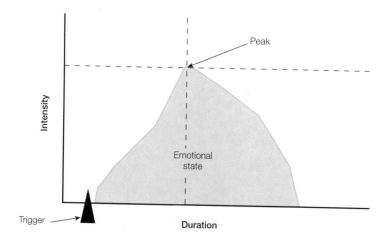

Emotional experiences have a beginning, build in intensity, peak at some point and then dissipate. For example, if you choose to allow something to enrage you, you get 'fired up', your rage reaches a high point and then you 'cool down'. The bell curve in the graph represents the point at which the rage was triggered, its building in intensity until you 'blew your stack', and the ensuing cooling off period until the rage receded completely.

If, during a period of rage, someone observed it closely and, as it reached its peak, clasped a firm hand on your left shoulder for a second, the chances would be high of your rage being 'anchored' to, or associated with, a firm clasp of the left shoulder. There would be a high probability indeed of triggering a return of your rage simply by walking up to you, clasping the same area of your left shoulder for a second and standing back to watch the fireworks.

This is no different from loved-ones and other significant people in your life learning how to press your buttons at will. Over time, they observe the things that stir you up and trigger various positive and negative emotional states. Often without fully realising it, they proceed to drop your anchors. You also have little or no conscious awareness of what has happened. All you know is that the offender 'made' you mad, laugh, melt, cry and so on.

The key to anchoring, then, is to observe an individual or group closely enough to notice when an emotional state is nearing its peak and then associate a sound, picture, object or touch with the state. The following diagram illustrates a window of opportunity for anchoring. While it is desirable to anchor an emotional state just prior to its peak, you can still install an anchor effectively within the range illustrated.

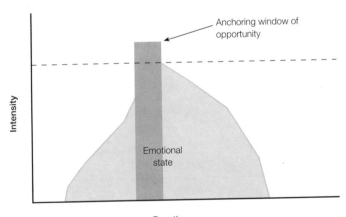

DROPPING ANCHOR

Sooner or later you may begin to think about practising the installation of anchors to demonstrate to yourself how effective they can be. As a party trick you may like to practise anchoring laughter, and here's how you do it. Find someone to talk with and, at an appropriate moment, ask them to recount a story that made them split their sides with laughter. You may like to begin the process with a commentary on how you feel that laughter can be the best medicine, and how it's a good idea when things appear dull or depressing to think back to a time when they laughed so much they could hardly stand up. Get them to recount the story.

As the story continues you will notice how easy it is to determine when the person nears the point where they laughed the most because they will show it physically by their eruptions of laughter. As they reach what you consider to be the peak of their laughter, and often they will break off the story and have a good laugh, naturally and effortlessly clasp their nearest elbow with your hand and laugh with them. Clasp their elbow for about a second or a second and a half, and let them continue the story. If they erupt into laughter again, clasp their elbow again in the same place while laughing with them.

Allow the story to finish and break the state of laughter or the anticipation of laughter by changing the subject. Then, choose to tell a story of your own, and as you say something like 'You know, your story reminds me of a time when I had a great belly laugh', laugh lightly while leaning forward to clasp the person's elbow in the same place you did when you anchored their laughter state. If you have effectively anchored the state, the person will break out into uncontrollable laughter very similar in intensity to that of the original experience.

This demonstrates that a response–stimulus episode can be created by using an 'internal' response, such as reliving a previous experience, with an external anchor, the clasping of a person's arm. Can you think of the opportunities this knowledge offers you in interpersonal relationships? An important factor in the souring of relationships is that key anchors are often associated with negative responses. In other words, you do something (stimulus) that evokes a negative reaction (response) in someone else, and you drop that anchor without ever being aware of its potential consequences.

Armed with the knowledge of anchors, you can develop an extraordinary sensitivity to the reactions of others. Having done so, you are in a position to reverse the process and anchor positive stimuli with something you do or say, immediately that positive emotional state reaches its peak. You do not have to be the cause of the positive state to anchor yourself to it.

SCOPE

A good way to investigate the use and benefits of anchoring is to learn by example. A key point to remember as you read about the ways other people anchor conducive states in groups and individuals is that anchoring often follows the following sequence:

1. An initial and useful emotional state occurs or is triggered.
2. The state is monitored until it reaches its peak.
3. A new association is made by the use of sound, touch, visual stimulus or the like.

Auditory anchoring

American comedienne Joan Rivers is a virtuoso in the art of covert anchoring, as are many other top-flight comedy performers. One of Rivers's most memorable anchoring routines is the 'Can we talk?' sequence.

A comedy performer's task is to make people laugh. The more people laugh and the better time they have, the greater the chance of a comedy performer reaching the top of the tree in their ruthlessly competitive profession. Joan Rivers reached the acme of her profession by using a combination of outrageously funny material and a devastating anchoring process that had people laughing before she even told a joke. A distillation of Rivers's sequence is as follows:

Hey, can we talk? [First introduction of the phrase is accompanied by the tonality of an innocent question. She then tells a three-step blow-out joke.]

[Step 1] You know, I'm a simple person, not at all hoity-toity. I call a spade a spade. And I'm not used to mixing in circles of the rich and famous. So when I heard I was to meet the Queen, I went into a tizz.

[Step 2] God, I wished I'd been to a finishing school, learned how to be graceful, learned how to mix easily, you know, swan around, be elegant.

[Step 3] So there I was, standing in line to meet the Queen of England! Thoughts were racing through my mind ... What to do? What to do? God, what to do? ... And there she was in front of me being introduced. I'd only ever seen the woman on postage stamps ...

[Blow-out] so I did the first thing that came into my mind—I licked the back of her head!

There was uproarious laughter, and as it was peaking, Rivers intoned 'I mean, can we talk, can-we-talk? CAN-WE-TALK here?'.

Rivers went on to tell several other Royal Family jokes, each time using 'Can we talk?' in the way described. Then, with the anchor fully installed, all she had to do was say 'Can we talk?', using the tonality of an innocent question, and the audience began to roll about in the aisles laughing. During the initial stages of her performance Rivers installed several other anchors. By the time she had reached a third of the way into her routine she was inducing 'pre-laughter' at will, firing the anchors she'd established in the initial stages of her performance. Suffice to say it was a riotously successful evening in the career of Joan Rivers.

Rivers used what are termed 'auditory' anchors to associate the state of laughter with her content. She triggered the initial laughter state with a funny joke, associated the words 'Can we talk?' at the peak of the laughter, reinforced it several times, and then tested and used the anchor throughout her performance. Auditory anchors involve the use of tone, key words and sound. There are many ways in which you can apply auditory anchors. From catch phrases to soft tonality, from a novel noise to a pregnant pause, you can anchor emotional states that provide a highly useful backdrop to the imparting of your key message points.

Visual and spatial anchoring

An important talent in conveying new ideas and information is the ability to imprint information when those listening are experiencing the most impressionable or inspiring emotional states. In a study into the impact of environmental factors on learning, a group of students learned a task in a classroom. The students were then divided into two groups to be tested by way of examination. One of the groups was examined in the classroom where it learned the task. The other group was examined in a different room. The results were surprising because the students who were examined in the same room where they learned the task did better than the students who were examined in a different room.

The point to be made here is that if you can create the optimum space, environment and state for learning and recall, your job as an educator, trainer or speaker can be made all the more effective. Think of some of the more resourceful states for learning. Curiosity, readiness to learn, creativity, intense concentration, heightened awareness and enjoyment, among others, have been found to increase memory and recall.

How would you go about inducing one of those states? Tell a story, create a cliff-hanger, point out significant personal benefits for the learner, do a creativity exercise, tell a secret, recount a joke, do an exercise that requires people to notice detail? You already know how to create numerous fertile states of mind. Your task is essentially one of finding the right anchor to associate the states you are able easily to induce.

Consider the teacher of an adult learning class who induces a state of curiosity by one of the above methods and associates the words 'green idea' to it. The teacher induces the state of curiosity by telling a story that incorporates rhetorical questions and cliff-hangers, notices the students' levels of curiosity rise and peak, and anchors their curiosity to the phrase 'green idea'.

This is an example of a visual-auditory anchor. The teacher uses green to reinforce the anchor and, on occasions when she has a really important piece of information to impart, will project a colour slide of green on the screen, invariably to a chorus of 'Green idea coming on!'. The students find it fun and never realise that their curiosity anchors have been fired covertly.

A number of high-level speakers and trainers use space to anchor attention and other fertile emotional states. When they have something important to say they will move to a pre-marked space, reveal the information in a solemn and earnest tone, with matching facial expressions and then walk away from the space and continue with the building of their argument or presentation. They repeatedly walk back into the 'let's get serious' space for all important revelations and points.

A senior executive of a telecommunications company uses space to great effect. In board and executive meetings he may once or twice get up out of his chair, put his finger to the side of his face, look intelligently thoughtful, say the most important things he has to say, and sit down again. Rarely does this technique fail to encourage agreement in those who observe this covert anchoring process.

Another technique involves the use of multimedia or overhead slides. The presenter or speaker broaches the idea and encourages those present by a variety of means (many of which are detailed in this book) to engage energetically in thinking about the subject material. At the peak of the participants' consolidation of their understanding, the speaker introduces a slide containing a few short points that illustrate the idea, thereby introducing a visual anchor that enhances the possibility of recall immeasurably.

Kinaesthetic anchoring

Kinaesthetic describes feelings, actual experience such as activity and doing things, and the sensation of touch. A useful way of anchoring fertile emotional states kinaesthetically is to invite your audience to go back to a time when they, say, felt really curious about something.

You invite them to associate into the experience of curiosity by asking them to feel what they felt when they were really curious. You guide them into their curious state with suggestions like 'There you are, sometime in your life, feeling really, really curious, and what is it you notice about the feeling? What are its qualities? Notice them', and so on. Instruct participants to touch their noses for a second to let you know when they have recovered the most curious state of mind they can achieve.

Having encouraged the group to anchor curiosity with the touch of the nose, you may then fire off the anchor at strategic moments, by pacing current experience, touching your nose and inviting any stragglers who haven't taken your cue to touch their noses. Be sure to give them something to be curious about. Interestingly, if you have established credibility and have demonstrated to a group that it can have harmless fun within a learning or speaking setting, the vast majority of people will accept your suggestions and directions, get into the spirit of things and have all the more fun doing so.

Another kinaesthetic anchor that is relatively easy to install is the 'pat yourself on the back' anchor. Applying the techniques of state elicitation, you can get an entire group to pat itself on the back for good work or for having solved an issue or problem. Review the process of what the group did, being careful to show admiration in the process, and then anchor the pat on the back at the point where you observe self-satisfaction swelling to a peak in those present.

RAISING THE ANCHOR

You have encountered a number of examples of how to anchor fertile states. Hopefully this chapter has encouraged you to become a people and group watcher so that you notice more carefully the emotions you can create in others and realise the potential to utilise them for good effect. As you become more sensitised to individual and group emotion you will begin to notice a smorgasbord of fertile emotional states to choose from. Your task then is to find a novel or effective anchor in which to associate those emotions.

Anchors are very powerful psychological tools. Often the most potent of all anchors are those that are covertly installed. The reason behind their power is that the process of associating an emotional state with an anchor you have chosen more often than not escapes the awareness of those who are thus anchored. Covert anchors can be extremely effective when individuals or groups get 'stuck' in patterned ways of thinking and behaving. As you have learned, charismatic communication is about offering choices, helping people expand their world views and bringing others to an *understanding* of your view of the world. Always have a clear purpose in mind before setting and firing anchors and ensure that your purpose embraces win– win.

16 CONQUERING STAGE FRIGHT

No passion so effectively robs the mind of all its power of acting and reasoning as fear.
Edmund Burke

People often associate the words 'die' and 'death' with public performance. Variations of 'She died out there last night in front of 600 people', 'I died a thousand deaths when I made that speech' and 'He performed ritual suicide in front of the entire executive team' are commonplace. A significant number of people would actually choose death and damnation now, rather than the hell on earth implicit in standing up and addressing a group. The thought of speaking in public, like the contemplation of death, seems to trigger powerful anxieties in a sizeable part of the population. Studies show that up to 85 per cent of people harbour a deep fear of public speaking. So, what are they scared of?

The idea of death makes many of us feel extremely vulnerable. Only the brave or the dim-witted could engage in a serious reflection on death and escape a state of intense trepidation. The idea of addressing a public gathering can also trigger feelings of dread and apprehension of similar intensity. We often feel highly exposed and threatened, alone and unsafe when we take those few steps towards the lectern or centre stage. Could an explanation of stage fright lay in perceived threats to the life of our public self?

Stage fright, or the fear of dying a thousand deaths in public, can be explained by exploring the internal processes you activate to produce it. Stage fright is something you do. It doesn't just happen by itself: you mentally create the conditions for stage fright to occur. Between the act of speaking in public and doing stage fright is a 'you', as visually represented in the following diagram.

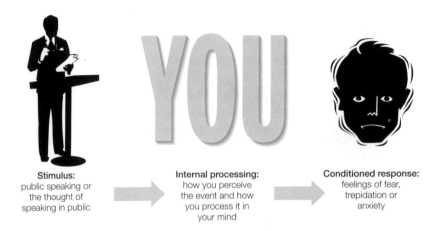

Stimulus:	Internal processing:	Conditioned response:
public speaking or the thought of speaking in public	how you perceive the event and how you process it in your mind	feelings of fear, trepidation or anxiety

In many cases, those who endure a 'thousand deaths' when they speak in public are unaware of the 'you' in the equation. Interestingly, many people start with dying a hundred deaths during their first public speaking experience and gradually improve until they reach four figures. You could say that it takes time and practice to achieve expert status in 'doing' fear to the point of dying a thousand deaths.

People who entertain general feelings of inadequacy often allow unsatisfactory public speaking experiences over time to build into a mighty snowball of self-condemnation: 'I am hopeless in front of a group', 'I'm a coward', 'There's a defect in my character that prevents me from speaking publicly', 'I just can't do it and there's nothing I can do about it'. Individuals so afflicted usually get worse with each speaking experience and often reach the point where their thoughts about their performance and themselves become hopelessly distorted. They give up public speaking without ever knowing that they have mentally created the conditions (the *you* part of the equation) for their perceived failures.

Andrew is a qualified and highly experienced technical expert. His expertise was highly valued by his employer and he was given the task of training technicians during a major technical refit. He assiduously prepared his content and presentation, but during the first training session his performance became progressively worse until a colleague stepped in and helped him through it.

During a post mortem Andrew expressed deep reservations about his ability to continue as a trainer, but he accepted his employer's assurance that he would get better with experience. However, with each ensuing experience he became more nervous, more muddled, until one day he literally froze during his presentation. Later, he recounted a growing hysteria during the presentation, his body drenched with perspiration, his breathing short and laboured, and an overwhelming feeling of 'losing it' until he reached the point of being unable to speak or move.

Andrew's initial discussions with colleagues failed to resolve his issues. He resisted any attempt at looking at the 'you' part of the equation, stubbornly insisting that he 'wasn't cut out for speaking in front of people'. He saw the problem as irreversible and allowed his experiences in public speaking to seep into other areas of communication. He reported that he felt 'a bit of a loser'. The longer the discussion continued, the more Andrew revealed a distorted view of himself and his abilities.

At that stage, Andrew had developed full-blown anxiety with textbook symptoms. Through one significant emotional experience at the beginning of his public speaking career (that of dying a hundred deaths in front of his students) he 'grew' his fear and responses over time until it reached a thousand deaths and he ceased to function in that environment. Andrew's supervisor referred him to a performance enhancement specialist who, after hearing Andrew's story, exclaimed 'Wow! How do you do that?'. The practitioner told Andrew he had a rare gift for building habits quickly. Andrew was stunned by the response. The practitioner went on to say that if Andrew could build bad habits so quickly, then chances were he could build good ones just as rapidly. At this stage, Andrew's perception of his so-called problem began to unravel slightly.

The practitioner was curious about how Andrew triggered his fear responses and invited Andrew to become his teacher. 'You do stage fright better than anyone I've encountered, and I want to learn how to do it with such virtuosity,' remarked the practitioner. It took less than an hour for Andrew to teach the practitioner how he did it.

Andrew's first thought when walking towards the lectern was that of seeing himself totally humiliated in front of his peers. He felt threatened and described the feelings of trepidation he experienced when seeing it in his mind's eye. He noticed what was happening to his body, worried that he was going to 'lose it', and perceived a deepening threat. He heard a strict and unforgiving voice chastising him for his folly and he began to internally focus on his worsening condition. He felt trapped in a loop and became ever more focused on his internal state, taking numerous external cues as evidence of a deepening predicament. He continued to 'feed' his anxiety, looping back to an escalating perception of threat, until it completely hijacked his attention. At that stage, he could neither speak nor move his body. The following diagram illustrates what happened to the 'you' part of Andrew.

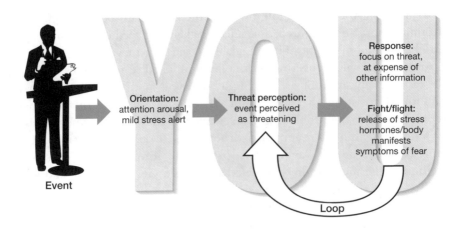

Many of the steps in Andrew's stage fright pattern were unknown to him until his performance enhancement specialist elicited them. Hearing his description of the process, Andrew began to realise the extreme self-prejudice that 'informed' his perception of being unable to speak publicly. He predicted personal disaster before his presentation even began! As he walked up to begin his lecture, he saw in his mind's eye a picture of himself in a state of total humiliation.

Commonsense will tell you that it takes an awful lot of work to be totally humiliated in front of an audience. Complete success in the total humiliation of the speaker would require a conspiracy between the speaker and the audience and both parties would have to work overtime to achieve the desired results. And yet, Andrew was deluded and obstinate enough to predict that he could do it all by himself, without uttering a single word. Delusions like Andrew's involve what are termed self-fulfilling prophecies (SFPs), and they're one of the most common and possibly destructive perceptual errors that public speaking novices make. SFPs amount to giving an instruction to the unconscious mind. If you approach any task with the expectation of failure, there's a very high probability you will fulfil the expectation. Andrew had already failed before he started. The way he perceived his task and the resulting internal pattern of doom guaranteed it.

How did Andrew overcome his public speaking anxiety? Essentially, he did it all himself. He learned and applied a technique that dramatically transformed his performance from one of inner chaos to one of relaxed confidence. He learned how to identify the point at which he perceived danger and interrupt the pattern before it became destructive. The following diagram illustrates the point at which pattern interruption is possible.

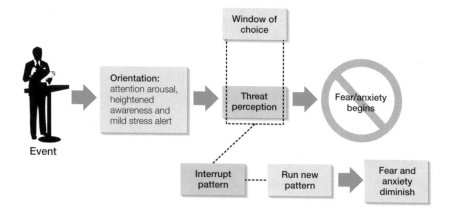

It's important to discover what triggers threat perception because the trigger represents the first step of a fear pattern. The dotted lines represent where perception of threat is triggered. In Andrew's case, it was the motion towards the lectern or centre stage that triggered his perception of impending humiliation. From there on, his natural flight/fight responses took over. All he could do after that was engage whatever coping mechanisms he had at his disposal in order to survive the ordeal.

ELICITING TRIGGERS

Think back to a time when you experienced a negative state of mind such as fear or anxiety. Take yourself to that event and see it through your own eyes, feel what you felt, hear any external or internal voices that you heard, and notice any movement that was present. Now, answer this question, how did you know it was time to have fear or anxiety? Tough question? If you weren't aware of the processes involved in doing fear, it may even be an unanswerable question. But, now you know that fear or stage fright is the *result* of the 'you' part of the equation— that it's something you do inside your head— you can realise that answering the question will give you the key to conquering your fear.

So, when is it time for you to have fear or anxiety? Examine the previous diagram again, and notice that fear occurs after you perceive a threat. The threat, or danger, doesn't have to exist in reality, but if you perceive it as a threat, then it's real. If it's real to you, your next response will be to do an emotional state such as fear. So, the answer to the question is that it's time for you to have, or do, fear when you have decided that you're in physical or psychological danger.

The key to interrupting a destructive pattern is to intervene at the point at, or just before, you begin to perceive the existence of a threat. When you have identified what triggers your internal perception of danger, it becomes a simple matter of designing a new pattern and rehearsing it until it automatically clicks in and overrides the old pattern. Follow the following pattern detection process to establish your fear/stage fright 'signature'.

Pattern detection

Have a piece of paper and pen handy when you engage in this process and write down your discoveries.

Step 1

- In your mind, go back to a significant time when you had to deliver a presentation, address a gathering or speak to the media.
- See the situation through your own eyes. This is critical if you are to observe your reactions during the event. What do you see? Write everything down that is visually associated with your memory of the event.
- As you see the situation, notice any sounds you hear and, most importantly, any feelings you have. Be specific. Write them down.
- Where are the feelings in your body? Where did you feel them? What sensations did you experience? Ensure you note the location, intensity and type of feelings experienced.
- Notice the position of your body. Were you moving or static?
- Are there any smells or tastes associated with this experience? Write them down.
- Once you have developed a full record of what you saw, heard, felt, smelt and tasted as you revisited the experience, review the list of things you did. Ask yourself if it is a reasonably complete description. Do you feel you have a good grasp on the experience as a history?

Step 2

- Go back again in the memory and ask yourself what happened just before you began to feel the sensations of fear in your body. Note it down.
- Keep going back in time, by asking yourself what happened just before that. Do make sure that you are seeing what you saw through your own eyes, feeling what you felt and hearing what you heard.
- You will reach a point where the feelings associated with the memory may change from fear to milder feelings of stress. This is the point just before you perceived that a threat existed.

■ Revisit that window where the feelings changed from fear to a milder stress alert to ensure that it's the point at which you begin to perceive the situation as threatening. The cut-out from the previous diagram illustrates the change point and the window of choice available to you.

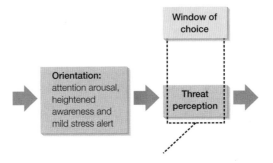

■ Revisit the point as often as it takes for you to have a clear notion of what you see in your mind's eye, the associated feelings and their location in your body, any sounds you hear in your mind's ear, and the smell and taste of the threat.
■ To use a culinary term, put them on the back burner to simmer while you continue with the process.

An important part of mastery over any internal limitation is to bring the limitation into your conscious awareness. It's extremely difficult to regulate and control an internal process as long as it remains unconscious and a mystery to you. As Andrew discovered, bringing a pattern into conscious awareness enabled him to better understand both its lack of logic and its destructiveness. If you have completed the exercise, you are now ready for the design phase in the process of transforming your fear into confidence.

DESIGNING RESOURCEFUL STATES

Think how effortlessly you spring into some of your most common negative moods or states when confronted by some unpleasant person, thing or event. You can fly into a rage, fall into depression, recoil in fright and jump to conclusions in the time it takes to blink, can't you? This is a very useful thing to know, because it proves you have the neurological capacity to pass quickly and smoothly from one state of mind to another. So, now you know you have the wiring in your brain to switch moods almost instantaneously, it becomes easier to see yourself effortlessly *leaping into a calm*, doesn't it?

The technique you are about to encounter works by using the point at which you perceive danger (threat) to induce a powerfully designed resourceful state. This has the effect of collapsing the negative state of mind and replacing it with a purpose-built state, giving you an instant rush of flexibility to deal with the things you had previously chosen to feel fear and anxiety over.

What kinds of resourceful states of mind would be handy to access when you confront a speaking engagement? Can you imagine what kind of calm you would need to leap into? A relaxed state of mind may be a good starting point, but you can appreciate you need something else to add vigour and energy to your presentation. Too much relaxation can produce complacency and inattention. Confidence may be a good additive. If you match confidence with the competence you will gain by structuring your presentation along the lines of Part 2 of this book, it can be a very useful resource to call upon.

So far, we have an imaginary state of mind that fuses relaxation and confidence. Let's call it relaxed confidence. You can probably recall occasions where you felt relaxed confidence. It's a positive state to experience and brings with it a set of comfortable feelings. Yet, you may need another constituent to allow you to have the degree of concentration and mindfulness you need to speak successfully in public.

Observe the cut-out below. It represents the first stage of a fear pattern. The act or prospect of public speaking evokes what is called an orienting response, triggering heightened awareness and a mild stress alert.

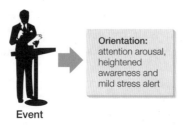

Event

Heightened awareness and a manageable infusion of adrenalin can be very useful when speaking in public, so hold in your memory the feeling of heightened awareness. As a state of mind, it feels very similar to a feeling you have undoubtedly experienced as 'being kept on your toes', or to use another cliche, 'being on the ball'. It may be beneficial to keep this part of your old pattern because a moderate level of stress can help you enhance your performance. If you add heightened awareness to relaxed confidence, what do you have? You have an amalgam of states that form a 'super-state' of mind ideal for speaking in public. Choose to remember the acronym RCA (relaxed and confident awareness) as a symbol for a powerful state of mind and being that will allow you to draw on whatever other resources are necessary to become a virtuoso in the art of public speaking.

BUILDING YOUR SUPER-STATE

The next step in taking control of the 'you' part of the equation is to amalgamate relaxation, confidence and awareness into one easily accessible whole. You'll learn how to instantly access this state further down the track, so let's concentrate on building it first. It takes a minimum investment of time to structure and practise your super-state. Once it is assembled, you will have a personal asset you can draw on for life, so it makes sense to attend carefully to its creation, doesn't it? First, you will build your relaxation component. The following diagram offers a visual example of the sequence to follow.

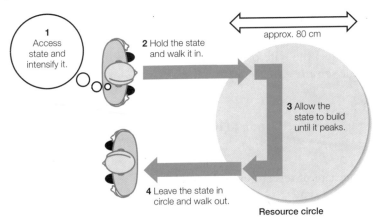

Building relaxation

Study the simple steps in the diagram, and then mark an imaginary circle on the floor, about 80 centimetres in diameter, about one half of a footstep in front of you. Stand outside the circle and follow this procedure.

Step 1

Can you remember a time when you felt completely relaxed? When your whole body felt loose, calm and balanced? It may have been with a group of friends, or it could have been a solitary experience, when your cares were banished for a time and you were comfortable and unperturbed. It could have been the sharing of a quiet moment with someone special. You know that feeling of serenity, don't you? Go back and experience the moment through your own eyes, ears and feelings.

Notice the nature and quality of the state of relaxation you achieved. What were the feelings like? Observe what was going on in your mind, and remember what inner sounds you heard, if any. What external sounds do you associate with the memory?

Where in your body did you feel the feelings of calm? What did your muscles feel like? What did both the outside and inside of your body feel like? What visual memories do you have of this state of relaxation?

Make sure you transport yourself back to the memory and experience it as it really was. Begin to build your memory of what it was like, noticing feelings, sounds, pictures, your rate of breathing and any other sensory experiences that are attached to the memory.

Step 2

When you feel the state of relaxation is at its peak, step into the circle and take all the sensory experiences with you.

Step 3

Allow the state of relaxation to build a little more.

Step 4

When the state of relaxation peaks, walk out of the circle leaving it behind in the circle.

Step 5

Stand in front of the circle again and walk into it. You can notice how the feelings of relaxation return as soon as you enter the circle. Saviour the experience and then walk out of the circle, leaving the state behind in the circle.

You may repeat this process, recalling different states of relaxation and taking them into the circle to join the existing ones. This will create a powerful alloy of emotions. When you are happy with the state you have created, move to the next sequence.

Adding confidence

Follow the procedure outlined in the last section and in the diagram, this time accessing feelings of confidence and walking them into the resource circle.

Please return to a time when you felt confident, when you felt entirely at ease with the task you were doing and could prophesy a successful outcome. Sometimes it's difficult to access confidence until you realise that it's a feeling you have quite often. Think back, for example, to the last time you may have noticed someone struggling with something and you said, 'Here, I'll do it', before easily and effortlessly carrying out the task.

Confidence comes and goes often without us noticing it. It's a feeling— isn't it?— no matter how fleeting, of our ability to successfully complete something. That feeling is a good place to start because you can amplify it or make it stronger simply by using your imagination.

Experience confidence through your own eyes and feel a taste of success on your tongue. Notice the quality of feeling and the internal voices you hear when you're doing confidence. Make it all bigger, amplify it, and walk it into the power circle.

Access a few different states of confidence you have experienced in your life and take them into the power circle. Notice, now, as you walk into the circle, how you can experience an amalgam of relaxation and confidence. The power circle is growing in intensity, isn't it?

Topping up with heightened awareness

If you did the first exercise to elicit your fear signature, you can know and remember the feeling of your attention being aroused, the resulting heightened sense of awareness and the mild stress associated with the experience. For good measure, you can add this state of mind to the resource circle you have created. So, following the instructions, go through the steps of adding heightened awareness to the mix. Be sure to recall the state through your own eyes when you go back and access it, walk it into the circle and leave it behind.

Test the mixed state to notice the subtle changes in the super-state you have created for as long as it takes for you to have it indelibly inscribed in your memory. Keep testing it to make sure it is well associated with walking into the circle.

TRANSFORMATION

Now we arrive at the stage where you will link the 'trigger' of your old fearful state to the new super-state of relaxed and confident awareness. In Step 2 of the pattern detection exercise on pages 304–5, you made a strong mental note of the point at which you began to perceive the speaking situation as threatening. It's worth remembering at this stage that a person doesn't invent a new fear pattern with each different speaking experience. Human beings are highly flexible as well as good at taking shortcuts, and the chances are high of your simply having used your old and trusty fear pattern in new situations. That's why it's important to find the trigger, or the first step, of the pattern. If you are sure you have identified the point at which you transform attention arousal and mild stress into a perception of threat, you are ready to continue the process.

Following is the final diagram detailing the process of transformation from fear to relaxed and confident awareness. Follow the guidelines to override your old pattern and install the new super-state.

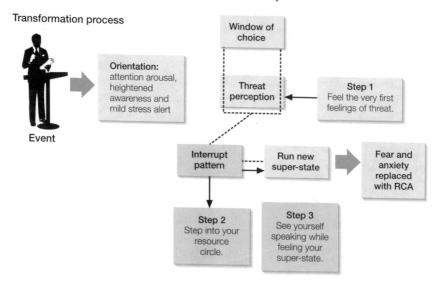

The diagram has become a little busy, but you can notice that there are three simple steps to observe in transforming fear into RCA. Follow exactly the process outlined.

1. DO YOUR PRE-FLIGHT CHECK

Using your abundant imagination, step into your resource circle to ensure that it's at maximum thrust and you feel the power of the super-state you have created. Having given yourself the all-clear ...

2. BEGIN YOUR LEAP INTO THE NEW SUPER-STATE

- Choose the most memorable occasion when you ran your fear pattern. Go back until you reach the point identified during the pattern detection exercise, that point at which you experienced the faint beginnings of feeling threatened. See things through your own eyes, paying particular attention to those now identifiable feelings.
- As soon as you feel the threat, take a half step into your resource circle and, as you notice how the fear suddenly transforms itself into confidence, begin to see yourself speaking fluently and confidently as you carry on to the end of your speech or talk.
- Repeat the process, and as you do you can probably notice the ease with which the transformation occurs. Continue to see yourself coming to a successful conclusion of the speech. Repeat this process about five times or only as long as it takes to instantly access your super-state with the mere thought and feelings of threat.

3. ACCESS OTHER NEGATIVE SPEAKING MEMORIES

Recall other occasions when you spoke in public and do the process detailed above, each time repeating it until simple recall transforms you into relaxed and confident awareness. Continue with the process until you have exhausted all memories of negative speaking experiences. Just imagine how things would have turned out if you had possessed RCA on those occasions.

4. PREPARE TO SPEAK

If you have a forthcoming speaking engagement, see yourself preparing to speak in front of the audience, notice if there is any perception of threat and step into your resource circle, feeling the full power of your super-state. Then see yourself successfully delivering your speech and add applause and hearty congratulations for good measure. Repeat this process until you can think about the forthcoming event at any time and feel empowered with relaxed and confident awareness.

The technique you have worked through will demonstrate to you once and for all that the 'you' part of the equation can be used to transform you into a highly resourceful and competent speaker. You can control your emotional states and enhance immeasurably your public performances by interrupting those crippling fear patterns that run beyond your conscious awareness and creating new and empowering states of mind. This is the pattern that Andrew learned and which signalled the beginning of a shift that went far beyond success in public speaking and lecturing. Having conquered his fear, Andrew went on to conquer other demons using the same method. He continues his steady rise in the company he works for.

A FINAL WORD

Never engage in a contest of wills with anyone unless you
can exercise both of them.
Anon.

You've covered much ground since the opening chapter. You've explored
three key variables of charismatic communication: who says it, how it's said
and who hears it. You've encountered a series of ideas, techniques and
models that will equip you to take the Path of Least Resistance and
support your goal of becoming a charismatic communicator and better
agent of influence.

You've learned that identity engineering gives you an opportunity to
build a stronger and more dynamic self around principles of integrity,
uniqueness, consistency and vision. You've seen how you can become a
more inspirational leader, increasing your ability to lead people beyond
narrow self-interest and towards a greater good.

You've discovered message characteristics and techniques that enable
you to say things with more clarity and more persuasiveness, and allow you
to create a shared space in which to negotiate meaning. You've found that
external focus on others allows you to gather a reservoir of information
about people and groups so as to communicate in accord with your
subjects' models of the world. And, you've discovered that it's not at all
difficult to share the spoils of the hard work and dedication you inspire
with those who have made it possible.

You have encountered numerous references to categorisation or
pigeonholing: the prototypes of success and leadership that people store in
their memories to streamline their perceptual processes. You have
discovered that sameness and similarity are important elements in shaping
how people will perceive you, and you have come to realise that you can
influence perceptual processes by demonstrating to your audience that you

are like them or that you match their prototypes of leaders and opinion-shapers.

You may, at times, have baulked at the idea of 'bringing yourself down to the level of others', and silently railed at the thought of conforming to the expectations of your audience. But, the thought can occur to you that you chose to read this book to improve yourself, to stand out above the crowd, to better express your individuality and to gain an edge in the fierce competition for attention and support in your area of endeavour.

If you are talented, have a good idea, have a winning proposal or a need to convince others of your merit and abilities, you can now appreciate the significance of separating means from ends, can't you? You've learned that ends are what you get after you have employed a process, and so it makes sense to adopt means that are known to be more effective in delivering the outcomes you seek. After all, if you succeed in persuading people to listen to and adopt your ideas, you will stand out, you will have gained an edge and you will have taken a major step in accomplishing some of the bigger ends you seek.

The aims, then, of matching the charisma prototypes outlined in this book are to get more than a good hearing and overcome the tendency people have of prejudging you on superficial grounds. People judge others in a fairly mindless fashion, as you have discovered, and in the highly competitive playing field of ideas you may find yourself concluding that it pays big dividends to conform to the mental pigeonholes people carry around in their heads. Matching the prototypes explored in this book will help you melt down resistance, gain attention and be truly heard.

If there are any remaining doubts lingering in your mind about beginning a journey down the Path of Least Resistance in your communications with individuals and groups, take stock of your jaunts down the Path of Greater Resistance. Notice the disappointment of being ignored, of being overlooked, of having good ideas sink in a sea of apathy, of being misunderstood, of people becoming more fanatical in their opposition to your plans and ideas because you confronted them head on. These are some of the obstacles you can look back on and see as problems of the past. For, who would want them to continue? Surely, it makes sense to embody models of persona and style that make it easier for people to lend you their ears and what's in between them.

Learning the ropes of charismatic communication is remarkably similar to the experience you have when learning the ropes of a new job. Can you remember what it was like to start a new job, entering a totally new environment, with new systems, new people, new practices and an unfamiliar culture? And remember how you went about adjusting and aligning yourself to your new circumstances. You probably took on the role of learner/observer, gradually unravelling the mysteries of unfamiliar practices and procedures, discovering the norms of the organisation, learning the more subtle elements of the culture, figuring out the power structure and getting used to a myriad of different customs and standards.

One day, however, you discovered yourself just doing the job without having to mentally rehearse everything. You mastered many things that, initially, would have appeared daunting and perplexing, and yet you came through. Over time you had assimilated enough information and experience in your new workplace to make the distinctions and decisions required to contribute fully to the task. How did you do that? The answer is, you practised and made the new approaches and behaviours habitual. You did it through an investment of your imagination, your intelligence, your memory and your time— resources we all possess in quantity.

And so it is with learning how to glide easily and effortlessly down the Path of Least Resistance. As you master each new behaviour or approach, your self-confidence will grow as it did during the early phase of a new job. You'll begin to observe that you have greater credibility with your peers, and your relationships will become more authentic as you begin to build trust-based bonds with people. You'll notice people listening more and acting on what you say, a powerful reward for your time and effort.

Use the model on page 315 as a constant reminder of the key discoveries you have made and the things you need to accomplish in your quest to develop a more dynamic and charismatic persona. Take the ideas, models and techniques in this book that align with your new persona and integrate them over time into your performances. Grant yourself the luxury of true scepticism and do what real sceptics do: investigate and try the techniques fully before deciding which ones suit your personality. Practise and form new habits of collaborative listening, try out new and simpler ways of structuring your message, build into your performance words that don't test the wills of those who hear them and begin to notice how your messages hit their mark.

In today's world, charisma is not a genetically inherited or God-given trait. What are fundamental to charisma and charismatic communication are the two-way rhythms that are established between leader and follower. Those rhythms are felt when you seek to negotiate shared meaning, when you incorporate into your message the beliefs, values, needs and aspirations of those with whom you establish a dialogue, allowing you and your

INITIATING THE CHARISMA EFFECT

Mental skills

- has strong identity and self-guide
- is optimistic
- has high level of empathy
- has high self-monitoring skills
- is emotionally mature: able to express appropriate emotions
- is consistent and visionary
- is able to crystallise ideas into symbols
- has high integrity and sense of morality
- is trustworthy
- is assertive
- has high curiosity and questioning ability
- has high abstract/concrete flexibility
- has high but managed and directed energy
- has strong sense of confidence
- is willing to take risks
- uses flexibility across contexts
- goes beyond self-interest
- has unique personality traits

Looks the part: grooming and style match expectations; looks healthy

Animated facial expressions

Eye contact

Relaxed posture

Animated but congruent body gestures

Delivery skills

- is highly articulate with strong message delivery style
- has unique argument style
- uses rhetorical devices such as analogy, story-telling and metaphor
- has high tonal flexibility/vocal animation
- has good vocal timbre and variety
- matches content with listeners' needs
- understands and effectively uses framing
- emphasises collective sense of mission
- is able to distil complex ideas into simple messages
- has remarkable skills in using the language of an audience

followers to elevate each other to higher levels of motivation and meaningful achievement.

Charismatic communicators recognise that taking the Path of Least Resistance leads them to better destinations in their relationships, delivering extraordinary opportunities, greater mastery of life's challenges and often profound success. Are you ready to follow in their footsteps?

INDEX